Jung, Irigaray, Individuatic

This work postulates a novel and unique relationship between Carl Jung and Luce Irigaray. Its central argument, that an ontologically different feminine identity situated in women's embodiment, women's genealogy and a women's divine is possible, develops and re-figures Jung's notion of individuation in terms of an Irigarayan woman-centred politics. Individuation is re-thought as a politically charged issue centred around sex-gendered difference focused on a critique of Jung's conception of the feminine.

The book outlines Plato's conception of the feminine as disorder and argues that this conception is found in Jung's notion of the anima feminine. It then argues that Luce Irigaray's work challenges the notion of the feminine as disorder. Her mimetic adoption of this figuring of the feminine is a direct assault on what can be understood as a culturally dominant Western understanding. Luce Irigaray argues for a feminine divine which will model an ideal feminine just as the masculine divine models a masculine ideal. In making her claims, Luce Irigaray, the book argues, is expanding and elaborating Jung's idea of individuation.

Jung, Irigaray, Individuation brings together philosophy, analytical psychology and psychoanalysis in suggesting that Luce Irigaray's conception of the feminine is a critical re-visioning of the open-ended possibilities for human being expressed in Jung's idea of individuation. This fresh insight will intrigue academics and analysts alike in its exploration of the different traditions from which Carl Jung and Luce Irigaray speak.

Frances Gray teaches philosophy at the University of New England, Armidale, NSW, Australia. She has contributed to the *Spring Journal*, *Cosmos and History* and *Australian Feminist Studies*. This is her first book.

Jung, Irigaray, Individuation

Philosophy, Analytical Psychology, and the Question of the Feminine

Frances Gray

Routledge
Taylor & Francis Group
LONDON AND NEW YORK

First published 2008 by Routledge
27 Church Road, Hove, East Sussex BN3 2FA

Simultaneously published in the USA and Canada
by Routledge
270 Madison Avenue, New York, NY 10016

Routledge is an imprint of the Taylor & Francis Group, an Informa business

Typeset in Times by Garfield Morgan, Swansea, West Glamorgan
Printed and bound in Great Britain by TJ International, Padstow, Cornwall
Paperback cover design by Lisa Dynan

This publication has been produced with paper manufactured to strict environmental standards and with pulp derived from sustainable forests.

British Library Cataloguing in Publication Data
A catalogue record for this book is available from the British Library

Library of Congress Cataloging-in-Publication Data
Gray, Frances, 1949-
Jung, Irigaray, individuation / Frances Gray.
p. cm.
Includes bibliographical references and index.
ISBN 978-1-58391-777-0 (hardback) – ISBN 978-0-415-43103-3 (pbk)
1. Irigaray, Luce. 2. Feminist theory. 3. Jung, C. G. (Carl Gustav), 1875–1961.
4. Individuation (Psychology) I. Title.
B2430.I74G73 2008
194–dc22

2007023916

ISBN: 978-1-58391-777-0 (hbk)
ISBN: 978-0-415-43103-3 (pbk)

For my great friend, mentor and teacher,
Maureen Flood, 1935–2005

The greatest concern of the human being is to learn how he should properly fulfil his station in creation and rightly understand what one must be in order to be a human being.

(Immanuel Kant: 'Selections from the Notes on the Observations on the Feeling of the Beautiful and Sublime', *Notes and Fragments* (2005) p. 6)

Contents

Preface

> You refuse to admit that the unconscious – your concept of the unconscious – did not spring fully armed from Freud's head, that it was not produced *ex nihilo* at the end of the nineteenth century, emerging suddenly to reimpose its truth on the whole of history – world history at that – past, present and future. The unconscious is revealed as such, heard as such, spoken as such and interpreted as such within a tradition. It has a place within, by and through culture.
>
> (Luce Irigaray 1991: 80)

This book provides a theoretical background to the thinking of Carl Jung and Luce Irigaray. It shows that they have a common grounding in philosophy, which provides a place from which we can begin to see their work in terms of overlapping concerns. I argue that Jung and Luce Irigaray's *œuvre* can be situated in a collectivist framework. The collective or social community is the birth site of community members who should be thought of as *potential* individuals. I argue that Jung and Luce Irigaray have a shared concern with the issue of how members get to be individuals, that is, the process of individuation. However, I argue that Luce Irigaray takes up Jung's idea, albeit unconsciously, of the individuation of group members in a collectivist context. The collective with which she is concerned is women. Using her idea that women must be emancipated from the masculine paternal symbolic, I argue that women can be individuated as specific members of a group only when the collective of which they are members is itself individuated.

I argue that collectives are ambivalently placed with respect to their members. On the one hand, the *ideal* of the individual – as an autonomous, responsible, choice maker – is promoted by the Western liberal democratic collective as a whole; on the other, specific collectives embody various practices of initiation, both conscious and unconscious, that assume and require sameness at a fundamental level. Much theory about the psyche assumes sameness: of experience, of categories and their applicability, of intent. Even the notion of individuation assumes sameness or similarity insofar as individuation involves development *from* a state of immersion and lack of individuated being, *to* individuated being marked by distinctiveness and integrity. Individuation, on this view, is an account of the lifelong process that the achievement of individuality is. Jung argues that 'individuation means becoming an "in-dividual," and, insofar as "individuality" embraces our innermost, last, and incomparable uniqueness, it implies becoming one's own self. We could therefore translate individuation as "coming to selfhood" or "self-realization"' (Jung 1966: 266).

My argument encompasses more than this, however. I introduce Luce Irigaray's mimetic critique of psychoanalytic theory and apply it to Jungian analytical psychology theory. Accordingly, I show that Jung's idea of individuation is limited by the masculine assumptions intrinsic to his figuring of the collective unconscious. I argue that individuation, like many other notions and processes which are developed and articulated by Jung, is a product of masculine symbolic understandings correlative with the collective unconscious and its archetypal structuring. I suggest that if we read Jung's work within this context, then we can see that his is not a neutral reading or construction of the psyche, but one which precludes the possibility of an authentic feminine voice. Individuation, I claim, is the *telos* of Luce Irigaray's ideal of a feminine-feminine symbolic/imaginary or system of meanings and significances which arises out of sex/gendered embodiment and collective responses to it.

Lest this reading of Jung be interpreted as reinscribing masculine notions of the feminine, I take a new look at the idea of essentialism which has plagued Jung's own theoretical construction of the feminine and 'woman', and also Luce Irigaray's approach to the woman question. Her work is important because it is a different woman's voice that challenges accepted understandings in a methodologically confronting way. Yet because she claims to be imitating the voice of the feminine as it is understood by men, her voice is quite familiar. It does not obey the 'rules' of discourse nor does it acknowledge, as and where it 'should', the dictates of allegedly 'good scholarship'. Her voice mirrors to us the feminine as perceived and constituted, (not always successfully) by the masculine symbolic/imaginary.

Having said all of this, I want to make some comments that relate to the epigraph which heads this preface. I recently attended a conference at which almost all of the keynote speakers in the plenary sessions were white middle-class male intellectuals and authors even though in the audience there was a number of white middle-class female intellectuals and authors. A lot of white middle-class women were at the conference and a lot of white middle-class women presented papers (and I was one of them). The conference began with three white middle-class men addressing us and finished with three white middle-class men addressing us. Yes, these white middle-class men knew a lot about the subject matter of the conference (and at times, I thought, about everything else); there was no question about that. Some of them were intelligent and witty and charming. But they seemed to be unaware of their privilege, their middle class-ness and its assumptions, and their men-ness. They expected to be listened to; after all, they were experts in their field. But did they expect to be listened to because they were experts or because they were *white middle-class male* experts? On the whole they were dismissive of the women in the audience, even though most of the women were white and middle-class as they were. At one stage I suggested to one of the famous that he read some Kant to help him with a difficulty he had with a theoretical matter. He did not say, 'That's an interesting idea. Can you say more?' or even 'Why do you think that?' He ignored my suggestion and asked, 'Do you teach somewhere?' (code for why should I listen to you and what would you know?) as if I could only be taken seriously if I had an academic job and some credentials to qualify as 'listenable to'. You might remark (and I have no idea if this is true) that, well, the famous are always being recommended this and that; and that it didn't matter that I am a woman, it's irrelevant: he would have responded to a man in the same way. Maybe, but that I doubt: he seemed not to engage with any of the intellectual material presented by any of the white middle-class women in the plenary sessions as either presenter or audience member. A number of women *did* speak in the plenary sessions but they were far outnumbered by men who continued to be seen as, and to represent themselves as, experts, as *the real* authorities.

What we got at the conference in the plenary sessions was interpretation and reading of white and middle-class theorists according to white middle-class men and women. Within that classist and 'racist' structure, a hierarchy operated which suggested that it is not *what* someone says but *who* says it that actually counts ('Listen to me because I am a man; and don't listen to her because she is a woman (unless of course, she is telling us where to get something to eat)'). But this small, influential, classist and 'racist' structure of which I was, and am, a privileged participant exists within networks of many overlapping classist and 'racist' structures. These structures work to maintain and foster their values (and conferences are often one way of doing this). The point I am making, though, is that these structures are negatively exclusionary and where there should be room for many voices, not only to be heard but also to be valued, there is not. And such valuing should be not on the basis of who they are but because of what they say.

We cannot and should not assume that every 'racial', class, sex/gender or age group shares the same or even similar interests and, on the whole, most of us probably do not make such assumptions anyway. Maybe the conference I attended was typical of any such interest group and that precluded other groups on the basis of very different interests and concerns. Paradoxically, however, the topics discussed during the conference seemed to me to have a universalising orbit: what was said was said *as if* there were no differences that could significantly contribute to, or even negate, the ongoing discussions and debates. Meanings were pre-established and predetermined and, basically, there was no room for otherness. And I think this is one of the things Luce Irigaray is saying.

The aporia of difference is captured in these considerations. First, had there been Australian Indigenous or South American or Chinese or African American or Lebanese speakers addressing us at the plenary sessions, it does not follow that what they said would be any more truthful or illuminating than what anyone else said. Truth and illumination as such are not the issue here, however. And secondly, the experiences of the white middle classes are not the experiences of everyone and in this *does* lie a question about representation and interpretation that *does* impinge on truth and illumination. On the whole, it would have mattered that Indigenous Australians or South Americans or Chinese or African Americans or Lebanese delegates were there, speaking in the plenaries, precisely because white middle-class experience is not universalisable, and because *the voices of others who are not us should be heard, should be listened to and should be taken seriously. And because a plenary session reflects the inspiration, the ethos, the affiliations and allegiances of a conference.* In the context of difference, this is not news: Frantz Fanon, Audre Lord, Alice Walker, Elizabeth Spelman, Aileen Moreton-Robinson, Iris Marion Young among many, many others have been saying these sorts of things for years (and years). Although we might tell ourselves that we do not make assumptions that erase difference, it seems nonetheless that many of us simply do not hear and attend to dissident voices; or to voices more or less the same as ours but which issue from a different kind of embodiment. So why do we continue to play out sex/gender, class and 'race' politics which marginalises some groups of people, among them women, and in the process renders women the utterers of dubious, unremarkable and thus insignificant opinions? And why do we do this not only with women, but with people who are themselves, and as such, very 'different from us'?

The politics played out during this conference (and many others like it which I have also attended) was methodologically, structurally and substantively misogynistic, classist and 'racist' – not intentionally but in fact. It assumes that some people – and women in particular and, again, any women whether black or coloured or white – have nothing much to say that can add to the incisiveness, expansiveness and general brilliance of white middle-class men's theory-making and analyses; it assumes that women have no real place in the structural hierarchy which orders privilege (and which needs to be reconfigured anyway, so maybe it's unsafe to let women in, just in case women start moving the furniture or throwing it out and buying new furniture); and it assumes that the content of women's thinking misrepresents and distorts 'reality' (whatever that is). This is not to say that women cannot and do not enact a similar politics (because we do, often on the basis of class and 'race').

In all of this, I am assuming the legitimacy of sex/gender politics and theory. Iris Marion Young argues for the necessity of understanding women as a social collective (Young 1994: 719). The relevance of her argument to the case presented in this book is clear not only from the perspective of the elites represented at the conference in which I participated, but to women who are made small and diminished by the supervening power structures which dominate this world we all live in. My hope is that these are some of the issues which this book either implicitly or explicitly addresses.

I honour Luce Irigaray by deferring to her preference to be called 'Luce Irigaray' (Hirsch and Olsen 1996: 5).

Acknowledgements

I thank the following for their support, assistance and loving kindness before and during the process of writing this book:

First, my wonderful children, Timothy, Alister and Madeleine, now adults, whose presence in my life has always given me a reason to live. Then, my partner, Peter, who is a gracious, loving and amazingly compassionate and tolerant man. Then, Susan Rowland, whose generosity of spirit and intellectual courage I truly and deeply admire. Then, Lesley McLean, graduate student, heart of gold and wonderful mind, who has read, and been enthusiastic above and beyond the call of duty about, this work. Then, Leslie Gardner for her encouragement and insight.

I would also like to thank Jay Garfield and the Smith College Colloquium for hosting me in 2003 when this work was beginning; Colin Hearfield for his good-heartedness and excellent editing skills; Peter Forrest and Drew Khlentzos, my colleagues at the University of New England, for their thoughtful comments on various chapters; Gina Garrett for her hospitality in London; Paul Bishop for his advice in a translation matter; and the former Burwood High School Library (Victoria, Australia) for having in its collection a biography of Jung which I read in about 1963 and which was my first exposure to his work.

And my cat, the hirsute Jung, for finding me, and for sitting on my lap and purring as if he is experiencing perfect bliss.

I would like to thank the editorial and production teams at Routledge, especially Kate Hawes, Jane Harris and Dawn Harris, the copy-editor Sue Dickinson for their care and attention in the preparation of this manuscript for publication, and Routledge's anonymous readers for their critical and constructive reviews of my manuscript.

Thank you all.

Introduction

LOOKING FOR RECOGNITION

> But equally, just as the individual is not merely a unique and separate being, but is also a social being, so the human psyche is a not self-contained and wholly individual phenomenon, but also a collective one.
>
> (Jung 1966: 147)

> How to articulate singularity and community?
>
> (Irigaray 2002: 13)

> The bud disappears in the bursting-forth of the blossom, and one might say that the former is refuted by the latter; similarly, when the fruit appears, the blossom is shown up in its turn as a false manifestation of the plant, and the fruit now emerges as the truth of it instead. These forms are not just distinguished from one another, they also supplant one another as mutually incompatible. Yet at the same time their fluid nature makes them moments of an organic unity in which they not only do not conflict, but in which each is as necessary as the other; and this mutual necessity alone constitutes the life of the whole.
>
> (Hegel 1977: 2)

In this book I develop some connections between the philosophical and psychological work broadly conceived of as both writing and practice, of Carl Gustav Jung and Luce Irigaray. I argue, although with modification, that there is a relationship between the two thinkers which can be thought of in terms of G. W. Hegel's Dialectic of Lord/Bondsman (or Master/Slave, as it is more popularly known).[1] The struggle for recognition found in the Master/Slave Dialectic is triply enacted by Jung and Luce Irigaray. First, it is enacted in and through Jung's notion of inferior and superior functions and 'characters' of the psyche, and the quest for self-identity which ensues. Secondly, we find the struggle for recognition in Luce Irigaray's radical critique of the foundational assumptions of Western philosophy and psychoanalysis. And thirdly, we see it when we compare them as, on the one hand, representative thinkers of a master masculine paternal symbolic (Jung), and on the other, the mimetic voice protesting the alleged creation and dependency of her identity or subjectivity through that master masculine paternal symbolic (Luce Irigaray).

It is clear that Jung's articulation of superior and inferior seen in his characterisation of, for example, anima/animus, introversion/extraversion, *puer aeternus*/wise old man embraces the twin ideas of recognition and struggle that we find in the Master/Slave encounter. Likewise, Luce Irigaray's re-writing of Plato, Sigmund Freud, Friedrich Nietzsche, Maurice Merleau-Ponty and Emmanuel Levinas among others, as she carefully dismantles what she argues is their methodologically masculine bias, announces her challenge to the hegemony of the masculine paternal. That challenge, then, is seen in the struggle for feminine individuation over and against the masculine, a struggle which calls for a recognition of masculine and feminine ontological difference.

We can construct a conversation between the two thinkers on this latter account, even though it is not one in which either has intentionally engaged. Rather, it is a conversation that arises because of the teleological nature of individuation common to both Jung and Luce Irigaray. Individuation aims at completion and wholeness of an individual self or subject once certain conditions, figured out by a subject, are met. Those conditions include assessing and then addressing one's own status as the subject of individuation: one is led to the individuating process by life's circumstances, by the need to identify oneself as an individual self distinct from one's life involvements. Jung's writings are replete with references to this process, its origins and effects.[2] For Luce Irigaray, whose work I interpret as offering a process through which women can become individuated, individuation is not simply a matter of conforming to the demands of some pre-set pattern exhibited in a neutral symbolic. Rather it means a radical reinterpretation and appraisal of that symbolic, its structure and contents. Her work extends beyond the individual, subjective level and takes account, directly, of the masculine nature of the social collective seen as the material expression of the symbolic. Thus individuation for women involves producing a feminine symbolic ontologically distinct from the masculine symbolic. Such a symbolic would evolve out of the struggle for recognition of feminine difference and can, therefore, be seen as a social collectivist instantiation of individuation. Luce Irigaray's work echoes Jung's own commitment to collective individuation in his critique of, for example, National Socialism. The need to dis-identify from mass-rule and mass-mentality, which commits a whole people to a path of self-destruction, became an important consideration for Jung (Jung 1968a: 97; 1966: 260ff). This is not only a matter between individual and collective, however; it is also a matter for the health and welfare of a whole group.

The foundations for a potential conversation between Jung and Luce Irigaray can be located in a careful examination and comparison of their respective commitments to both the intra- and intersubjective, the struggle for recognition and the role sex/gender plays. My book is an initiatory site of this conversation: it brings the conversation into being and then mediates it through exploration of philosophical orientations germane to their theorising.

Before we go any further, let us take a brief look at the Master/Slave Dialectic as reminder of – or perhaps an introduction to – what is at stake here in my use of it. We should be aware that my reading of Hegel is not Wolfgang Giegerich's. His claim that the 'dialectical process does not begin with Two, but with One, with a *Position*. There is no opposition to this position, no alternatives, no "dynamic relationship"' (Giegerich 2005: 5) is not how Hegel constructs the Master/Slave Dialectic, as we shall see. That there is a 'position' might be the case. Giegerich seems to envision the (original) position as a stand taken by the mind, out of which the possibility of an alternative arises because the position proves to be untenable (so the original position A engenders non-A) which in turn is negated (non(non-A)) and so on (Giegerich 2005: 6). Thus, in his view, dialectic is a series of negations of an original position.[3] This, indeed, is a version of dialectic but it is not faithful to Hegel's Master/Slave. Further, Giegerich's privileging of One (the Position) iterates Luce Irigaray's claim that the masculine valorises an Economy of the Same in which the Phallus is the primary signifier, a claim I explore in Chapters 4, 5 and 6.

On the other hand, Giegerich's contention that dialectic, read as thesis–antithesis–synthesis is '(a) historically and philologically speaking not Hegelian, (b) in itself mindless, mechanical, unthinking and (c) views what it calls thesis and antithesis, from outside, like objects that need to be reconciled or united' (Giegerich 2005: 4) does seem to capture something of the 'popular' view of dialectic. But that it is popular does not entail (b) and (c) as a version of dialectic. I make these comments in passing, and return to the notion of dialectic in Chapter 2.

HEGEL'S MASTER/SLAVE DIALECTIC

Hegel argues in *Phenomenology of Spirit* that human consciousness cannot exist in and of itself. Consciousness, as self-consciousness, can exist only through another and that other is also a self-consciousness (which also exists because of an other). In other words, he argues that self-consciousness is relational. He contends that '[s]elf-consciousness exists in and for itself when, and by the fact that it so exists for another; that is, it exists only in being acknowledged . . . Self-consciousness is faced by another self-consciousness; it has *come out of itself*' (Hegel 1977: 178–9). In coming out of itself, self-consciousness, a property only of living and human beings, finds its identity in another whom it needs to recognise as recognising it. Self-consciousness moves between another self-consciousness and itself, as it affirms its own being.

Hegel describes this as a process of loss and supersession: in finding itself in an other, self-consciousness moves out of itself but it also has to overcome or to supersede the other in order to see its own self (Hegel 1977: 179). The bi-conditionality of human self-consciousness emerges in self-consciousness' ontological dependency on the play of difference expressed in two-ness and mutuality. Hegel argues that each self-consciousness in the moment of mutual recognition is 'equally independent and self-contained, and there is nothing in it of which it is not itself the origin' (Hegel 1977: 182). Because each self-consciousness is independent (yet, paradoxically, *inter*-dependent), it cannot use the other as an object of its desire: each mirrors the other and any action on the part of one is an action on the part of the other. Each self-consciousness preserves itself and the other in its respective action, while at the same time acting as one. Hegel refers to this as the double movement of self-consciousness: it is itself through another yet is not the other even in the exact imitation of the other.

To begin with, being-for-self as an individual must negate the other, the object whom it does not see as essential to its own being. But since the other is also a self-consciousness, the two 'are for one another like ordinary objects, *independent* shapes, individuals submerged in the being [or immediacy] of *Life* – for the object in its immediacy is here determined as Life'. Each self-consciousness needs to become certain of the truth of itself but this occurs only when it is certain of the other. The 'pure abstraction' of being-for-self is achieved only when 'each is for the other what the other is for it' through the total complementarity seen 'only when each i[s] its own self through its own action and again through the action of the other' (Hegel 1977: 186). Self-consciousness realises itself as an independent individual only when it can see itself as ontologically distinct from the other (self-consciousness). At some point, though, the action of the other means that each will begin to seek the death of the other and a life-and-death struggle will develop. Hegel maintains that the truth and self-certainty that is supposed to arise from this struggle results in the realisation that 'life is as essential to it as pure self-consciousness' (Hegel 1977: 189) and the struggle ends up in the disruption of the original mutuality. This is superseded by an inequality and opposition, expressed in a new relationship of an independent consciousness – the Master – and a dependent consciousness – the Slave.

The relationship between the Master and the Slave becomes mediated by something external to each. The Slave works for the Master. The Master does not work, but relates to the Slave through the objects produced by the Slave's work. The objects produced by work are what the Master desires and has power over. The Slave as worker, who produces what the Master desires, is now constructed as other. The Slave is held in subjection by the Master. Thus the Slave works and the Master enjoys the fruits of that work, but it is the Slave who mediates the Master's desire for the objects which emerge from the work done. In this process the Master comes to 'achieve his recognition through another consciousness', to become dependent and not to achieve the truth of self-certainty. It is the Slave who, through his direct relationship with the object, achieves the truth of his own self-certainty. Ultimately then, the consciousness of the Master 'as a consciousness forced back into itself . . . will withdraw into itself and be transformed into a truly independent consciousness' (Hegel 1977: 193). The dynamics of the Dialectic recommence once more.

There are many interpretations and criticisms of this Dialectic. Jacques Lacan, for example, interpolates *jouissance* into the life-and-death struggle and argues that the Slave chooses work as *jouissance* rather than death. He also takes Hegel to task for assigning no place to the unconscious, since Hegel focuses, instead, on self-consciousness.[4] Tom Rockmore maintains that, although Thomas Hobbes had pre-empted Hegel in pointing out our social interdependence, from Hobbes' perspective this was on account of our need for protection, and not for recognition as it is in Hegel. Rockmore also underscores the importance of Hegel to Marx in terms of the value Hegel places on work.[5] Initially, my triple figuration of Jung and Luce Irigaray shadows some of the debate about the meaning of the Master/Slave Dialectic which, I take it, is to be read at the level of metaphor. The metaphorical nature of the Master/Slave Dialectic is partly responsible for its polysemous nature. For now, I propose that it can be read, metaphorically, as an account of the internal processes of the psyche thought of as both conscious and unconscious, in spite of Lacan's claims with which I shall also deal; it can also be read as an account of the relationship between an individual and her social group. Thirdly, as an account of the material conditions of the socio-political sphere between social groups, it has been seen by Marxists, for example, as a proper characterisation of class relations between worker and bourgeoisie.[6] On any reading, the struggle for recognition is central. Indeed, we are all aware of our need for recognition in its many forms: as children, students, workers, lovers, business partners, and so on. Who does the recognising and why opens up the question of the power relations in which we become involved.

From a clinical perspective, our initial recognition of own problems or issues is the impetus for our seeking a solution, so that we can become happier, more balanced, less aggressive, more creative, less tied to old forms of being and doing, or whatever it is that we need in order that we might become more whole human beings. A skilled, insightful practitioner who can recognise our needs, who can recognise our situation, *who can recognise us as we are now and as we might be*, can be the catalyst for the adventure intrinsic to the individuating process. Jung seemed to be particularly skilled at this, at the vocation of recogniser. But because we place ourselves in the clinician's care, we become, in a sense supplicants: we acknowledge our fragility and, in doing so, we acknowledge the insight of the person to whom we commit ourselves for care – we acknowledge the explicit power relation in this situation, here, now. The object with which we are concerned is our very own psyche. Because of the relationship we embark on with the clinician, we go out of ourselves and begin to see ourselves through her/his eyes. We work on the object that is ourselves. We mediate our own psyches, choosing what work to do, but concurrently attending to the wisdom of the clinician whose desire it is that we find ourselves in the objectification of ourselves: in speaking, in writing, in painting, in our exposed imaginations. We see ourselves anew as we go out and then return, as we mark the moments of ourselves that once were and are now superseded. The life/death struggle is generated in the room that becomes a confessional where we seek absolution and affirmation, simultaneously. Ultimately, we need to untie ourselves from the clinical situation, both for ourselves and the clinician, who cannot be tied to the work we do. A hiatus is created where we both turn our backs and retreat; in this, we each achieve aspects of our own individuation, freed from each other, yet bearing the imprints of the struggle and its resolution. In all of this, we have had to relinquish some aspect of who we are in this power dynamic: unless we do that, the process fails.

The Master/Slave Dialectic gives us pause to meditate on what it is that we do in this clinical situation, or in any situation that requires an openness to an other. It suggests a means by which we are called to heightened self-awareness and to radical self-critique as either Master or Slave. So while my characterisation of the clinical situation might seem Utopian, it nonetheless sketches the possibilities for embodied understanding of the Dialectic. I have more to say about dialectic, albeit in an alternative form, in Chapter 2.

The struggle of the psyche within itself seen in the tension between conscience and desire, between the ego and the self, between the conscious and the unconscious, for example, can be seen as instances of the Master/Slave Dialectic in the intra-psychic domain. The intersubjective should be thought of in two ways: between individual subject and individual subject, and between individual subject and collective. The former covers our day-to-day relationships but includes, as a special case, the relationship between therapist or clinician and patient, extending to the notion of transference. The latter is illustrated in the struggle of the psyche to define itself over and against its collective(s). We should note that both the intra- and inter-psychic are aspects of the process of individuation.

Because I take the view that groupness or collectivity pre-exists the individual, the kind of account I give of the intersubjective will have important ramifications for the intra-subjective, for the development and growth of the psyche. I argue that Jung and Luce Irigaray also hold that the collective is the ground of being for the individual. However, Luce Irigaray's insistence on the importance of the sex/gendered body brings a fresh perspective to the debate. Just as Jung maintains that a 'fundamental change of attitude (*metanoia*) is required, a real recognition of the whole man' (Jung 1970: 719) if there is to be an increased valuation of the individual, so a fundamental change in attitude to what has been seen as sex/gender neutral theory is argued for by Luce Irigaray if there is to be an increased valuation, indeed a *re-valuation* of woman. I argue that Luce Irigaray's work picks up Hegel's identification of the submersion in Life of the being of the object, where the two self-consciousnesses 'are, *for each other*, shapes of consciousness' (Hegel 1977: 186) and that this moment reflects the registering of the sex/gendered body. The recognition of similarity that accompanies the recognition of sex/gender is, simultaneously for human self-consciousness, the recognition of difference.

PSYCHO-SOCIAL RAMIFICATIONS OF THE MASTER/ SLAVE DIALECTIC

My argument in this book does not start and finish as a philosophical position relevant only to a metaphysical understanding of the psyche. For Jung and Luce Irigaray, the relationship between individual and her/his collective origins is the background and the impetus for individuation; and that the process of individuation is an instance of the dialectical struggle for recognition. This is not, of course, simply a matter for philosophical speculation. There are, as I suggested earlier, social and clinical ramifications of the philosophical argument because Hegel's position can be seen as a description of 'the way things are' for all of us. If it is the case that self-consciousness develops and positions itself in the Life-world in the way Hegel suggests, then our experience of both ourselves and others, and of Life, is fundamentally dialectical, involving loss and supersession. The notion of recognition embraces affirmation and denial, acknowledgement, the gaze of the other. This fluid engagement of self-consciousnesses traces the dynamics of interpersonal, personal/social and intersocial relationship as our original condition: we are always already in the world, in social relation, and this has a profound existential impact on us. As a consequence, we can better grasp the importance of heightening our awareness of the Dialectic which subtends the binary nature of human being.

To this end, we might consider Jung's deliberations on the nature of the psychology of complex phenomena. The description he develops here is an almost perfect mapping of Master/Slave. 'And once the complexity has reached that of the empirical man, his psychology inevitably merges with the psychic process itself. It can no longer be distinguished from the latter and so turns into it. But the effect of this is that the process attains consciousness' (Jung 1969: 429). Methodologically, we find Jung employing the language of Master/Slave either consciously or not, even when he sees in Hegel the final downfall of reason and 'the European mind' (Jung 1969: 353).

Further examples will throw even more light on this. At personal/social and interpersonal levels, the Master/Slave Dialectic provides a cogent means by which we might understand the concept of projection. In going out of itself, we can see that self-consciousness as a mode of psyche collapses the boundaries between itself and the other so that it can eventually return to itself. This generates a moment of insight that in turn creates the need for survival and re-formation: self-consciousness achieves identity through dissolving the projection: its going out of itself. This is precisely the movement Jung describes in his analysis of projection, as we shall see in Chapter 3. Furthermore, we can reflect, as I did before, on the idea that therapist and patient are involved in a dialectical relationship in which recognition of the subjectivity of each is crucial. Jung's own analysis of transference is testament to this. Lastly, Luce Irigaray's demands for a feminine symbolic can be seen as a moment when the Slave realises her own self-certain truth, that her identity need not be conceived through the identity of her work for the Master, that she is independent. This is a moment that is couched in terms of recognition on the part not only of the Slave, but also of the Master. If we take Luce Irigaray's critique seriously, then both the social/material and clinical implications are very clear: a radical reconfiguration of how we live is in order. Such a reconfiguration cannot, however, be merely lip-service. Something of the power of the Master must be ceded. In my view, this remains work in progress to this date. I explore this theme fully in Chapters 4, 5 and 6.

Subtending the arguments of my book is the idea of difference and how it might be dealt with in relation to individuation. Both Jung and Luce Irigaray's work reveals a preoccupation with difference. Specifically, each is concerned with the role that paired contraries like male and female, masculine and feminine, man and woman, play in the creation of, and ground, our symbolic systems. Such symbolics both influence and construct, and are influenced and constructed by, personal human identity. Individual human agents do indeed affect the identities and operations of collectives (think of national leaders like Gandhi, Joseph Stalin or Pol Pot, and of Sigmund Freud and Carl Jung). Even so, these identities are themselves formed within overlapping socio-cultural contexts that sit in even larger, more elaborate overlapping collective frameworks.

Hegel's Master/Slave Dialectic assumes difference as a founding moment of identity, and the expression of that is desire. Since self-consciousness requires the recognition of an other who is not itself, that other must be different from it. Hence an axiological dimension of difference can be seen in the Master/Slave Dialectic. Difference is configured through various relations of domination and subordination, and privilege at an inter-psychic and intra-psychic level in relation to individuation. I develop these themes in greater detail in Chapter 5 in particular.

COLLECTIVE BEING AND THE INDIVIDUAL

As I noted earlier, both Carl Jung and Luce Irigaray hold that the groupness of social being pre-exists individual existence: one becomes a self within a lived-in collective and because of that lived-in collective: this is a profoundly important aspect of the processes of becoming a self or a reflective human being who is aware of her/his subjectivity. Becoming a self is a process undertaken at first without knowledge and with limited, embryonic choice. The moral and cognitive growth of the individual at some point takes a reflective turn such that it is possible for the growing self to examine critically her/his life, her/his lived-in collective and collectives other than her/his own. It is then that consciousness might become deepened and more aware; it is also then that the self might realise the degree to which she/he is engaged with processes and events and histories of which she/he is not at all conscious, but which make their presence felt in her/his life.

The relationship between self and lived-in collective is compounded in its complexity when we consider where the self begins and ends, where lived-in collective begins and ends. For it appears that one can identify an apparently private and isolatable aspect or aspects of oneself, which can take a moral and cognitive stand distinct from the domination of the lived-in collective.[7] If one takes such a stand then this means that the trajectory set for a collective member by her/his community is interrupted and questions are raised about the member's being in the collective. Some of those questions have to do with the member's own authenticity, with their integrity and autonomy. These moments of often radical doubt and re-evaluation are the first conscious steps in the individuation process. They are also issues that are fundamental in the thinking of Carl Jung and Luce Irigaray in their articulation of individuation. The Master/Slave Dialectic can help to explain these critical moments from either a Jungian or an Irigarayean perspective because it suggests how important recognition is to the achievement of psychological independence. An unindividuated psyche is a psyche dependent on objects external to it and over which it has difficulty in attaining control. For instance, the pull of the collective mass and its material enticements (as Jung would have it) will bind a collective member to her/his collective as if she is indistinguishable from the mass collective. Or, as Luce Irigaray would have it, where the feminine remains identified with the masculine symbolic, there is no freedom.

Our original state, then, is as a member of a collective, a state in which we are minimally individual and from which we become individuated. This might be compared with Hegel's idea that at the beginning, being-for-self is an individual. We have a specific physical uniqueness at birth which does not guarantee psychological uniqueness. (We can imagine a world in which there are physically unique bodies who 'share' a common psyche.) Although it seems obvious in some ways, the acceptance of our collective origins can be difficult to get our heads around. If our origins are in the collective, how can we ever be independent in any plausible sense? How can we achieve the recognition that is needed to attain the self-certain truth of our being, and what does that mean anyway? These questions are not entirely theoretical. Indeed, they are questions with huge existential import and Jung's analytical psychology has provided practical means by which answers can be found. That is the work of analysis. So if we look at Jung's 'Study in the Process of Individuation' (1968a) we find the existential process that is individuation illustrated by his patient, with his accompanying descriptive analysis. The Master/Slave Dialectic is detectable at different points throughout Jung's analysis.[8]

What will count as Master and what as Slave is contentious. The unconscious, in demanding to be integrated into consciousness, the resistance of the conscious subject, the effort of the unconscious to 'catch up' with consciousness, blurs the boundaries between Master and Slave. Yet the Life/Death struggle that is explicit in the Dialectic is explicit in Jung's assessment: 'How can consciousness, our most recent acquisition, which has bounded ahead, be linked again with the oldest, the unconscious, which has lagged behind? The oldest of all is the instinctual foundation. Anyone who overlooks the instincts will be ambuscaded by them, and anyone who does not humble himself will be humbled, losing at the same time his freedom, his most precious possession' (Jung 1968a: 620). The *kind* of analysis developed by Jung assumes the actuality of the collective and the possibility of genuine individuation. His and, to this day, our recognition of this struggle finds its home in the Master/Slave Dialectic. I explore these ideas more fully in Chapter 3 when I look at the issue of projection.

It also seems to be the case that collectivity – the group-ness of social being – is seen as contrary to the individualism proclaimed by liberal democratic societies. Recent legislation in Australia which focuses on workplace reform, for example, is aimed at reducing the potential for collective bargaining by unions; the term 'union' has been reinscribed by the current government to suggest that somehow 'union' and the notion of the industrial outlaw go hand in hand. To that end, student unions, the site of activism, social opportunities and student services like second-hand bookshops, have been forced out of existence through federal legislation. Such anti-collectivism reflects, in part, our unwillingness to accept the fact of our collective origins. Yet, as I am arguing, collectivity as the condition of human being is, paradoxically, the condition of individuation, of becoming an individual. One cannot become an individual without being a member of a collective, or, indeed, of multiple collectives. This extends beyond the realm of the conscious and is captured beautifully in Jung's notion of the collective unconscious.

We should be aware that the process of individuation entails an ethics or practices, habits, attitudes and values that promote the good in terms of human development and flourishing. That 'ethics of individuation' in turn entails considered engagement with oneself and with the lived-in collectives: the communities or groups with which one is concerned and with which one shares concerns. For this reason, the ethics of individuation involves the development of a political awareness which exceeds the narrow concerns of an individual subject or self, terms which I use more or less interchangeably in this book.

We do need to note at this point that talk of the self has been partly eclipsed by talk of the subject in recent theory, especially through the work of Foucault. A self may be both subject *of* and subject *to*. 'Subject *to*' evokes one's situatedness in a way that 'subject *of*' does not. One is subject to the laws, practices and social constraints and liberties of one's communities. Classical statements about the self such as those found in Descartes' *res cogitans* (the notion that one is primarily a thinking thing and that thinking is the essence of being human) do not put the self in this kind of context: the self is introspected, a subject turned inwards on itself, distinct from any external engagement, and thinking. This is a limited view of self which reduces self to psychological properties. But, as we shall see in Chapter 1, even the self as introspected is subject to the unconscious and this is clearly demonstrated in dreaming.

The idea that the self is situated, which we saw, initially, in Hegel's setting of self-consciousness in Life, creates a space for reflection about my proposed conversation between Jung and Luce Irigaray. This conversation is not unjustified even though one might raise an eyebrow at the coupling of these two thinkers. Yet the coincidences of their own lived experiences, their foci on the feminine and the masculine as ontologically separable, their commitments to questions of religion and their interests in Eastern philosophies make them, oddly enough, complementary theorists and practitioners.

Carl Jung was a man of the nineteenth century as much as the twentieth, the founder of analytic psychology, Swiss, a one-time colleague of Sigmund Freud. Luce Irigaray is a woman of the twentieth century and now the twenty-first, a psychoanalyst in the Freud–Lacan lineage, Belgian, a student of Freudian and post-Freudian theory. These facts serve to distinguish as well as to connect the two. But there are further connections in their appreciation and use of philosophy and, indeed, Plato and Nietzsche have deeply influenced each thinker. Luce Irigaray's use of Maurice Merleau-Ponty and Emmanuel Levinas as points of departure for her writing on the flesh and ethics distinguishes her idiosyncratic refiguring of some of the fundamentals of philosophy, the place of woman being central in these ruminations. She is sceptical about the possibilities that are offered for either men or women if the insistence on the neutrality of the symbolic is maintained. Jung does not engage in any discussion of sex/gender neutrality: why would he? His is a Master status in relation to his work and the community of analytical psychologists and as a world figure in the later part of his life. But much of this is superficial comparison and contrast. The conversation I envisage assumes this territory, but it also relies on the mobilisation of Jung's and Luce Irigaray's resolve to draw attention to the importance of the masculine and the feminine in theorising the psyche.

It is apparent, for example, that Jung gives a voice to the feminine. But he is in a long tradition in which the feminine voice and the voice of women is ridiculed and trivialised. As we shall see, this is the case for Plato but Plato is just one of many Masters who cannot abide the voice of their female Slaves. Jung was very familiar with Arthur Schopenhauer and cites him with approbation in many places, especially in his discussions of the Will.[9] Yet Schopenhauer's views on woman are notorious and Jung, unfortunately, echoes enough of Schopenhauer's misogyny to make it worthy of comment. But Jung, as we shall see, is ambivalent about both the feminine and woman. Even so, Schopenhauer remarks that '[o]ne needs only to see the way she is built to realize that woman is not intended for great mental or for physical labour . . . Women are suited to being the nurses and teachers of our earliest childhood precisely because they themselves are childish, silly and short-sighted, in a word, big children, their whole lives long . . . Thus it lies in the nature of women to regard everything simply as a means of capturing a man, and their interest in anything else is only simulated, is no more than a detour, i.e. amounts to coquetry and mimicry' (Schopenhauer 1972: 80–6). Compare this with Jung's claim that 'It is woman's outstanding characteristic that she can do anything for the love of a man' (Jung 1970: 243) and '[i]n the place of parents woman now takes up her position as the most immediate environmental influence in the life of the adult man . . . She is not of a superior order, either by virtue of age, authority or physical strength' (Jung 1966: 296). I am not claiming that Jung was directly influenced by Schopenhauer in respect of these views, nor that their views were identical. But as with many of Jung's ideas, it is easy to see evidence of its prior articulation in the work of his predecessors. The value of women and the feminine has had a bad press for millennia and there is no reason to suppose that Jung's socialisation would escape cultural and historical bias; I take up some of these issues more thoroughly in Chapter 1.

In his review of Henri Ellenberger's *The Discovery of the Unconscious*, an exploration of the origins of the development of theories about the unconscious, John C. Burnham advises users of Ellenberger's book 'not to accept without grave reservation any assertion that a particular thinker influenced any other thinker unless this is based upon hard, specific evidence;

otherwise the relation is probably logical rather than actual' (Burnham 1971: 528). The distinction between 'actual' and 'logical' is curious. But I take it to mean that there is an actual relation where a thinker is explicitly influenced by someone's ideas from an earlier time (as Plato was by Socrates); and a logical relation where one can trace the development and perhaps the origin of an idea or set of ideas because of what those ideas look like (as there is between Hebrew/Christian Common Testament conception of the Creator God and the Hindu conception of Brahma). We can further distinguish between direct influence when an idea is actually attributed by one theorist to another, and indirect influence where some ideas prevail over others and are dominant and popular and are in general use. (Who 'invented' the idea of social constructionism so prevalent, dominant and popular in our current climate?) We might bear this in mind when we consider what influenced Jung's attitudes to women and the feminine and, more broadly, what influenced some of his key ideas such as the archetypes and the collective unconscious.

Jung acknowledges many thinkers in his work either through affirming their stances or rejecting them (he regards Hegel, for instance, as a dangerous threat to reason and to Germany) (Jung 1969: 358–9). We can see in Jung a thinker who sifts through 'positions' and takes from them what is agreeable to him, and leaves what is not. But sometimes Jung is not very specific about the origin of his ideas and maybe that does not matter all that much. In the first place ideas then, as now, would have been in general circulation. So who first thought of a particular idea might not have been known and attribution of origins might not have been considered important at any rate. If we think about the nature of Jung's audience, he may well have assumed that it was unnecessary always to identify where an idea came from: perhaps the ascription of authorship of an idea is more important to our contemporary audience, an audience informed by ideals of liberal individualism, than it has been in the past. But sometimes Jung is very specific. We might think about these points in light of Ellenberger's concerns with the genesis of psychological concepts and German Romanticism.

Ellenberger attributes the origin of the anima/animus distinction to the German Romantic concept *Urphänomen* (primordial phenomena), specifically to the myth of the original human nature, the androgyne that is found in Plato's *Symposium*. Ellenberger also argues that *Urphänomen* 'not only reappears in Jung's work under the name "Archetype," but is also found in Freud's as well' (Ellenberger 1970: 203–4). And Ellenberger also notes that along with the idea of the unconscious, 'there is hardly a single concept of Freud or Jung that had not been anticipated by the philosophy of nature and Romantic medicine' (Ellenberger 1970: 205). Gottfried Leibniz, Gustav Fechner, Theodor Lipps, Friedrich Schelling, Gotthilf von Schubert, C. G. Carus, Ignaz Troxler, Eduard von Hartmann and Arthur

Schopenhauer are all listed as possible sources of Jung's ideas. But it seems to me that Jung is careful to acknowledge these early articulations of the unconscious.[10]

What can we make of all of this? Only that Jung needs to be seen in a theoretical context which was deeply philosophical in which he situated himself and that clearly was very influential in the development of his thinking – and which he acknowledges up to a point. He asserts that 'Leibniz, Kant and Schelling had already pointed to the problem of the dark side of the psyche . . . [but] it was a physician who felt impelled, from his scientific and medical experience, to point to the *unconscious* as the essential basis of the psyche'. The two men to whom he then refers are C. G. Carus and Eduard von Hartmann. Interestingly, he claims that medical psychology as it developed 'approached the problem of the unconscious without philosophical preconceptions' (Jung 1968a: 259). I wonder whether Jung actually believed this? Or was Jung here attempting to address the issues that, for him, framed the idea of analytical psychology as an empirical science distinct from philosophy? After all, who is immune to philosophical preconceptions?

I maintain throughout this book that psychology *in general* owes much to philosophy: in a sense, philosophers were the earliest psychologists: they dealt in matters of the soul, the mind, the spirit and they were later joined by theologians; and that today, all of us are still influenced by the philosophies of the past which live on into today, as well as by new philosophies. We need also to think about these points in relation to what a thinker *does* with an idea. Here Jung shines. He had the opportunity, the insight and genius to *apply* what he came across as he read and studied, observed, listened and reflected and learnt from his patients and the empirical data he developed. Jung's claim that he was an empiricist and not a philosopher, about which I have more to say later, signals his belief that he was practising a science of the psyche, a science embedded in philosophical speculation and early attempts to heal the psyche.[11]

The story of Luce Irigaray is very different. She wants to be identified as a philosopher and complains that her work is misinterpreted because its philosophical core is ignored by many scholars, a complaint I return to in Chapter 5 (Hirsh and Olsen 1996: 2). As a student of Jacques Lacan, thus of Freud, Luce Irigaray's intellectual heritage is in the psychoanalytical tradition. The voice she wants to give to the feminine is an ironic re-reading of the kind of voice we find in Jung's anima.

Luce Irigaray recognises that women's position in relation to the symbolic and thus the unconscious is not irrevocable. For her, the symbolic/imaginary is mutable and is historically produced and situated (Irigaray 1991b: 38). That the symbolic is masculine, one of her important claims, is therefore a contingent matter and open to change. But a *change* in the symbolic/imaginary order is *not* what Luce Irigaray wants: she wants difference and ontological difference at that. Without a speaking voice, without a gender of a specific sexuate-ontological kind, ontological difference is not possible for women. So Luce Irigaray does not want to introduce sexual difference into the masculine symbolic, but she wants to use the masculine symbolic to create an *alternative* feminine-feminine symbolic, *a symbolic other than, different from the masculine symbolic.* She wants women to have a *genre.*[12] She argues that there is no neutral symbolic which could be ruptured by the introduction of feminine difference.[13] Indeed, hers is an anti-Platonic view that does not presuppose the existence of an *a priori* collective unconscious and Forms or archetypes. She does not posit the symbolic/imaginary in these terms. Her view is discordant with Jung's notion of the collective unconscious even though there is significant overlap between collective unconscious and symbolic/imaginary.[14] Claims about *change* in the masculine symbolic are understandable given that feminine difference already exists.

Luce Irigaray argues that feminine difference is really a mode of masculine sameness, since its source is the economy or the logic of the Same. The operation of a reductionist logic in which one-ness is not only privileged, but appropriates the very possibility of difference, frames and gives substance to the feminine (Irigaray 1985b: 74). On Luce Irigaray's understanding, acknowledgement of difference in being is partly a matter of re-visioning women (and we women must do that for ourselves). Re-visioning has its origins in the subversion and dissipation of the logic/economy of the Same, and the job of mimesis is to assist women in this process. But difference is not straightforwardly decidable – it is a polemical matter.

For her, women and the feminine are opposed to the original position we saw expressed in Giegerich's analysis of Hegelian dialectic; the feminine and woman are constructs of a dominant symbolic system in which they are subservient and through which their identities are constituted. Women, in her view, have no voice of their own making. Her re-reading of the major figures of the psychoanalytical tradition (Freud and Lacan) appropriates and then inverts their claims. *Speculum of the Other Woman*, for example, contains a long and complex study of Freud's analysis of feminine sexuality (Irigaray 1985a: 11–146). In other words, she interrogates the basic assumptions of psychoanalysis which, she maintains, are unremittingly masculine, but she nonetheless uses psychoanalysis as, for her, it has a compelling explanatory power when it comes to understanding 'patriarchal forms of subjectivity' (Grosz 1990a: 169). As we shall see, she uses language as a tool of disruption, that is to say, mimetically, to connote the male construction of women and their feminine identity. 'Her assault on patriarchal language consists in showing that those discourses which present themselves as universal and neutral, appropriate to all, are in fact produced and maintained according to male interests. In questioning this neutrality,

Irigaray poses the question of sexual enunciation: of who speaks, for whom and with what interests' (Grosz 1990a: 177). Luce Irigaray, like Julia Kristeva, who is also a psychoanalyst, takes Lacan (and through him, Freud) as her starting point and from this perspective these two theorists can be aligned. It must be stressed, though, that they are opposed in the way in which they read and interpret Lacan, as Grosz points out (Grosz 1990a: 149). Lacan proves to be an important link not only between Luce Irigaray and Kristeva, but also between Luce Irigaray and Jung. How is this so?

Grosz argues that 'Lacan's work also helped to introduce questions about sexuality to legitimized academic and political discourses . . . Lacan inserts the question of sexuality into the centre of all models of social and psychical functioning. To be a subject or "I" at all, the subject must take up a sexualised position, identifying with the attributes socially designated as appropriate for men or women'. Grosz also notes that Foucault, too, had raised this issue (Grosz 1990a: 148). In my view, Jung's work pre-empted both Lacan and Foucault when he articulated the importance of the persona and then the anima/animus distinction, as we shall see in Chapter 3. In any case, Jung's reading of sex/gender seems to be a reiteration of Plato's view of the gendered nature of the soul, as we shall see. It was already there in philosophical and analytical psychological work, well before Lacan's pronouncements. This was also the case with a similar claim made by Grosz that 'Lacan denounces the illusory mastery, unity and self-knowledge that the subject, as a self-consciousness, accords itself. For him, consciousness is continually betrayed by the evasion typical of the unconscious' (Grosz 1990a: 148). We find in Jung's work frequent references to the subjectivising disposition of the unconscious over consciousness.[15]

While these comments about Lacan might seem like quibbling (especially in light of what I was arguing earlier), I think there is something more at stake here: that is, that Jung has been systematically overlooked in 'legitimate' academic and political discourses. His work has been trivialised as unworthy of serious academic consideration, the less worthy brother of Sigmund Feud. Debates, and there are many of them, about their split often 'side' with Freud as if there is no 'case' to be put for Jung.[16] Because of Jung's interest in religion, mysticism, occultism, synchronicity and alchemy, he has been seen as a crank.[17] The attribution to Lacan of views about the sex/gendered nature of the psyche already proposed by Jung is worrying even when, from a methodological perspective, Lacan's analysis focuses on language. The fact is that Jung had already, in his account of anima/animus, introduced the idea of identification with a compulsory sexualised position in society and, indeed, this forms the basis of the work he did on individuation, as we shall later see.

Luce Irigaray does not come to the question of sex/gender through Jung but through Lacan. Her concerns are with Lacan's idea that there is no woman and thus no feminine subject.[18] My intention in this book is to offer an alternative reading of Luce Irigaray which locates her in a symbolic/imaginary framework different from that with which she is usually identified. If we can see Luce Irigaray's work as the work of individuation in the Jungian sense to be developed in this book, then her claims that there is no feminine subject and that women need a feminine divine take on a different complexion. As a consequence, the place of ethics accorded by Luce Irigaray to the relations between women and men, and the place of ethics in political practice, conceived of as the workings of the collective and the individual together and apart, will need to be refigured outside the Freud–Lacanian framework in which she is usually interpreted (Deutscher 2002; Hollywood 2001; Chanter 1995; Burke, Schor and Whitford 1994; Whitford 1991; Grosz 1989). Certainly, this is not the only framework within which she operates: her work is a response to Plato, Aristotle, René Descartes, Baruch de Spinoza, Maurice Merleau-Ponty, Immanuel Levinas and Martin Heidegger. We see in her responses a profound understanding of their various positions on love, on the body, on the other, on seeing woman as the means to producing a son for the father, on constructing woman fundamentally as mother.[19]

Lastly, Friedrich Nietzsche is a thinker who has clearly had a deep impact on both Jung and Luce Irigaray. The notion of individuation (*principium individuationis*) plays an important role in the distinction between the Apollonian and Dionysian in *Birth of Tragedy*. Nietzsche relates this idea to Schopenhauer (Nietzsche 1967: 1). Jung's lectures on Nietzsche's *Zarathustra*[20] and Luce Irigaray's poetic essay, *Marine Lover of Friedrich Nietzsche* (Irigaray 1991a), draw out evocative responses to Nietzsche's manic brilliance. The genealogical lines are clear when we consider all of these influences on both Jung and Luce Irigaray; they become clearer in the pages of this book.

Perhaps one of Carl Jung's most controversial distinctions is that between the individual and the collective unconscious (although Freud's notion of 'unconscious instinctual impulses' can be interpreted as an allusion to a collective notion of the unconscious) (Freud 1961: 39). We will not find this distinction in Luce Irigaray's work yet her reading of the Lacanian symbolic and the imaginary suggests that there is a correlation between the two sets of concepts. To this end, I argue that Luce Irigaray implicitly adopts and adapts Carl Jung's notions of the collective unconscious and individuation.[21] We need not see Luce Irigaray's work only through the lens of her Lacanian lineage. The possibilities for interpreting her work more broadly are considerable, especially when we take into account the factors I have been talking about above. I shall argue that only then can we redeploy the terms of the masculine symbolic of which she is so critical – its appropriating and universalising aspects for instance. Once that is done, her insistence on a *feminine*-feminine (the feminine conceived of and embodied by women) can be revisited as an attempt to understand the collective unconscious. Luce Irigaray's distinction between the *masculine*-feminine (the feminine conceived of and embodied by men) and the feminine-feminine is, as I shall argue, central to a robust theorisation of sexual difference. Further, the analysis of Luce Irigaray's notions of the feminine will help to re-examine Jung's foundational work on the feminine, work that has led to accusations of essentialism in much the same way as has Luce Irigaray's.

My exploration of the work of both Carl Jung and Luce Irigaray and the connections I set up as part of the conversation I am initiating has begun rather sketchily. Theirs is a complex relationship that I shall construct through their complementary philosophical interests and forged in their experience as practising interpreters and therapists of the psyche. The implicit and sometimes explicit philosophical character of their thought is the fertile ground of their theory-making. Their common philosophical heritage in the genealogical links of psychological and philosophical literature needs recognition. The following pages are an attempt at this recognition in the hope that we will gain a richer appreciation of these two remarkable thinkers.

Chapter 1

The dreaming body

Dreaming might seem like a strange place to start up the conversation between Jung and Luce Irigaray. Yet it brings together Hegelian Dialectic, the unconscious and the body. Once we encounter the body, we need to imagine what kind of body we are engaging with; and since bodies are not neutral with respect to their material properties, their social locations and how they are valued, then we are on the road to exploring just what is entailed in the dreaming process. In the first instance my discussion explores Carl Jung's idea of the collective unconscious by examining his notion of dreaming. I argue that Jung understands dreaming as both a collective affect and as a personal or individual response to one's lived-in world which is structured by and structures, in part, the collective unconscious: the relation implied here is dialectical. The focus on the collective unconscious draws attention to the role the body plays as a limit of both consciousness and the unconscious. I then propose that the body question provides a link to Luce Irigaray's work because her conception of the body is never simply 'body' but always 'sexed' body.

The argument I advance about dreaming and the unconscious constitutes a significant intervention in our considerations regarding our embeddedness in the world, as both conscious and unconscious selves. It raises some salient questions about the mode of embeddedness, viz. as bodies that are lived-in bodies and the kind of effect that has on us. Carl Jung's insight regarding the restricting role the body plays in the production of consciousness out of unconsciousness, and the ubiquitous presence of unconsciousness, requires careful deliberation, however, because, as we all know, our bodies are sites of differences as well as similarity. His theory misses out on an important feature: it speaks in generalities; it is not specific to sex/gender, race, age or class. The repercussions of a theory which fails to take cognisance of these specificities are clear: if we are to take seriously the idea of collective constitution then we must likewise take cognisance of difference as difference is manifested through constitution. Importantly, too, acknowledgement of the role of the lived and living body, in the elaboration of consciousness and unconsciousness, means that we must reorient our thinking around the relevant relationships we are socialised into, and/or internalised by them, through our collectives.

THE COLLECTIVE UNCONSCIOUS

Carl Jung claimed that:

> [t]he collective unconscious is a part of the psyche which can be negatively distinguished from a personal unconscious by the fact that it does not, like the latter, owe its existence to personal experience and consequently is not a personal experience . . . The personal unconscious consists for the most part of *complexes*, the content of the collective unconscious is made up essentially of archetypes.
>
> (Jung 1968a: 42)

He goes on to remark that:

> [i]n addition to our immediate consciousness, which is of a thoroughly personal nature and which we believe to be the only empirical psyche (even if we tack on the personal unconscious as an appendix), there exists a second psychic system of a collective, universal, and impersonal nature which is identical in all individuals. This collective unconscious does not develop individually but is inherited. It consists of pre-existent forms, the archetypes, which can only become conscious secondarily and which give definite form to certain psychic contents.
>
> (Jung 1968a: 90)

This might appear to be a pretty unfashionable thesis by today's theoretical standards.[1] The thesis invokes notions such as universality and innateness which intellectual fashion dictates are politically and intellectually suspect. But Jung's claims give a serious account of the unconscious collective aspect of what it means to be a human being and his realisation of collective influence on the individual psyche pre-figures the social-constructionist turn of the past fifty years. Friedrich Nietzsche has been a big influence on the turn to the body and social constructionist theory and he was also a major influence on Jung in this respect.[2] I begin my exploration of the collective influence with a short discussion of dreaming and the unconscious because, as Jung also remarks, the main source of knowledge of the archetypes, hence of the unconscious, is dreaming (along with active imagination and paranoid or extreme psychic state delusions (Jung 1968a: 100–3). The discussion of dreaming will bring into focus the important role of the lived-in body in the work of Jung, an importance which cannot be gainsaid given the refiguring of the mind–body problem over the past one hundred or so years. It also brings into focus the binary nation of the psyche, as both conscious and unconscious.

One of the major difficulties in understanding dreams and dreaming is that the conscious and the unconscious seem inevitably to be invoked: when we are awake we are conscious, when we are asleep we are unconscious. What 'conscious' and 'unconscious' are, however, is difficult to discern, particularly in the context of dreaming, because dreaming does not occur during waking life, during conscious life. 'Waking life' and 'conscious' seem to go together, just as 'sleeping life' and 'unconscious' seem to go together. Yet some would argue that they are conscious of having dreams when they dream: they feel emotions (of elation or fear or anger or love), for example, of which they are conscious while they are dreaming. They do not wake up and *then* become afraid or feel happy when they remember that they dreamed. Rather they wake up *already* feeling afraid or happy because their feelings are continuous with what has been going on for them while they were asleep. One view of this suggests that there is a sense in which we are conscious while we dream during our sleep.[3] Dreaming and dreams are a way of sorting out what might be the implications of such a view. Descriptions of consciousness and the unconscious provide the basic data of any conclusions one might draw about the nature or ontological status of the mind. How consciousness operates in the world is the only evidence, the only experience, we have of the mind. A satisfactory account of the mind of the unconscious and consciousness has to be, minimally, phenomenological and this applies to dreaming as an important function of the psyche.[4]

That said, a good account of dreams and dreaming thus will have the following features:

1 it will not overlook or eliminate the subjective, that it is an embodied subject who dreams
2 it will acknowledge its objective grounding in socio-cultural factors which are collective
3 it will be subtended by a satisfactory account of the conscious and the unconscious, the mind and
4 it will attend to the dialectical nature of dreaming, to the intrusion of the unconscious into consciousness.

A good account situates the dreamer at the centre of the dreaming process. It takes, as primary material, the experience of the dreamer as an embodied, situated collective member. Further, such an account would be both phenomenological and analytical; which is to say that such an account is not simply descriptive but also deals with the relations which might be exhibited in the dreaming process. For example, that the dreamer is an embodied social being, in a social network with specific structures and arrangements, illuminates what is going on in the dream (and I assume that *something* is).

So a good account will also display its awareness of the dreamer's social context, the dreamer being seen as a product, to some extent, of her/his world environment and lived experience in that environment.

Freud attributed the existence of the unconscious to repression.[5] In Freud's theory, we see the imbibing of the self's local domain as a moral issue: unconsciousness is produced through the persuasions of the collective's sanctioning some possibilities, prohibiting others. For Freud, the unconscious is a domain constituted by the effects of prohibition. Coming to know what is prohibited, and the frustration of desire associated with that, contributes to the making of the self. Frustration and disappointment emerge in dreaming, a psychic activity by which the unconscious makes itself known to the self as an aspect of herself. The subject finds herself immersed in her outer world, her local domain, and by her inner world, both circumscribed by collective objectivity, history and culture. She learns the rules of sanction and disapproval; she does not arrive in the world with a pre-inscribed set of rules with which she judges that world. The unconscious is manufactured from the subject's own experience of the world, from what is acceptable and not acceptable, from what can be encountered openly and what needs to be repressed. Yet even as Freud argued for three aspects of the psyche: the conscious (*Cs.*) the preconscious (*Pcs.*) and the unconscious (*Ucs.*), he further distinguishes between two kinds, and then three kinds of unconscious: 'there are two kinds of unconscious, but in the dynamic sense only one . . . We still recognize that the *Ucs.* does not coincide with the repressed; it is still true that all the repressed is *Ucs.*, but not all that is *Ucs.* is repressed. A part of the ego, too – and Heaven knows how important a part – may be *Ucs.*, undoubtedly is *Ucs.* . . . When we find ourselves thus confronted by the necessity of postulating a third *Ucs.*, . . . we must admit that the characteristic of being unconscious begins to lose significance for us' (Freud 1961: 15 and 18).[6] So Freud's account is not limited to repression as an explanation of the *whole* unconscious, yet he does not seem to know what to do with the apparently unrepressed elements.

Jung's account of the unconscious retains elements of repression, but attempts to account for anomalous material that appears in dreaming (like how one can have dreams containing apparently ancient symbols of which one has no lived-experience, no imaginary or actual encounter). We can imagine that he does this by attending to those aspects of the unconscious which have lost significance for Freud, those aspects which are 'unconscious instinctual impulses'. The instinctual impulses appear to be structural. Jung's account is both structural (he talks about the archetypal forms, for example) and is also content based (it 'contains' pictorial images and sensations). Such material is anomalous because it is not locatable in the subject's personal history and experience of the world. On this view, what transpires in dreams is irreducible to lived experience either directly or derivatively through association. Hence some dream material might be thought of as existentially anomalous.

To account for that anomalousness, Jung suggests that the unconscious is supra-personal as well as personal. The supra-personal he called the collective unconscious.[7] The collective unconscious pre-exists the individual unconscious *and* the individual conscious. There is thus, to the unconscious, a bipartite configuration, a double aspect, collective and personal. The intersection of these aspects, the encounter between them, their relation one to the other, produces the content of dreams, produces the phenomenon of dreaming. But it also produces the self, in conjunction with the conscious, that about which the self is aware. From this perspective, the self is a relational entity, not only because it is in relation to the world, and the world to it, but because its internal aspects, as heterogeneous, are also in relation with each other. On this view, the self is a product of dialectical relations. We may think of the self as a synthesis of the kind which Giegerich disdains. The notion of sameness, of internal coherence and identity, is absent from this conception of the self.

The unconscious, collective or personal, has a temporal immediacy, a constant presence that consciousness does not have. Owen Flanagan proposes that 'we are always, while alive, conscious' (Flanagan 2000: 68). Is this claim consistent with the idea of the constant presence of the unconscious? That depends on how we figure the complexity of both conscious and unconscious and their relations. We need, therefore, to address their temporal dimensions evident in intentionality, or the directedness of mental states and mentation more generally.

Consciousness is marked in its directedness towards an object (Brentano 1973: 88). But consciousness is limited both in content and directedness while simultaneously always directed. The operativeness of consciousness suggests that a necessary condition of its being is that it is not autogenic, not self-engendering. Consciousness always and everywhere requires an object external to itself, in order to operate, in order to *be* consciousness. We miss out on a lot of what is going on around us, in part because of the directedness of consciousness and for the sake, I suggest, of our sanity.[8] We need to distinguish between the directedness of consciousness (consciousness always has an object: there is always something there, external to consciousness, responsible for 'activating' consciousness) and the awareness of that directedness. We are certainly not always aware of that directedness (mostly we take it for granted). Hence the notion of directedness is ambiguous. Most of a subject's life is spent with marginal awareness of both the cause and effects of one's conscious existence. Immanuel Levinas writes of this very phenomenon:

> The comedy begins with the simplest of our movements, each of which carries with it an inevitable awkwardness. In putting out my hand to

> approach a chair, I have creased the sleeve of my jacket. I have scratched the floor, I have dropped the ash from my cigarette. In doing that which I wanted to do, I have done so many things I did not want. The act has not been pure, for I have left traces . . . We are thus responsible beyond our intentions. It is impossible for the regard that directs the act to avoid the nonintended action that comes with it . . . That is to say, our consciousness and our mastery of reality through consciousness do not exhaust our relation to reality, to which we are always present through all the density of our being. Consciousness of our reality does not coincide with our habitation of the world.
>
> (Levinas 1996: 4)

Our habitation of the world is primarily *unconscious*: we are only momentarily conscious. Consciousness itself is an effect of limitation. Indeed, Jung argues that restriction, as constraint, is of the essence of consciousness: 'you must be able to exclude many things in order to be conscious. So restriction is the very being, the character of consciousness' and, as we shall see in a moment, the body is important in the restricting of consciousness (Jung 1998: 94). Jung's notion of consciousness focuses on discrimination, discernment (Jung 1998: 243). Furthermore, 'the conscious mind can claim only a relatively central position and must accept the fact that the unconscious psyche transcends and as it were surrounds it on all sides' (Jung 2002: 215). The psyche is fundamentally intentional and this entails that *both the conscious and the unconscious exhibit intentionality*. The discriminating activity of the mind suggests intentional activity of which one is not conscious and could not be conscious. In other words, the directedness of the mind is discoverable through both its conscious and its unconscious contents, including dreams.

THE CONSCIOUS, THE UNCONSCIOUS, WAKEFULNESS AND EXPERIENCE

The extent of the unconscious as an aspect of the mind and of social inheritance, the idea that mind in its fullness is intentional, gives some insight into the issue of the relationship between experience, consciousness and wakefulness.[9] What follows is a version of a philosophical argument about the relationship between consciousness, wakefulness or being awake, and experience. The philosophical arguments can be seen as an attempt to examine the cogency of various views of conscious and unconscious experience and the relation between them. Experience (what happens, what we do, what we know and believe, who and what we are in the world and our awareness of all of these) and consciousness go hand in hand. If you are not conscious, then you cannot experience, a point made by the philosophers Norman Malcolm (1959) and Daniel Dennett (1977) among others. Hence one widespread but contested philosophical construction of experience, of consciousness and being awake, is that:

- in order to experience, one must be awake
- to be awake is to be conscious, and
- to experience is to be conscious

and for being asleep or asleepness, that:

- to be asleep is not to experience
- not to experience is to be unconscious
- to be asleep is to be *un*conscious.

Dreaming, it is held, occurs during sleep.[10] What is the experiential status of dreaming? Does dreaming have such a status? On the basis of the above argument, it is not possible for a dream to be an experience, because experience requires waking consciousness. Since discrimination, restriction and constraint affect consciousness, and we do not perform these activities when we are asleep, then being awake looks at least a necessary but perhaps not a sufficient condition for both consciousness and experience. Discrimination can be enacted only at a conscious, wakeful level, it would seem. Experience happens as a consequence of being conscious, of consciousness: one of the 'tests' of experience is epistemic. Can I be said to have had an experience of which I was not aware, about which I did not know? On the view of mind I am proposing above, let us call it the awash-with-intentionality view, yes, one can experience without awareness, without knowing that one is experiencing. The activities of mind are both conscious and unconscious and the discriminating activities of mind need not be conscious, indeed are not conscious if consciousness emerges as an effect of discrimination.

But what this suggests is that one can have an experience of which one is not aware. The claim of the dreamer, on the other hand is that she/he was asleep and was aware of the activities of her/his mind during sleep, even if that awareness is recalled upon waking. There seems then to be a relationship between the dream experience and its vocative nature that involves some kind of temporal gap, for dreams are reported in the past tense. To a great extent, the vocative nature of the dream is the evidence that one has dreamed, but need not be so (Malcolm 1959). Many people say that they have dreamed but they cannot recall what it is they have dreamed. This involves a modal dimension that should be emphasised: dreaming is to be thought of as conscious awareness during sleep with the *possibility* of recall and re-tell at a later stage. Whatever the case, that people even report dreams tells us something significant about the psyche because of the sleeping state they are in when *whatever it is* occurs.

CONSCIOUSNESS AND THE BODY

We are *always* unconscious and *sometimes* conscious, yet we know about the unconscious because we are conscious. This immediately suggests the dialectical nature of both consciousness and the unconscious. Consciousness is produced through the imposition of boundaries on the unconscious; consciousness is always bound. What binds consciousness, what triggers the imposition of boundaries, thus what produces consciousness, is the essential directedness of the mind towards an object, that the mind is awash-with-intentionality. If that is the case, consciousness is relational. But what else is interesting here is that the conscious as the boundedness of the unconscious provides an alternative reading of the idea of the experiencing self. Waking life exhibits consciousness through awareness of the world in which the subject finds her/himself; the exhibiting mechanism being intentionality.[11] The realm of intentionality could be understood as only the realm of consciousness: if one is conscious then one is conscious of something and awareness sometimes accompanies that consciousness. Mental activity, the directedness of the mind or the psyche towards an object, is constitutive of consciousness and the unconscious. I am claiming that the unconscious affects the mind so that the mind becomes 'visible' to itself by its essential directedness. The mind is awash-with-intentionality, and that one experiences during sleep and also that one remembers some mental, internal experience during sleep suggests that intentionality is not exclusive to waking life. The sphere of intentionality, in other words, is both conscious and unconscious.

In waking life, the unconscious permeates the self's experience, providing a ubiquitous, potent and subliminal backdrop for the experiencing subject. In sleep, aspects of the subject which are unknown in waking life, that is to say, of a subject's unconscious and of the collective unconscious, become known. Dreaming provides the opportunity for the unknown to become known. What this says, though, is that the unconscious is, *in practice*, knowable. *Note that there is a distinction between the unknown and the unknowable.*[12] The unconscious is the unknown, aspects of which may become known: in that sense it is knowable. Christopher Hauke says, following Jung himself, and most Jungians, that '[u]ltimately all these so-called *unconscious contents and unconscious processes are all, and always, unknown*' (Hauke 2000: 200) (Hauke's italics). However, that the unconscious is *unknown* is incoherent if we are to make sense of dreams and dreaming, or any psychological phenomena at all. It is not *unknown* – after all it is the subject of this discussion. Perhaps there is a slip here between what is unknown and what is unknowable, but even then 'unknowability' needs to be qualified, since presumably we can get to know something of the unconscious through dreaming: the archetypes for example are manifested during dreaming. Even though as *a priori* structures we cannot know archetypes, we see their effects and to that extent they are *known*. While we cannot know the unconscious *in toto*, we can know parts of the unconscious. Further, we might distinguish between the French *connaître* (to be acquainted with something) and *savoir* to know a fact: we may know the unconscious in the first but not the second sense. We certainly seem to know the unconscious in terms of our being acquainted with it; but we do not know *facts* about it. I return to this point at the end of this book.

And sleep is a mechanism for this epistemic occurrence. Where previously it has been thought, then, that sleep must be the absence of awareness, this view suggests that sleep has the function of permitting awareness, not through conscious control, but through dissipating resistance to the contents of the mind. Awareness, in this respect, is an attribute of consciousness and the unconscious, which may be either absent or present.

On this reading, dreaming is intentional, aware experience, had while one is *unconscious* or not responsive to external stimuli. The dream emerges from the unconscious, albeit as an experience of which the sleeper is aware while she/he is unconscious. The self becomes aware of itself, it becomes aware of its own mind differently during sleep because it has access to its unconscious that it usually cannot have. Sleep and dreaming are a means of self-revelation.

One might think of dream situations as the site of nocturnal admissions, where fantasy and fact, poetry and pain confront the sleeper. One might also think of this as a revelation of subjectivity, a revelation which, in its capacity for awareness during sleep *and* its memorability, is experiential.

Jung suggests this in the context of his claim that consciousness is restricted by the body, if consciousness is to be acute. His insightful discussion of the body in relation to consciousness is critical to an understanding of dreams and dreaming. He recognises that the body, the living body, is in time and space, and that time and space are an aspect of the restricting function of the body over consciousness. This spatio-temporal situating of the living body in relation to consciousness also situates the body in relation to *unconsciousness*, for the unconscious, like its excluding partner, consciousness, is also embodied by individuals. Jung remarks that 'the ego consciousness is exceedingly narrow; it contains only a few things in the moment and all the rest is unconscious' (Jung 1998: 93). This applies not only to the personal unconscious but also to the collective unconscious which is in excess of the individual. That excess is explicable in terms of the always there-ness of the unconscious.

In dreaming, one becomes consciously aware of unconscious aspects of the psyche. Dreaming is an opportunity, in other words, for the unconscious, collective and/or personal, to make felt its always there-ness. It is the awareness of the unconscious in operation; and it is a mode through which the self to a fuller extent than is possible only in consciousness can place itself in the given-ness of the world.

DREAMING AND THE COLLECTIVE

The theme of always there-ness of the unconscious, collective or personal, and the relatively limited nature of consciousness evokes the idea that we live *in* a pre-established, albeit mutable world, a world already given. That world, however, need not be a fixed and complete world, a world which is predictable and unchanging. Jung speaks of the collective unconscious as objective psyche. 'Objective psyche' is to be understood as the already given-ness of the world in so far as the self finds itself in a world, as Jung, Heidegger, Levinas, and Foucault, among others, emphatically announced. 'Objective' has to do with the existence of a world, and thus a psyche, beyond the control of the self.[13] It is primarily an ontological term or a term to do with being, rather than an epistemological one or term dealing with knowledge, when used by Jung *in this context*. But the objective psyche is relational, to be elucidated in terms of relations between the embodied nature of the self and its in-the-world status. We are not disembodied psyches floating around attached epiphenomenally to bodies.

Our meanings arise from our embodiment. Embodiment is a *material* or *physical* embodiment in a material world. I, as a self, dream. I do not dream because I am a self: I dream because I am a *self immersed*. I tell my dream. In telling my dream, I use language. The telling of my dream further exposes my immersion in webs of relations, exemplifying those webs of relations in which I am engaged, which are producing me. Without that immersion, there would be no self that is identifiable as the I that is me. The I that is me is a specific cultural product, albeit an embodied, fleshy existent, contingent upon socio-cultural and biological relations. Yet I am not merely the sum of those relations. The 'gestalt' that is me, the whole me which seems greater than the sum of my parts and that is expressed in the use of I and other transposable pronouns, is not reducible to a collection of social relations. This is the case no matter how detailed the descriptions and analyses of those relations might be. Of themselves, those relations are greater than I am, greater than my dreaming. But I, too, am greater than those relations.

In my dreaming, I am instantiated as that socio-cultural product, just as I am in my waking life. Hence both my waking life and my sleeping life instantiate me as a specific token of my culture. But the dreaming in my sleeping and my waking life fails to completely instantiate me: there is a more-ness to me that exceeds simple token-ness. My dream and my waking life are to some extent all that I am, but are also simply a mark or a permeable limit of what I am. My dreaming, my dream and my waking subjectivity are fragments on a mirror ball: this tiny mirror that is me reflects a world far in excess of this identifiable I, identifiable, in part, through my specific embodiment.

In the particularity of this dreaming that is mine and no one else's, my dreaming expresses a point of view unique to me, a point of view which emerges because of my embodiment: my dream is a product of this I and no other, a product in which I have active engagement through my unconscious. My unconscious, my mind, in a profound sense, *makes or produces or even provides an active vehicle for* my dreams: we *make* as well as have dreams.[14] Once we think of *making* our dreams rather than having dreams, then the notion of something passively happening to us is obviated. We become active constructors, through our unconsciousnesses, of our psychic lives: we are agents in dreaming. However, the activity of archetypes in the collective unconscious also places me *beyond* agency and, to that extent, the dream makes me.

What comes together in the dreaming and is told in the dream narrative is an expression of me, which nonetheless is fully me in the experiencing of the dream. In dreaming, as in any experience, I am fully that experience, but simultaneously not reducible to that experience because there is always more to me than this experience, here, now. Dreaming pinpoints the experiencing subject in a somnolent mode, highlighting the persistence of selfhood in multiple modes of being (waking, sleeping, semi-conscious). Dreaming bridges the gap between the awareness of the conscious and the awareness of the unconscious, which by their very natures are also both greater and lesser than their manifestations in the subject.

Foucault draws attention to the identity between the subject and her/his dream when he contends that:

> The subject of the dream, the first person of the dream, is the dream itself, the whole dream. In the dream, everything says, 'I', even the things and the animals, even the empty space, even objects distant and strange which populate the phantasmagoria . . . To dream is not another way of experiencing another world, it is for the dreaming subject the radical way of experiencing its own world. The way of experiencing is so radical, because existence does not pronounce itself world. The dream is situated in that ultimate moment in which existence still is its world; once beyond, at the dawn of wakefulness, already it is no longer world.
>
> (Foucault 1954: 59)

The subject and the whole dream are one and the same: the dreaming subject *is* that subject at that moment. The dreaming subject is performing its being in dreaming. Note also that it is unproblematic for Foucault that the dreaming subject is experiencing. Dreaming is figured as a mode of experiencing similar to the way in which Jung suggests. That the dream and the subject are one and the same implies a necessary connection between dreaming and the self, dreaming and the subjective. *If the self is dreaming and is unconscious, then from a phenomenological perspective the subject is identical with her/his unconscious at that moment, just as, phenomenologically, the self is identical with her/his unconscious when she/he is awake.*

The phenomenon which is the dreaming self, the dreaming subject, and which is identical with her/his unconscious, is an embodied phenomenon which utters itself in the first person, in self-conscious, first-person utterances as ‘I’. The subjective, and subjectivity, bespeak that I-ness. In the dream, the ‘I’ which is said, the spoken-ness of the ‘I’, performs itself in the unboundedness of the unconscious, the domain of sleep. As first-person utterance, however, that I-ness is neither completely, utterly isolated, autonomous, nor sacrosanct. It is, after all, an embodied ‘I’, an embodiment which renders complete isolation and autonomy impossible. Embodiment entails relationship: interdependence and reliance on community. The explicit speakability of the ‘I’ always already situates it in a socio-cultural matrix of language speakers. That there is *this* ‘I’ means that there is *that* ‘I’, and *that* other ‘I’ over there. The indexicality of the I suggests the simultaneous uniqueness and sameness of each user of the term. The condition of sameness and uniqueness is embodiment, and embodiment is not only socio-cultural but historical and collective.

Earlier, I mentioned that Jung conceived of the collective unconscious as objective psyche. The socio-cultural and the historical are the ground of Jung’s ‘objective psyche’. Jung’s awareness that the self is constituted through her/his interactions with the present and the past as members of communities with specific cultural features and that one is who one is because one is permitted to be so, by that world, evolved in his writings. For him, one instantiates the world in which one lives and the world that has preceded it. The socio-cultural constitutes the collective of ‘collective unconscious’ and ‘collective conscious’. The socio-cultural nature of the collective unconscious echoes, symbolically and actually, the history which has preceded it. What is more, the historicity of the socio-cultural continues to inform the collective in total, both conscious and unconscious. The nature of the collective unconscious is such that its structuring motifs transcend the individual experiences of any one self. Jung saw those motifs as archetypes. For him, archetypes are tendencies of the unconscious to ‘translate’ the experience of the culture into self-awareness. The picture that emerges then, from Jung, is that, for the self, the body is the limit of the conscious and the unconscious and that the self is as much a ‘product’ of its socio-cultural location as it is of its individual embodied-ness. The self internalises its engagement with its context, making itself consciously and unconsciously as a relational entity. And it does that structurally, through the operation of archetypes.

In Jung's view, as we have seen, our habitation of the world is exceeded by our unconsciousness, by the given-ness of that world and the structural role that archetypes play in the collective unconscious, and in therefore contributing to the self. The French anthropologist and sociologist Pierre Bourdieu elucidates the collective in a specific, socio-symbolically embracing way which he calls *habitus*: [15]

> The structures of a particular type of environment (e.g. the material conditions of existence characteristic of a class condition) produce *habitus*, systems of durable, transposable *dispositions*, structured structures, that is as principles of generation and structuring of practices.
>
> (Bourdieu 1977: 72)

If we think of the collective unconscious in this way, as a kind of collective memory, the psychological imprint left by history and interpreted symbolically, then the collective unconscious can be interpreted as a kind of *habitus* not inconsistent with Jung's view that the collective unconscious is inherited. Rather, it provides a way of interpreting that inheritance as an historical remnant, recallable without direct volition. Just as *habitus* functions at every moment, so the unconscious, so the *collective* unconscious. 'At every moment' is inclusive of sleeping life as well as waking life. The body continues to be an organic, living organism when it is asleep as much as it is when it is awake, only differently so. The idea that the unconscious brings the given-ness of the world, its present and its past, into the mind of the dreamer through mythological, fantastic and poetic images makes the dreamer aware in ways not possible in waking life, and gives a richer tone to the experience of dreaming and to its theorisation. What is more, the intersecting of the individual self with her/his socio-cultural context is made visible once we can give an account of dreaming that shifts the focus away from a mono-focus to a bi-focus. This bi-focal nature of dreaming, the foci being the individual and the socio-cultural within history, emancipates dreaming from the narrowness of Freudian-inspired interpretations. And that can only be a good thing, no matter how brilliant his groundbreaking work.

A good theory of dreaming will take all of this into consideration. It is a subject, an embodied self in context who dreams, who continues as an experiencing, living individual during sleep. The world, culture, history, relations do not disappear during that time. The dialectic between subject and the world in which a subject finds her/himself, figures the subjectivity, the I-ness of that subject. In dreaming, that which might be forgotten is remembered, remembered without the constraints of waking consciousness.

The collective *intrudes* into the sleeper. The self is dreamed through the activities of unconsciousness during sleep as much as it is actively constructed and constituted in conscious, waking, wakeful life.

Recall that Lacan was critical of Hegel's neglect of the unconscious in the Master/Slave scenario. We can characterise dreaming as I have outlined it above, as a process cognate with the Master/Slave Dialectic. We should be aware, however, of taking the Master/Slave Dialectic too literally here. Two self-consciousnesses do not face each other and there is no struggle unto death. But two aspects of the psyche, the conscious and the unconscious, 'face' each other and there is a struggle for recognition. A struggle is evident between the conscious and unconscious minds: the unconscious intrudes into a 'passive' consciousness. The unconscious acts on the conscious, calling it to a recognition that it is not all that there is from a psychic perspective. The recognition is as successful as what is learned from it. What is also evident is the situation of the dreamer in her/his collective(s), analogous to Hegel's drawing our attention to the embeddedness of his two self-consciousnesses in Life. By extending the metaphor that the Master/Slave expresses, we can see the struggle of the unconscious for recognition played out in the psyche. But dialectic as a logical process has a long history prior to Hegel's elucidation of the Master/Slave. We find it in Greek philosophy and we find it in the playing out of the male/female oppositional pairing. In the next chapter, then, I examine how dialectic was pre-figured by Socrates and Plato in their argument and philosophical method.

Chapter 2

The philosophical Jung

INTRODUCTORY REMARKS

Everyone makes philosophical assumptions, no matter how naïve or how complex. We all have views about the structure of reality, what exists and what does not, whether or not there is a divine and/or a malignant being, what is good and bad, what is beautiful, whether or not we should eat animals, the differences and similarities between men and women (and the why of this). And we act on the basis of these beliefs and assumptions. In this sense we are all of us philosophers. But most of us do not read the philosophical canon where we will find the 'greats' (and not-so-greats) who are considered to be the 'true philosophers'. As I argued earlier, Jung's and Luce Irigaray's work is deeply philosophical in a way that many of us can only begin to imagine for ourselves, but which is, nonetheless, very clear when we begin to read what they have written. Their engagement with the canon is not only obvious, but very deep. Indeed, the philosophical canon is part of what brings them together. Plato's philosophy is of particular interest to both of them especially around the question of women and the feminine. Methodologically, the mode of argument we find in Plato is also apparent in their work, even though it is subverted, as we shall see, by Luce Irigaray.

It is arguable that Jung had a somewhat ambivalent attitude to philosophy in spite of his use of both its content and methods. Indeed, many of us would be familiar with Carl Jung's claim that he is an empiricist and not a philosopher (Jung 1971: 320). Jung obviously believes that a distinction can be made between empiricism and philosophy, and that the two are in some way exclusive of, or incompatible with, each other. But as we know from David Hume (1962), Immanuel Kant (1930) and John Stuart Mill (1957), philosophy and empiricism can be comfortable bed-fellows.

We can therefore think of some philosophy as *empirical* philosophy which we develop out of our experience of the world, its effect on us and ours on it, as distinct from philosophy developed out of *a priori* principles of reason, as in the philosophies of G. W. Leibniz and Baruch de Spinoza. In their original senses, science as knowledge (Latin: *scientia*) and philosophy (Greek: *philos*: friend, or lover and *sophia*: wisdom) are not incompatible, the suggestion implicit in Jung's comment. One can develop a relationship with wisdom out of one's encounter with, and experience of, the world.

What Jung means by 'empiricism' is not at all clear, but it seems as if he might be making a distinction between empirical science and empirical philosophy where 'science' connotes a more modern understanding of science as a rational set of procedures which gives to us an objective and verifiable knowledge of the world or a body of facts. His claim, then, might be seen as a claim that he is not doing empirical philosophy, but is, instead, working at empirical science: he is working at producing knowledge out of experience, out of his encounters with the world, with fellow human beings and objects in that world. He employs objective and verifiable procedures and produces facts about the human psyche. Hence his distinction invokes empiricism as a scientific idea distinct from philosophy. He does not, in other words, acknowledge the original inseparability of philosophy and science.

Implicit in the scientific idea of empiricism are questions of evidence, testability, verifiability and repetition which have become indispensable to modern understandings of empirical research. As Jung appears to have seen it, his work was concerned with just those questions. But as Susan Rowland has pointed out, Jung's 'empirical evidence and facts are psychic images, dreams and psychological symptoms' (Rowland 2002: 106–7). Their status as empirical, scientific data is therefore problematic as much psychic or mental activity does not satisfy evidential requirements of empiricism. On the other hand, Jung's use of art, cultural artefacts and texts from the public domain does satisfy these requirements (Jung 1966) and his work in relation to the word association test, for example, is certainly able to be laid out in empirical scientific terms (Jung 1973). Jung evokes the polysemous nature of the empirical, on the one hand alluding to the scientific credibility of his work in an environment of scientific realist commitments, and, on the other, broadening what might count as 'legitimate' data of research and theory-making. For him, experience, thus the empirical, exceeds the limitations implicit in a scientific realist model of 'reality'.

IRRATIONALITY, THE FEMININE AND MIMESIS

But my concern here is not to debate the philosophical status of Jung's work. Instead, I look at Jung's use of philosophical concepts and the way in which his conceptual framework has been influenced by those concepts. I do not claim that Jung always consciously used these concepts, nor do I want to make any particular claims about the identity of those concepts and Jung's own. Rather, and apropos of my remarks earlier, I show that some of Jung's arguments and assumptions bear a strong resemblance to philosophical arguments and assumptions that have also been the centre of some important philosophical debates over many, many centuries. Many of those debates, and their assumptions and the beliefs that inform them, are still alive today.

Jung's concept of the feminine, for example, is very close to Plato's. On the other hand, the Platonic concept is rejected by Luce Irigaray because of ubiquity either in or behind theories of the subject that suggest the feminine is the irrational. In her early work, *Speculum of the Other Woman* (1985a), she, as a feminine other, a slave to the master philosopher, challenges the Platonic conception of the feminine as disorder. We will see that her challenge is also a challenge to Jung's notion of individuation. The conceptual, thematic closeness of Plato's, Jung's and Luce Irigaray's works opens the possibility of dealing philosophically with some of the issues (such as constructions of the feminine) that are found in Jung.

Plato is only one philosopher whose presence we can trace in Jung's work. The idea of individuation, concerned as it is with the disengagement from projection and thus identification, can be seen in Immanuel Kant and Ludwig Feuerbach as an ideal of reason. Jung's notion of individuation amounts to a rejection of the feminine in pursuit of that ideal of reason. Jung also seems to be following in Nietzsche's footsteps here. Oliver, for instance, argues that for Nietzsche 'birth is a process of individuation . . . For Nietzsche, individuation always covers over the chaos and arbitrariness of what was before individuation', which was union with the mother. 'The indeterminate identity between mother and child is too much to bear, especially for the male child.' Oliver also points out that Nietzsche held that 'our relationship to women is determined by our relationship to our mothers' (Oliver 1994: 58–60), a theme we will see recurring in Jung's anima feminine. On the other hand, Luce Irigaray reclaims the terrain of the feminine and the maternal, and inverts the notion of individuation as a masculine ideal. She redeploys that ideal as a feminine possibility.

As I argued in 'Plato's Echo: A Feminist Refiguring of the Anima' (Gray forthcoming), Jung represents the feminine as anima feminine and as maternal feminine. Within each of these representations, we find sub-representations which nearly always suggest a contradiction inherent in the feminine. Whether or not the contradiction reflects and represents what is the case is moot. Luce Irigaray's risk in miming the feminine, as we shall see, aims at disabusing us of our commonly held conceptions of the feminine, among which is the idea of disorder represented in intrinsic contradiction. In 'Plato's Echo' I maintained that the irrational, or soul disorder, which we find in Plato's account of the feminine, is a feature of Jung's rendering of the anima. But whereas Jung at least attempts to characterise the feminine sympathetically, Plato is uncompromisingly critical in his account. I argue throughout this book that Plato's idea of mimesis or imitation is incorporated, either consciously or unconsciously, into Jung's account of the development of the soul. We see in *The Republic* that Plato demonises the mirroring of women's chaotic and uncontrollable desires and passions. And repeated in Jung, we find that an anima feminine as the basis of moral inspiration is to be avoided. The anima feminine seen as a source of moral caution mimics the role of the irrational or womanly in *The Republic*: look to women to see what you need to steer clear of if you would acquire moral, and thus civic, virtue. Luce Irigaray's defiance of this injunction from Plato and its repetition in Jung gestures towards the possibility of a different kind of individuation, one that is emancipatory for women. Thus Luce Irigaray's provocative rejection of Plato can be seen as a response to Jung's idea that it is sometimes appropriate, and always necessary, for a woman to liberate herself from the binding shackles of a needy and dependent man.

I suggested that in *The Republic* Plato distinguishes between simple narration and imitative narration and raises the question of the moral worthiness of imitation or mimesis. Plato argues that the guardians or rulers of the republic should only imitate those whom they are potentially like, those whose professions they will become a part of because 'each man can practise well one profession but not many, and that if he attempts more, and meddles with many, he will fail to attain any credible distinction' (Plato 1992: 194e). Imitation is therefore important in the development of a person, but who one imitates is crucial: one should imitate those who embody the best character as it relates to one's potential professional life. This applies through education: pedagogically, one privileges the best and resists the worst: guardians, on this story, should 'know madmen and bad men and women, but they must neither do nor imitate any of their actions' (Plato 1992: 396a). Since poets are exemplary imitators – that is what they do as a living – the character of poets is morally problematic given their potential influence. Thus the kind of poetry they produce and the kind of character they are are morally significant.

The problem with poets, however, Plato later argues, is that, as imitators, they do not represent reality: the imitative man, of whom poets are exemplars, has 'no knowledge of any value on the subject of his imitation; [and] that imitation is a form of amusement and not a serious occupation' (Plato 1992: 602b). Poets are three times removed from the truth as all imitation 'produces work that is quite removed from the truth, and also associates with that element in us which is removed from insight, and is its companion and is friend to no healthy or true purpose' (Plato 1992: 603b). In Plato's tripartite soul, which I shall shortly be discussing, reason brings us closest to truth: passion assists reason in its apprehension of truth, and desire is the errant factor of the soul which leads us astray. The element in us which is removed from insight is, then, desire. Desire is the least worthy aspect of the soul, obfuscating and leading us astray. To be ruled by desire is to be womanly and unreliable and, indeed, Plato holds in contempt those governed by desire.

For Plato mimesis is one of the elements that is fundamental to our character formation. Mimesis as imitation 'brings about' who we are: we imitate and internalise what we imitate and so develop our own moral characters which we can then represent in our moral imaginations and the actions that emerge as a result of these imaginations. So, for example, when we imitate goodness or badness, or encourage others to do the same thing, our moral characters are enabled. So mimesis does (at least) two things: it distances us from truth, because it is imitation, but mimesis also helps us not only to understand but to see what goodness and badness are actually like as practised by those we imitate (Griswold 2005).

One of the effects of poetry is that it represents to us aspects of ourselves of which we might be ashamed; and in so doing, it forms our imaginations by allowing us to think and feel in ways we would not readily admit to. This is one reason we need to be wary of poets. They enact mimesis in their work and, while acknowledging their influence, we cannot be certain of the precise nature of that influence, whether it is good or bad.

Plato's directive that we should know what is bad and mad without imitating them is instructive here in terms of gender conceptions. His examples of the mad and the bad, you will have noted, allude to women and what we might think of as anima feminine properties. The properties Plato ascribes to women, young and old, that men, especially guardians, should avoid imitating are simultaneously the feminine properties characteristic of Jung's conception of the anima, and of the bad. Plato's view is that women are bad because they have disordered souls. The exception is women who have manly souls ordered by reason.[1] Women with *manly* souls can become guardians. Since most women are ruled by desire rather than reason, and are thus irrational, most women are bound to the bad and are unworthy of imitation. Woman, the bad and the irrational form a 'triumgynate', the imitation of which leads to moral unworthiness, moral failure and immoral character.[2]

When we turn to Carl Jung's discussion of identification as imitation we can see that it has resonances with Plato's analysis of imitation as a mode of mimesis. We find that Jung argues for identification as unconscious imitation and is thus an integral constructive mechanism of the psyche. Jung also argues for a notion of conscious imitation very like that which Plato claims for the poets and for the development of a good moral character (Jung 1971: 738).[3] In 'Plato's Echo' I pointed out that imitation initiates and reveals the dialectical relationship between a subject and her world (Gray forthcoming).

I also proposed that the moral dimension of individuation is highlighted by the play of mimesis in which modes of behaviour appropriate to sex/gendered bodies fall under a masculine ideal that valorises manliness and the masculine, and deprecates womanliness and the irrational feminine[4] and that Jung iterates the very same sex/gender values as Plato. Again, we find in Jung these prejudicial notions at work in his conceptions of anima and animus (Jung 1966: 296ff).[5] One might wonder, on this basis, about the gendered nature of individuation.[6] If there are attitudes and dispositions brought to bear on individuation, thought of in terms of liberation and wholeness, for whom is wholeness the existentially important process Jung claims it to be? Plato's idea that the ordered soul matches a masculine ideal of reason seems to be what Jung is attuned to rather than a balance of both manly and womanly properties. Of course, one could argue that the ordered soul is nothing more than the balance brought about through the mediating influence of reason. Reason functions then, on this account, as the fulcrum around which the masculine and the feminine are poised in equilibrium.

But this overlooks the manliness of the soul governed by reason, itself a masculine aspect of the soul. Positive psychic characteristics are always weighted in favour of the masculine and the manly, because the feminine is positive only in so far as it is a catalyst for change to the masculine, the manly and the ordered. In other words we find in both Plato and Jung, a preference for abandoning what is considered to be feminine or womanly. The adoption of masculine or manly psychic characteristics is what will ensure moral order and increase the chances of becoming individuated.[7] The feminine is castigated as a genuine mode of being that is capable of producing *directly* either moral development or individuation. Desire tips the balance in favour of disorder and, as it happens, in favour of construing the soul as a womanly soul.

DIALECTIC AND OPPOSITION

We need to be very careful in our articulation of what is going on in Plato's and then Jung's elucidation of the feminine. Plato is not arguing that the feminine is to be equated with desire. Rather, Plato's point is that when desire predominates, then the result is a womanly soul. Womanliness or the feminine is thus an effect of the interplay between the three elements of the soul as they relate to each other. Womanliness or manliness is an attribute of the soul *overall* and not an attribute of one aspect of the soul. On the other hand, Jung attributes to the anima feminine the capacity to bring disorder. In other words, the anima feminine is already in principle a feminine attribute of the psyche. The feminine is not an effect of the overall composition of the psyche as is the case in Plato. It would be fair to say, however, that both Plato and Jung are working within a framework which employs oppositional concepts like order and disorder, masculine and feminine and that very clearly they align or group together some concepts which they then privilege over others.[8] This struggle between order and disorder, for example, which can be expressed in the notion of dialectic, is the inspiration founding philosophical dialectical method.

Dialectic is at work in Plato's texts; and in Jung's work, dialectic emerges as both a methodological device, which articulates the logical relations between some of his central concepts, and as relationship, which emerges in his discussion of concepts such as collective and personal forms of the unconscious. So let us, in our Platonic mapping of Jung, distinguish dialectic as method and dialectic as relationship. We have already seen one use of the term in Hegel's Master/Slave Dialectic, but let us return to an earlier period, when it was not interpreted in that form.

Dialectic as method

Dialectic as method has a long philosophical history and involves both affirmation (of a proposition or set of propositions and their conclusion in an argument) and negation (of those propositions and rejection of their conclusion). The aim of dialectical argument in this sense is to explore the consequences of holding specific views in relation to discovering the truth about some concept like beauty or justice. Arguments advanced and countered become the testing ground for exploring how one might best conceive of that concept. The best conception will not only be the best logical case, but will also be the best possible understanding a concept might be given within the context in which it is discussed and argued. One proceeds through a series of arguments and counter-arguments to arrive at the truth of a matter. Typically, examples are drawn from the lives and experiences of the advocates and antagonists. Central to this conception of dialectic is the idea of opposition contained in affirmation and negation: I assert 'X' and you assert 'non-X' by offering an example either contrary to, or contradicting, what I have just affirmed. Your retort results in my defending my position with the addition of new propositions; you respond, and so on.

This sense of dialectic occurs in Plato's dialogues and may be loosely called 'Socratic' dialectic after Socrates, who argued in just this fashion. Characteristically, Socrates poses a problem, for example, 'What is justice?', the central question of *The Republic*. The various characters in the dialogue then put forward answers which Socrates refutes by arguing against either their whole answer or some of its premises. Dialectic in this case is the posing of a question, an offering of an answer and then an attempt at its refutation: in essence it is philosophical argument. It is what Giegerich is referring to when he claims that dialectic is one, is a Position, the original position. Dialectic as method has to do with practice: how we argue, how we attempt to influence the opinions of others and to persuade them that something is or is not the case. Fundamentally, it is linguistic practice, practice that evolves with our learning to speak and to use language as a tool of communication. In using dialectic as method, we continue, as

Socrates did, to call upon the world as exemplary of that about which we speak. Philosophy as empirical practice is embodied in this idea of dialectic. How things are and how we might like them to be are often the grist of dialectical method. In this sense dialectical method can reflect dialectic as relation, to which I now turn.

Dialectic as relationship

In the 'Physics', Plato's former pupil Aristotle argues that 'everything that comes to be or passes away comes from, or passes into, its contrary or an intermediate state. But the intermediates are derived from the contraries – colours, for instance from black and white. Everything, therefore, that comes to be by a natural process is either a contrary or a product of contraries' (Aristotle 1941: 22–6). One and many, rest and motion, Love and Strife are all contraries or opposites for Aristotle.

The pre-Socratic philosophers Anaxagoras and Empedocles each tell different stories about the origins of rest and motion, which are conceived of as opposing states. Each suggests that rest and motion are the effect of activity. In the case of Anaxagoras, Mind (Nous) acts to disrupt and to separate an original one-ness at rest, which produces motion, a view reminiscent of Giegerich's. Empedocles, on the other hand, argues that originally there are two opposing trends, rest and motion. Motion is caused by the activities of Love and Strife and their involvement with the one and the many. For Empedocles, Love strives to make one out of many, and Strife attempts the opposite, to make many out of one. Lack of activity by either Love or Strife results in rest. Thus, in his discussion of motion, Aristotle observes:

> If then it is possible that at any time nothing should be in motion, this must come about in one of two ways: either in the manner described by Anaxagoras, who says that all things were together and at rest for an infinite period of time, and then that Mind introduced motion and separated them; or in the manner described by Empedocles, according to whom the universe is alternately in motion and at rest – in motion when Love is making the one out of many, or Strife is making many out of one, and at rest in the intermediate periods of time.
>
> (Aristotle 1941: 21–9)

On this reading of Anaxagoras and Empedocles, we can see two possible origins of the notion of dialectic: in singularity and in duality. This fundamental principle of contraries or opposites sees paired 'things' in tension with each other, a tension that means one is possible only through the existence of the other; but what relates them is negation, not strictly as a logical term, but as a logical relation by virtue of the way things are. First, opposing pairs are related through negation because each is not what the other is. Secondly, the negation of either 'thing' (not-white, Aristotle's example) implies both the existence of white and not-white. 'Not-white', as Aristotle points out, might imply either black or any other intermediate colour. The negation of something might mean either its absolute opposite or something intermediate between that opposite and the thing opposed. If we follow Aristotle here, we can see that negation of the term 'masculine' would imply both the existence of masculine and not-masculine as absolute opposites but would also allow feminine or something intermediate between masculine and feminine.[9] In other words, Aristotle's construction of opposition allows for both contraries and contradictories as possible oppositions.

This is an interesting turn, for the binary pairing of, for example, masculine and not-masculine ties the affirming and negating terms into a mutually exclusive relationship. Jung's assessment of homosexuality fits into this binary opposition (Jung 1968a: 356), yet his distinction between the 'primitive' and the 'civilised' seems more in sympathy with Aristotle's idea of negation as intermediate possibility. Whatever the case, difference is the pivotal idea here, for to say that something is or is not (something) is to differentiate or ideate it from other 'things'. We will see in Plato's discussion of the soul that reason and desire are engaged in struggle and that passion's role is to assist reason. This struggle is exemplary of dialectic as relationship: it is also Hegel's idea found in the Master/Slave. We might think of this as a struggle for recognition between elements of the soul. Where reason dominates, the soul is ordered; where desire dominates the soul is disordered. The disordered soul, the feminine or womanly soul, is seen as contrary to the order of the rational masculine or manly soul. Because desire is always present as an element of the soul, there is an ongoing relationship between it and reason as reason strives to maintain order.

Both dialectic as method and dialectic as relationship are exhibited in Jung's work. Jung uses dialectical method in extrapolating the archetypes, in his discussion of psychological types and as a means of identifying the collective unconscious as distinct from the personal. His mode of discussion and argument is, overall, couched in dialectical terms: comparison, contrast and evaluation. Simultaneously, he employs dialectic as relationship in the way he establishes his specific psychological categories and concepts. Furthermore, Jung uses dialectic as relationship in both senses: as oppositional and as intermediate possibility. The notion of individuation, for example, assumes the idea of flux where self is fluid and has the potential to be transformed. On this view, self can have no fixed and unchangeable boundaries and therefore exemplifies dialectic as intermediate possibility. Self is never what it is but it is also never not what it is. In its fluid mobility, self engenders from its internal makeup and its external engagement with the world the two-ness necessary for dialectical method and relationship. These two terms become the relata of change.

I have already argued that Jung's reading of the anima feminine as something to be overcome since it embodies disruption is close to Plato's notion of the feminine as disorder of the whole soul. I want now to turn to some more general observations about the philosophical tracings of Plato in Jung, whose interpretation of the self as sex/gendered echoes Plato's conception of the soul or mind. Jung's familiarity with Plato is evident (Jung 1967 and 1968a). Indeed, a reading of Platonic texts reveals a remarkable coincidence between aspects of Jung's psychological typology and Plato's faculty psychology expressed in the existence of a tripartite soul, much of which can be mapped onto the sex/gender cultural stereotypes found in both Plato's and Jung's cultures. For example, the idea of the transcendent function in Jung closely resembles Plato's rational part of the soul, as I have already suggested; and the irascible feminine or anima in Jung's work evokes the wantonness of Plato's account of the irrational, disordered soul ruled by desire. But let us see how this is played out between the two thinkers.

HUMAN NATURE AND THE PLATONIC SOUL

As I have been arguing, Plato's writing is primarily in dialogical form: dialogue between protagonist and antagonist is the means through which dialectic as method is expressed. As I have just noted, the dialogues explore questions posed by Socrates, who then engages in conversation with one or several other discussants.[10] It is generally agreed among scholars that Plato's dialogues can be divided into early, middle and late periods. The early and middle periods are held to most closely resemble the views of Plato's teacher, the historical Socrates. Socrates was indicted by Meletus for impiety, for being 'a doer of evil, inasmuch he corrupts the youth of Athens, and does not receive the gods whom the state receives, but has a religion of his own' (Plato 1970a). The events surrounding Socrates' death are found in the early dialogues, *Euthyphro*, *Apologia*, *Crito* and *Phaedo*. These early dialogues foreshadow the complexity, depth and breadth of Plato's philosophical interests which culminate in the *Laws*, his last book. Many of the issues Plato discusses are still modern debates both within and without philosophy, for example the existence and nature of the mind or soul (psyche). Plato's own philosophical views are evident in the later dialogues although, chronologically, it is never clear where the line between the historical Socrates and Plato can actually be drawn. For this reason, my use of 'Plato' should be interpreted as having an ambiguous referent in Socrates/Plato.

In *The Republic*, a dialogue from Plato's middle period, he sets out to define justice.[11] Plato develops a theory of community or collective, the individual soul and the relationship between them. He argues that a community's origins are in individuals' awareness that they are not self-sufficient. Individuals pre-exist communities, and collectives are formed around the exchange of labour and goods between individuals. In this sense, communities or collectives are based in economic need. 'People become involved with various other people to fulfil various needs . . . And people trade goods with one another, because they think they'll be better off if each gives or receives something in exchange, don't they?' (Plato 1992: 369b–d). Not only that, Plato also argues that some people are more suited to some occupations than they are to others because they have the kind of nature which predisposes them to performing a specific type of work: people are innately oriented towards medicine or philosophy or rhetoric, for example. Such a nature, then, 'is relevant to identity of occupation . . . We want for example, that a man with a medical mind and a woman with a medical mind have the same nature' (Plato 1992: 454c–d). Plato uses the idea of a just or moral community as a potential model for the just or moral individual. He argues that '[i]t's not impossible, then, that morality might exist on a larger scale in the larger entity and be easier to discern . . . [w]hy don't we start by trying to see what morality is like in communities? And then we can examine individuals too, to see if the larger entity is reflected in the features of the smaller entity' (Plato 1992: 369a).

There are three things to note here:

i Plato is making a claim about individual psychology. Individuals come to the *realisation* that they are needy and better off with the help of others.
ii Plato is suggesting that community is formed through economic need based upon the recognition that self-sufficiency is not possible. Hence he is suggesting that there is an intrinsic relationship between individual psychology and economics.
iii Plato is suggesting that it might be possible for a just individual to mirror a just community, a point to which I return below.

Plato argues that there are three classes of community members: workers, auxiliaries and guardians, each of whom has a different function in a community, to produce and sell, to protect, and to rule.[12] A community is just or moral when each member and each class performs its function to its best capacity. He also argues, as I noted above, that a just or moral individual will be like a just community. Since communities are composed of three classes, so individuals will have the same three classes in themselves. And here is the rub: Plato concludes that the composition of the community reflects the features and characteristics of its constituent members. In other words, communities have three constituent parts because their individual members *already* have three constituent parts: 'I mean where else would they have got them from?' (Plato 1992: 435e–436a).

Communities are, for example, passionate, lovers of knowledge or mercenary because that is what their members are like. Hence communities are as they are by virtue of the characteristics of their members: the morality or justice of a community reflects the collective morality or justice of individual members. Collectives or communities are mirrors of their members and as such are mirrors of their members' souls.

We can see from this why it is that Plato is so concerned about poets and about imitation. The success, moral or otherwise, of a community really depends on the characteristics of its individual members, all of whom should endeavour to do that for which they are best suited. They learn how to do this from others who are similarly possessed of the same kind of soul. That being the case, members need to act as exemplars of the best moral characteristics for they will be imitated by younger members who are learning how to be good, *the best* members of the collective. Economic need brings communities into existence, while the characteristics of the individuals concerned determine the kind of community that will result. For Plato, justice, love of knowledge, self-discipline, courage and wisdom are properties or characteristics of soul or mind that will produce individuals who will produce harmonious communities. Given this, psychological capacities and characteristics of community members are qualitatively fundamental to community. Individuals who realise their human inability to be self-sufficient in the first place suggest the existence of thoughtful and judging aspects of their souls.

The Platonic soul is tripartite and consists of desire, passion and reason (rational part). Like their community equivalents in workers, auxiliaries and guardians, each of the three parts of the soul performs a different function. As in the community, the soul works best when each part works at its highest level, doing what it should do. An analogy that Plato employs in a later dialogue, *Phaedrus*, where he suggests that the true nature of the soul 'would be a theme of large and more than mortal discourse', is helpful here; this is also an analogy to which Jung refers on several occasions.[13] Plato compares the soul with a 'pair of winged horses and charioteer joined in natural union' (Plato 1970b *Phaedrus*: 246a). He draws a comparison between the gods and humans and their respective tasks as charioteers and argues that, comparatively speaking, the gods have an easier undertaking as charioteers than do humans. This is because the natures of their respective pairs of chariot horses are different. On the one hand the gods' chariots are driven by paired horses both of which are 'noble and of noble breed', and on the other, humans have great difficulty in managing chariots driven by their 'mixed', paired horses. Plato maintains that only one of the two horses of which a human charioteer has charge is noble and of noble breed. The other is 'ignoble and of ignoble breed' (Plato 1970b *Phaedrus*: 246b). Plato intends us to think of the charioteer as analogous to reason; the noble horse to passion, the auxiliary of reason; and the ignoble horse, to desire. The triadic nature of the chariot mirrors the tripartite nature of both the soul and the republic. The charioteer is to reason what reason is to ruler or guardian; the noble horse to passion as passion is to auxiliary; and the ignoble horse to desire as desire is to worker. Plato's description of the task that must be undertaken by a charioteer reflects that of reason and of ruler in their respective functions. The work of each part is similar in each of the three cases.

Hence the actions of the charioteer, aided by the noble and controlled horse, in keeping the unruly, ignoble horse under rein when it runs wild, illustrate the harmonising work of reason in the soul and the disruptive nature of desire. Just as the auxiliaries aid the guardians in the city to control the workers, so the charioteer (reason) and the noble horse (passion) work to control the feistiness of the ignoble horse (desire) which has the potential to destroy the whole chariot. This characterisation of the soul and Plato's assertion that the republic mirrors the souls of its citizens have some interesting consequences with respect to women.

Plato, then, argues in *The Republic* that 'every individual has to do just one of the jobs relevant to the community, the one for which his nature has best equipped him' (Plato 1992: 370a–c, 374a–d, 433a). One's nature decides the kind of occupation that one should engage in. For example, a cobbler has a cobbler-nature and should cobble, a doctor has a doctor-nature and should practise medicine and a guardian has a guardian-nature and should become a guardian. Each person is naturally suited because his/her soul is naturally disposed to performing the tasks associated with each occupation and to performing those tasks well. Biological features do not count when it comes to determining what occupation a member of the republic should pursue. And socialisation through mimetic education serves to develop innate characteristics an individual might have. Thus characteristics of the soul are supremely important. Not only that, the ordering of the tripartite soul determines its quality. The best-quality soul is one where reason harmoniously rules passion and desire and is thus a masculine or manly soul.

We have seen that the function of the guardian in the collective is to rule and to maintain harmony, as is the function of reason in the soul. One becomes a guardian because one has a guardian-nature; and a guardian-nature is identifiable through the qualities of a particular kind of soul. Significantly, philosophers turn out to be those who most clearly embody the kind of soul that is a prerequisite for becoming a guardian: one of Plato's radical conclusions in *The Republic* is that it is philosophers who are most fit to rule because they are 'sightseers of the truth' (Plato 1992: 475e). And at 484b of *The Republic*, Plato argues that 'philosophers are those who are capable of apprehending that which is permanent and unvarying, while those who can't, those who wander erratically in the midst of plurality and variety, are not lovers of knowledge'. Philosophers are qualified to rule because they can perceive and contemplate the Forms, the unchanging reality subtending plurality and variety. So philosophers can see things as they really are. In the philosophers, the rational part, or reason, 'is wise and looks out for the whole of the mind' and so has the role of ruler. The number of individuals in whom such a soul is present is very small. And to train and live as a philosopher is an extraordinarily difficult task.[14] Importantly, philosophers will take turns at guardianship. Plato regards ruling as 'an obligation, not a privilege' so that the actual practice of ruling, when philosophers become involved in the affairs of state and everyday life, is taken on as a necessary part of their lives, and one to which is attached a certain amount of resentment (Plato 1992: 540b). The primary task for a philosopher is to contemplate the Forms and to train others who will inherit guardianship. Fulfilment of the guardian role means that one's communion with the Forms is disturbed.

SEX/GENDER AND THE SOUL

Very clearly, Plato is proposing a class system, determined by soul type (and birth) in which guardianship is the pinnacle. However, it is not only men who can become guardians and rulers. Plato argues that, although women are physically inherently weaker than men, some of them will nonetheless be naturally predisposed to being guardians because they will 'have the required natural abilities'. They will have philosopher-natures: and the having of the same natures is equivalent, for Plato, to having the same kind of soul (Plato 1992: 451a–458, 540c). That is to say, if women possess harmonious souls that are ruled by reason rather than by either passion or desire and if they have all of the other skills required of a philosopher, then they are eligible to become rulers. The function of women in the republic, then, is determined by the quality of their souls in the same way as it is for men. In a discussion of the role and identity of women in the republic, Elizabeth Spelman examines Plato's apparently enlightened view of women (Spelman 1988). But, as Spelman points out, the idea of Plato as a proponent of liberation for women is misguided.

Spelman reiterates Plato's view that it does not matter that a cobbler might be hairy: she/he can be a good cobbler regardless of hairiness or baldness. What makes someone a good cobbler is not related to this specific quality (hairiness or baldness). It is a quality of the soul or a talent for being a cobbler that make someone a cobbler. Similarly, a person's sex/gender is a physical feature not relevant to good governance. Indeed, Plato argues that 'if we find either the male or the female sex excelling the other in any art or other pursuit, then we shall say that this particular pursuit must be assigned to one and not to the other' (Plato 1992: 454e). Being biologically male or female is analogous to being hairy or bald in relation to one's occupation. On the whole, physical characteristics and properties are to be discounted as irrelevant to one's occupation. Spelman notes that in Plato's republic the behaviour of men and women is an important determinant of anyone's nature. The hairiness of a cobbler might not affect his capacity to fulfil his role as a cobbler. But that he cobbles – what he does, how he behaves – indicates that he does not have the nature of a philosopher. 'Doing what a cobbler does cannot be the expression of a soul contemplating the eternal forms; thus the soul of a philosopher cannot be expressed in the life of a male cobbler. And though it can be expressed in the life of a woman, this is only so long as she acts in particular ways and engages in particular pursuits' (Spelman 1988: 31).

Thus *what one does* as an occupation and *who one is* in the republic is quality-specific, but that specificity must be relevant or appropriate to the task under consideration. Farmers and cobblers (whether hairy or bald, tall or short) do not have the kind of soul that is capable of contemplating the eternal forms. Most females will be precluded from guardianship as they simply do not behave in the relevant ways and therefore do not possess the same nature as the philosopher. Spelman argues that, although in *The Republic* not all women are inferior to all men and that some women are equal to the best of men and in fact superior to other men, this reflects a system of class privilege based on allegedly innate characteristics of the soul. She suggests that in the best and most widely governed state, we can expect to find women as well as men among the ruling class (Spelman 1988: 34). Relatively speaking, the number of women who have the potential to be rulers is small because the possession of the relevant kind of soul by women is very limited (as it is also in the case of men, but women are on the whole a much smaller proportion of the total possible guardians).

It is important to stress here that Plato's individuals are not monistic: they are not composed of one single substance, but of two, body and mind or soul. The relationship between the two is such that the body reflects the soul: you can tell what a soul is like by how a body behaves. In *The Republic* there are clear suggestions that Plato has little time for most women. He argues that if boys are 'to grow up good' then they should be encouraged to imitate men and not women. He tolerates the idea of women guardians because they possess the souls of philosophers, or, as Spelman calls them, *manly* souls.

Spelman argues that Plato treats souls 'as if they are gendered' (Spelman 1988: 34). In the *Timaeus*, for example, Plato remarks that:

> of the men who came into the world, those who were cowards or led unrighteous lives may with reason be supposed to have changed into the nature of women in the second generation. And this was the reason

> why at that time the gods created in us the desire of sexual intercourse, contriving in man one animated substance, and in woman another . . .
> (Plato 1970c: *Timaeus* 90e–91a)

The transmigration or movement of the soul from its former body to a new one once death occurs, and its subsequent rebirth, is alluded to in this passage, as is the idea that souls are judged once their mortal body dies. Salient to our purposes, though, is the idea that souls are gendered and can change from one sex/gender to another upon rebirth. A cowardly man's soul will change to a woman's soul and he will be reincarnated as a woman when he is reborn. Spelman, however, has a more interesting interpretation of what is going on here. She suggests that four different sex/gender combinations of body and soul are possible for Plato:

a Manly soul/male body
b Manly soul/female body
c Womanly soul/male body
d Womanly soul/female body (Spelman 1988: 32).

That a man is a coward suggests a mismatch of body and soul: cowardice, like courage, is a state of the soul. So that if a soldier is cowardly it is because he has a womanly soul. His is a soul ruled by desire and for him there is an improper fit between his soul and his body. A cowardly soldier has a womanly soul and a male body. Reborn as a woman, the soul of a cowardly soldier achieves a proper fit, so a womanly soul in a female body best represents what really is the case. On this view, a woman with a philosopher's soul is represented in b (above). But as Spelman also points out, there is a difficulty with the question of fit. 'Despite the demand for a "fit," there doesn't have to be a male body in order for a manly soul to be recognized, nor does there have to be a female body for a womanly soul to be recognized' (Spelman 1988: 33). In terms of sex/gender, the soul expresses itself through the body of that in which it is found. A manly or a womanly soul confers manly or womanly characteristics onto the body to which they are attached. Hence a manly soul elevates the ranking of a female body; and a womanly soul demotes the ranking of a male body. So if we think of sex/gender as conferring a *type* on both body and soul, then it does two things. First, sex/gender is the ground for distinguishing what sex/gender a soul really is. A soul that is rational, ordered, courageous and moral is a manly soul. A soul that is irrational, disordered, cowardly and licentious is a womanly soul. And secondly, the manliness or womanliness of a soul is, very clearly, the basis for the attribution of value to souls and their bodies. A manly soul is the more valued soul and the combination of manly soul and male body is more valued than other possible combinations. As we saw earlier, to be a woman or to have womanly soul attributes is to be regarded as both morally and existentially inferior. Fortunately for those women born with a manly soul, there is a way out through transmigration of the soul and the possibility of reincarnation in a man's body where proper fit will be achieved. A womanly soul will achieve a proper fit through transmigration and reincarnation but the resulting complex of body and soul will be inferior to the complex of male body and manly soul.

This construction of sex/gender type pre-figures Jung's analysis of the relation between body and psyche. Obviously, we cannot transfer all of Plato's account of the republic, the individuals of whom it is composed, and their origins, to the Jungian corpus. But we can use elements of the account in a dialectical interpretative framework in which we might locate some of Jung's philosophical understandings that find themselves transformed in his analytical psychology. The relationship, as we shall see, between individual and collective is strikingly different in Jung's and Plato's accounts. For Jung, the existence of the individual is an effect of collective activity on a biological, social and symbolic body which is coupled with the development of consciousness. For Plato, a collective (the community or republic) grows out of economic necessity based on the realisation that no one is self-sufficient. Furthermore, Plato's account suggests that individuals are most truly their souls, souls that transmigrate and are reborn in a body that is appropriate to soul type as a reward or as punishment for good and bad deeds. Individuals pre-exist the community and it is the job of the community to develop the soul as it should be developed in terms of the one thing it can best do. The role of the body seems to be, on Plato's account, as a conduit for the activity of the soul and as a sex/gender type indicator of the soul. The role of the body, the flesh and blood of which humans are made, as a sex/gender type indicator and the relationship between body and soul are more ambiguous in Jungian psychology. We need now to explore the ways in which Jung thinks of the body and its relation to the psyche. And because the body is *in* the world, in a community, we need also to explore the way in which Jung understands the relation between body and community or collective.

Chapter 3

Locating identity

Individual and collective matters

> We do not begin as individuals and become members of a collective; we begin as members of a collective and become individuals . . .

For whatever reasons, and whether we like it or not, either through nature or nurture, or both together, the world is divided into men and women who are initiated into male or masculine, and female or feminine, roles in life. There are two things to consider here: what men and women are like, and what men and women *do*, given what they are like. 'What we are like' is a reference to the sex/gendering of us as human beings based on what *our bodies are like or are perceived to be like*, and how they are interpreted by our birth collectives, as our bodies – and we – are groomed to be men and women through the social processes of those collectives. It is an indisputable fact that 'men rule the world': men are more visible in the public sphere in politics, religions, sport, senior management, business, the arts and sciences as 'decision makers and shakers'. Men are glorified in violent cultural productions in film and television, in wars and in the authority of their opinions. Their visibility symbolises their power. Lest you think you have just travelled back thirty-five years to some feminist consciousness-raising text, watch your television tonight, read your newspapers, see who predominates in the telecasting of sporting events. It is not women you will come across (although they[1] may be incidentally important, and even intrinsic to, the grand narrative that persists, in spite of all attempts to dislodge or disavow it). On the other hand, women are visible, yes: but as adornments, as love-struck and then abandoned stars, as unhappy ('real' or pretend) princesses, or 'older women who still manage to look young', as failures or successes in high or low culture. Where do these women come from and how are they related to the visibility of men? And what is a woman, and what is a man, anyway? Furthermore, how are individual women and men related to the generalisations we make about them given their differences, cultural diversities and sexual preferences?

The arguments about collectives, cultural embeddedness and situatedness which we explored earlier give us a 'way in' to answering these questions. If men and women and the major cognate terms associated with them ('male', female', 'masculine', 'feminine') emerge from collective cultural understandings, then we need to turn to the collective rather than the individual, to figure out their origins. That, indeed, is what has happened with the appearance, from the middle of the twentieth century, of the work of Martin Heidegger, Jean-Paul Sartre, Simone de Beauvoir, Maurice Merleau-Ponty, Emmanuel Levinas, Jacques Derrida and Michel Foucault. Their work highlights the shift to the collective as the site of origins of human being.

The political, legal and moral ramifications of the collectivising of individual origins have yet to be seen. How responsible, morally and legally, is an individual for her/his actions if she/he is an effect of socio-cultural processes? What obligations do collectives have towards their members over and above the settling of their rights and responsibilities? Are collectives politically, legally and morally bound to provide the very best circumstances that will lead to the flourishing of both individual and collective? Are collectives obligated to eliminate all forms of oppression, actual and potential, so that their members will have the best possible life opportunities? And what role does the unconscious play in all of this?

Most of these questions, and their answers, are far beyond my scope in this book, yet it is important to acknowledge the delicate, yet robust, underpinnings of identity if we are to see the solutions to some of these issues. That is what recent feminist theorising, in particular, has attempted to do: to look at the foundations and to do the important work of understanding the psycho-social and psycho-cultural assumptions that determine the ordering of the social world and the making of individual persons. So, for example, if we consider the wraith-like models and their 'opposites', the overweight bodies whose images frequent popular media, the debates about women's bodies and bio-technologies such as IVF, breast implantations and cosmetic surgery, then our reflections might lead us to ponder the preponderant attitudes to women and their bodies so evident in these images and issues.

The attitudes are not new: indeed they are very, very old: they are articulated in and through the pages of philosophy and they emerge in the social representations of women and their bodies. We can see this if we look at women's magazines and the portrayal of women, for example, in popular television and film. The study of the psyche, because it has been so pervasively influenced by philosophy, has assumed many of these attitudes. More disturbingly, they are attitudes that are insidious and still operative, generally, in Western democratic societies, the 'things that are taken for granted' as foundation myths (for instance that women are more sociable than men, that women are more caring than men, that men and women reason differently or that men attain at a higher level in mathematics than women, who are 'better at language' than men). Philosophy and psychology, both psychoanalysis and analytical psychology, reflect and then inform some of those myths which in turn reflect and inform philosophy and psychology. A dialectic of the common and popular on the one hand, and the specialist and the 'expert' exists here, with projection and counter-projection trading places for recognition. In all of this, the body is basic, as is the role of the unconscious and its manifestations. This chapter opens up discussion on both of these elements. I begin with the body.

BODY-TYPE AND PSYCHE

The distinction between manly and womanly souls, and male and female bodies, their match and mismatch, to which Elizabeth Spelman draws our attention in her analysis of Plato's *Republic* is echoed in Jung's understanding of men and women and the masculine and feminine. Plato's mind/body dualism is obvious with the requisite privileging of mind over body that sees mind contributing its qualities to the overall value of the mind/body configuration. Needless to say, it is not so obvious that Jung is dualistic in this Platonic sense, although what *is* clear is that Jung does not unambiguously associate the masculine and feminine with body-type.[2] On the one hand, Jung works with the assumption that one takes oneself to be, primarily, of one sex/gender. On the other, he argues that the anima feminine is an *a priori* given, a natural archetype that 'is not characteristic of unconsciousness in its entirety. She is only one of its aspects. This is shown by the very fact of her femininity. 'What is not-I, not masculine, is most probably feminine, and because the not-I is felt as not belonging to me, and therefore outside me, the anima-image is usually projected upon women' (Jung, 1968a: 58). The conscious subject of this assertion is masculine, a subject that can dis-identify from its unconscious feminine aspect. Not-I is the contrary or counter-sexual of the sex/gender identified *primary* conscious subject. So that men consciously think of themselves *primarily* as masculine/male and women consciously think of themselves *primarily* as feminine/female.

This is not merely a matter of sex/gender of soul or mind, however. Men's and women's understandings of themselves as men or women arise through their conscious and unconscious experience of their bodies and how they figure their bodies by virtue of their experiences in their communities or collectives. We are told that the sex/gendered body plays an important role in Plato's philosophy – the body suggests the kind of soul that someone *should* have where there is a good or right match of soul and body. A female body points to a feminine soul and a male body to a masculine soul. The body acts as a gross indicator of an expected sex/

gender in Jung's work as well; and from the perspective of everyday lived experience, he is committed to the importance of the sex/gendered body as a mediating ground for the relation between the self and the collective. We see this operating in the development of the persona. The link between persona and sex/gendered body manifests itself in the domain of choice about one's role in the social world. And just as the soul is innately masculine or feminine according to the order it manifests, so the innateness of the feminine is explicated through Jung's analysis of the role of the anima feminine in its relation to the persona. The idea that the body operates as a gross indicator of sex/gender is primary and operative until this day, as it may well remain. But more needs to be said about the body and sex/gender identity than that.

Plato urges, as we saw, that men should not imitate women. Women as women are identified first and foremost through the type of their embodiment, as are men (presumably via their genitalia). Both women and men learn to imitate modes of behaviour appropriate for their sex/gender type. On this model, girls will imitate both the female-ness and the womanliness of adult women where there is an appropriate fit between body and soul; and boys will imitate the male-ness and manliness of adult men where there is an appropriate fit between body and soul. On this conception of sex/gender type, both learning and innate dispositions contribute to the making of men and women. Plato discourages boys from imitating both femaleness and womanliness where these are thought of as characteristics of body and soul respectively. It is possible for a boy to imitate a woman with a manly soul on this characterisation of psychic and bodily dualism, a prospect Plato does not really contemplate. And that, surely, should be encouraged. Plato is mute on this point although it is implicit that such women would provide good role models for boys (and girls). On the other hand, a boy should be discouraged from imitating the womanly soul in a male body (boys should not imitate a cowardly soldier as a cowardly soldier has a womanly soul).

Jung's idea that the feminine is initially an 'imprint' that results from a child's relationship with his mother is an extension of the innateness of the manly and the womanly, but from a very different perspective. His idea incorporates the notion of mimesis because he relies on the idea of imitation as unconscious copy in what is suggestive of a quite literal reading of the relationship between mother and child. The maternal feminine literally leaves an imprint on the child because of the child's existence in the mother's body during pregnancy. Jung relies on an idea of the innateness of the feminine not as soul disorder *per se*, but as a disruptive anima feminine in relation to the persona. Let us follow the steps of his argument here.

In 'Anima and Animus' (1966) Jung describes the role of the anima feminine in 'rescuing' the self from its persona entrapment. Jung's anima feminine is an innate disposition of the psyche that in its initial activity compensates for the over-valuation of the persona. The persona is an archetypal structuring of one's presentation of oneself to the world. In part, this involves conforming to the expectations that the collective has of specific sex/gendered embodiments. We can see empirical examples of this in our ordinary everyday lives and indeed the expectation of conformity often begins at birth. In Australian hospitals, for example, newly born female bodies are wrapped in pink blankets and newly born male bodies in blue. These sex/gender marking practices aim at the symbolic identification of this body as a girl child and that body as a boy child; girl and boy bodies will ultimately develop into women and men. Girls are given a girl's name, dolls, ribbons, frocks and are handled gently. Boys are given a boy's name, cars and trucks and trains, trousers and are handled less gently than their sisters. These practices are oriented around cultural assumptions about the meaning of being a girl and the meaning of being a boy. Collective meanings may not coincide with the meanings ultimately developed by a specific man or woman, but they do mould any individual's self-presentation. To put this in a Platonic context, sex/gender marking practices are derivative of perceived innate dispositions borne by female and male bodies and assumptions about womanly and manly minds. What one can be, what one can do, how one can engage with the world are always already prescribed in the meanings of specific sex/gendered body-types. The persona is a response to how the collective sees and understands a specific sex/gendered embodiment (and its social situatedness).[3] What one can be, who one is, is always tied to these meanings, even if one is able to rupture the socio-cultural threads that bring meaning. The persona is then, to a large degree, a reflection of a collective's attitudes to the kind of embodiment that one has, an extraverted response to one's place in the socio-cultural world.

Jung's concept of the persona contributes to an explanation, and highlights the role, of the collective origin of an individual, which I shall be dealing with more extensively in the next chapter. Briefly, the story is this. During early life and young adulthood, the persona develops as a response to the demands and expectations of its collective and the world. It becomes a person's mode of being in the world. As an apparently 'mature self', a man might identify with his persona, as masculine, and according to Jung, usually does (Jung 1966: 'Anima and Animus'). Unconscious identification with the persona, which as we saw is mimetic, causes a man to generate a 'false' sense of himself as an individual: the persona seems to be him, the I that he is, but actually turns out to be something from which he can distinguish himself, a not-I in the same way as the anima feminine is not-I. A man can therefore be both not-I feminine (anima) and not-I masculine (persona). He can think about who he is in the world as an entity distinct from what he takes himself to be. Who he is *to* the world and to himself is a mode of his subjectivity. Correlatively, who he is *in* the world is a subject position that enables him to locate himself in his social reality. The conscious realisation that he occupies various subject positions enables a man to see that his persona, as a mode of subjectivity, can be retreated from, is something with which he need not identify, and thus to realise he is *other apart from* such subject positions. That is to say, it highlights his ego function, basically through negation: his persona as a mode of subjectivity is indeed a not-I.

Jung says that the persona is 'a mask that feigns individuality, and tries to make others and oneself believe that one is individual, whereas one is simply playing a part in which the collective psyche speaks' (Jung 1966: 245). The persona is a construct, a system of relations that produces the illusion of individual I-ness. In analysis, Jung claims, that illusion is disrupted as the collective nature of the self is discovered. But the persona is 'only a secondary reality, a product of compromise, in making which others often have a greater share than he' (Jung 1966: 246).

But, Jung suggests, there is a moment when, with the prompting of the anima, a man can no longer give himself over to the persona's worldly orientation. A 'voice' interpolates itself into a man's psyche. Significantly, this is the voice of the anima feminine which Jung describes as disrupting and unhappy. An analogous process takes place in a woman with what Jung sees as a masculine voice, the animus, insisting on its presence in a feminine subject. These voices, Jung claims, are as much aspects of the self as they are personae.[4] He calls the voices *contra-sexual* because they are the sexual opposite to what the subject takes to be his/her sexual identity.

Given this, we are immediately in the Platonic domain of differently sex/gendered bodies and minds or psyches. Jung's twist on this, however, is to suggest the co-presence of both manly and womanly characteristics in the one psyche. So not only are the voices contra-sexual in the sense that they are the opposite of the sex/gender one takes oneself to be, they are internally contra-sexual. What one takes oneself to be psychically or mentally, as far as sex/gender is concerned, on this basis, must be indeterminate. One is neither psychically masculine nor feminine, but is both. The corollary of this, and it is a corollary unrecognised by Jung, is that the feminine must be overcome. However, let us see where Jung takes us with his understanding of the sex/gendered nature of the psyche as a contra-sexual agent of change that symbolises the resistance of the self to the collective.

We might note that where a collective is deeply invested in the radical dichotomy and exclusiveness of masculine and feminine, male and female, the recognition of a contra-sexual voice is potentially subversive, just as it was in the work of Plato. But in contrast to Plato and although Jung assumes that the self is sex/gendered according to its body-type, a male body guarantees not a masculine self, but a self that is both masculine and feminine. This is also the case with a feminine self and female body: feminine sexed embodiment does not guarantee a feminine self but allows for the possibility of a self that is both feminine and masculine.

Jung argues that men have a psychic aptitude for the feminine that prepares them for relationships with women, which in turn prepares man for his conscious acquaintance with the collective feminine, the anima. On this account there is a deep connection between the mother, hence woman and the feminine, to which a man is ontogenetically tied. The feminine exists in man by virtue of his maternal, material origins. Indeed, the feminine, the trace of which is borne by the soul, is the precondition of man's existence. Woman's body is seen as the matter of life, her trace in the flesh and spirit an archaic reminder of her feminine immanence.

Jung argues that:

> the form of the world into which he is born is already inborn in him as virtual images, as psychic aptitudes. These *a priori* categories have by nature a collective character; they are images of parents, wife, and children in general, and are not individual pre-destinations. We must therefore think of these images as lacking in solid content, hence as unconscious.
>
> (Jung 1966: 300)

The idea of psychic aptitudes as images is clearly misleading if we think of images as icons or pre-formed pictures. Jung seems, here, to be construing 'copy' as form such as we find in the Aristotelian distinction between form and content. The copy of the feminine, which exists in a man, might be more properly thought of as a map or formal copy, a codex pointing to the existence of an innate feminine. On this argument, the grounding of the feminine in a man through the mother is both pre-discursive and pre-cognitive. Men unconsciously imitate the maternal feminine because of their originary exposure through their mothers' bodies; they are bathed in their mothers' bodies, fashioned and nourished by the maternal feminine. The imprint of the maternal body is a copy, an imitation which is an irresistible condition of men's being in the world.

Mutatis mutandis the argument Jung develops with respect to the relationship between a man and maternal copy applies equally to a woman. A woman, too, shares precisely the same prenatal conditions as does a man: she bathes in the mother's body, is produced as an effect of her mother's body and inherits her mother's genetic material. What is different, what change is necessitated in the case of the woman, is her very own embodiment: she is a woman body-type quite distinct from the man body-type from which emerges the male/masculine. Luce Irigaray picks this position up and it becomes the basis of her radical critique of masculinist theory. The body of the woman child, the girl, the daughter is not the body of the man child, the boy, the son. Boy and girl are always already different, albeit marked by their experiences in the body of the mother, marked by their mother's body as woman-type in her engagement in and with the collective and her own deep being. The body of a girl is a material copy of the body of the mother in a way that the body of a boy is not and cannot be. Likewise with the body of a boy and his father: the boy's body is a material copy of that of the father in a way that a girl's is not and cannot be. Psychic aptitude for the feminine is born in the body, feminine or masculine, with the traces of futurity immanent in its sexed fleshiness. Body-copy perpetuates body-type and its presence in the world.

Thus the notion of copy is doubly figured: the boy's body is a material copy of its father's body and simultaneously imprinted with a codified copy of the feminine; the girl's body is a material copy of its mother's body and simultaneously imprinted with a codified copy of the feminine (and a codified copy of the masculine, inherited from the father?). Codification of the feminine arises as an effect of experience of the maternal body, a remnant of originary exposure which grounds and anticipates the feminine in the lives of boys and girls. Yet the precise mechanism of codification is unclear. While genetic inheritance might be responsible for material copy, both the masculine and feminine are, in this analysis, not material, but psychic or mental.

If the psychic or mental is reducible to the material, then we might be able to give an account of the feminine and masculine in materialist terms which can then be extrapolated as genetic inheritance. If not, we need to be able to account for a non-material innateness principle from which arises psychic properties. Body-copy, like body-type, is not, however, reducible to sexual organs. The fabric of embodiment is woven genetically, its sexual organisation an effect of chromosomal structuring. The body that emerges from this process *remains* in process, nurtured by the symbolic existence into which it is initiated and by which it has already been influenced in its being in the body of the mother. Blue and pink blankets and naming augment this initiation. Body-copy enables identification with either mother or father, doubly figuring an eternal return to the parents. The body becomes a site of reminder and memory which brings with it the possibility of the future.

Yet the mother's body takes ontological precedence as the originary site of both anima feminine and maternal feminine. The female body becomes the medium through which the feminine is established and interpreted. One might wonder at the prospect of the father's body being understood as the site of the originary masculine, the medium through which the masculine is established and interpreted. The ejaculating penis in the mother, it might be argued, symbolises this originary site.[5] Hence, marked, too, by the body of the father, the bodies of men and the bodies of women bear the image of the father. This sex/gendered marking is subtle in its manifestations: a father's smile in the face of his daughter, a mother's sense of humour in her son. We see here, as we articulate the masculine and feminine as origins, a coalescence of the material and the symbolic, the literal and the metaphoric, the biological and the psychic. The theoretical distinctions emerging do not, however, contribute to a neat and tidy theory. To the contrary, they serve merely as descriptive possibilities from which we might develop a hermeneutic of feminine and masculine, of mind and body, of conscious and unconscious.

There are blurred boundaries between body and psyche, as this interpretation of Jung implies. For both man and woman the feminine and the masculine are necessarily mediated by the experience of their embodiment. Both I and not-I permeate their sexed embodiment, each interactively fabricating who each subject is. Their selves are (partially) a complex of sexual and contra-sexual interactivities, variously displayed and expressed through their modes of subjectivity and multiple subject positions. Both the collective, through unconsciousness and consciousness, and individual men and women (fathers and mothers) are the origins of the masculine and the feminine. Psychic aptitude is grounded in innateness, but activated by response from and to the collective and individual members of the collective. On this basis, modes of subjectivity are open to difference and mutability. But mutability is constrained by hegemonic forms and practices, symbolic or otherwise, which permeate the foundational relations with which we are here dealing. Jung's theorisation of the feminine and the self is, after all, developed from and through a masculine paternal perspective which does little to address the hierarchical asymmetries constitutive of those relations. This is the major critique that Luce Irigaray makes of theories of subjectivity and I shall return to her point at length in Chapter 4.

In Jung's assessment of the masculine and the feminine these asymmetries are clear. As I have already argued, his discussion of the anima/animus sees the feminine as a corrupting influence on the masculine. The masculine in a woman, the animus masculine we might call it, is a corruption of the masculine ideal of order and reason. The feminine in a man, the anima, is unsettling and disagreeable. That is to say, the animus masculine is compromised when it is present in a female body and the anima feminine corrupts when it is present in a male body. There is no suggestion that the anima feminine is compromised by its presence in a male body or that the animus masculine corrupts when it is present in a female body. Although the boundaries between body and psyche are blurred, body-type becomes a value determinant for the anima feminine and the animus masculine. The potential for mutability of subject position if and when it can occur is limited to the ontological and precluded from the affirming axiological so long as the body is thus interpreted. When Luce Irigaray claims that any theory of the subject has been appropriated by the masculine, it is, I shall argue, this kind of interpretation to which she is alluding. The feminine is axiologically appropriated by the masculine with ontological consequences that debilitate the feminine as a positive influence.

COLLECTIVE ONTOLOGIES AND SEX/GENDER

We can see from the argument of the previous section that, for Jung, the anima feminine acts as a counter to the assumed manliness of the man-subject and that the animus masculine acts as counter to the assumed womanliness of the woman-subject. The anima feminine and the animus masculine allow Jung to develop a concept of the self which is neither masculine nor feminine, but both. This radical conception of the self takes body-type as fundamental to the identity of the ego, but interpolates its opposite sex/gender into the psyche. That is to say, innate somatic male and female attributes ground the ego, sex/gendering the I, but innate psychological masculine and feminine attributes begin to bring the multiple nature of the psyche into focus. However, this is not a purely interior and private matter: the domain of the exterior and public, the collective or community, responds immediately to body-type (thus the declaration 'it's a boy/girl' and the ensuing blue/pink blanket). In its response to sex/gendered embodiment, the community doubly figures the masculine and the feminine as both innate and as *a posteriori*.

The conceptions of feminine and masculine, female and male that become operative are an interplay between body-type, assumption and social practice. Indeed, the attribution of the terms 'masculine' and 'feminine', 'male' and 'female' alerts us to the specific mechanisms of sex/gender stereotyping that communities use to identify and label community members.[6] Those mechanisms are sophisticated, powerful and effective. They operate before, and as a condition of, bodies' becoming conscious subjects. Although bodies can usually be identified as male and female, bodies are sometimes sexually ambiguous. This has profound consequences, as we shall see in Chapter 8, in terms of both physical and psychic identity. In the case of unambiguously sex/gendered bodies, we saw in Plato's discussion of the cowardly soldier his claim that male children should not be exposed to the hysteria of women; and we saw that women who are courageous and have philosopher or manly souls would be elevated in the hierarchy.

The social context of this characterisation needs to be taken seriously for it is within a social context that these categories and their instantiations are created. Jung does not employ Plato's conception of the relation between individual and collective as the basis of his social ontology. Recall that in the Platonic republic, individuals are drawn together through economic need and relations of exchange: Platonic social ontology is individualistic. Contrary to this individualistic ontology, the Jungian individual only *potentially* exists at birth because one is born into a collective. On this story, Jung utilises a collectivist and not an individualist ontology. One emerges as an individual from a collective and it is the journey of psychological development that precipitates this emergence. Jung's inspiration for his collectivist ontology is Lucien Lévy-Bruhl, but we find evidence of collectivist ontologies like this in many twentieth-century social theories. Let us see how such ontology works.

We all are born in, and belong to, collectives. Now 'collective' is a rubbery term, often used as a contrary to 'individual', and often associated with anti-liberal-democratic philosophies such as some forms of socialism like Communism and Nazism. My use of the term is not meant to evoke such negative connotations. Rather, I use the term as a socio-ontological category which helps us to understand the origins of individuals. In this, I take my cue from Iris Marion Young's articulation of the social group, which she argues is a specific kind of collectivity. She argues for the dialectical nature of social groups, that one group presupposes the existence of another and that such groups are 'differentiated from at least one other group by cultural forms, practices or ways of life' and that their 'members have specific affinity with each other prompting them to associate with each other more than those not identified with the group' (Young 1990: 43). One of the most important features of the idea of affinity is that it has the character of 'thrownness': one finds oneself as a member of a group which one experiences as always having been (Young 1990). Young argues that social groups are different from aggregates and associations which emerge out of the bringing or coming together of individuals. Aggregates are based on the idea of classifying individuals according to some arbitrary bodily feature such as eye or skin colour. Associations, on the other hand, are organisations, for example, knitting or cricket clubs, corporations or political parties which people join.

Social groups, aggregates and associations are all forms of collectivity, modes of collective coming or being together. Whether one's entry into a form of collectivity is by choice, by attribution of values associated with specific characteristics, or by birth, one's identity is variously constituted through these multiple modes of collectivity. Very broadly, I conceive of these modes of collectivity under the rubric 'collective'. I use 'collective' in both its nominal and adjectival forms, *the* or *a* collective and *the* or *a collective* X respectively.

I identify three constituent modes of expression of the collective, which are intertwined but nonetheless distinctive. Here is a very general outline of how I intend them to be understood:

1 Symbolic – 'Symbol' and its cognate 'symbolic' are mimetic terms: they are the means by which we represent the world to ourselves and to others and are thus a mode of expression. Symbols are epistemic mediators that inform what we know and believe. According to Jung, symbols are different from signs where a sign or system of signs (or the semiotic) has fixed meanings; and the symbolic or a system of symbols has complex, flexible and changing meanings.

In Luce Irigaray's work, we find her using a Lacanian notion of the symbolic that should always be read in conjunction with another Lacanian term, the imaginary. The symbolic is an order of representation, a manner in which we 'see' and interpret our worlds. It is 'the junction of body, psyche, and language' (Whitford 1991: 38). Luce Irigaray argues that women have no symbolic of their own, that the symbolic through which women represent and interpret meanings is masculine and patriarchal, and assumes women's sameness rather than women's difference.[7] The masculine symbolic is patriarchal,[8] because it represents power relations among and between men, who exchange women as commodities in a society dominated by the Law of the Father.[9] The imaginary or the order of unconscious phantasy is also dominated by masculine images which the symbolic structures. The principal and originary symbols in the symbolic/imaginary nexus[10] are the Phallus and the Father.[11]

2 Social – The social is a system of relations and associations among groups of people and their members, mediated by contingent practices such as law, ritual, religion, politics, dress, diet, birth and death memorialising, and education.
3 Biological – The material conditions of life supported by the elements: earth, air, fire, water. The biological is the absolute ground of being for both the symbolic and the social without which neither could exist.

The relationship between a collective and its members incorporates the symbolic, the social and the biological, not always equally, but as always dependent on what is important at specific moments. As humans we emphasise each constituent mode depending on circumstance. In Western, developed collectives, the biological might take precedence in illness when the body is treated as a living organism that will respond to surgical intervention and prescribed, sanctioned medication; on the other hand, the symbolic might take precedence in a collective where Western medicine is unavailable and tradition deems that certain 'magical' procedures can cure and enhance a life. The social takes precedence when a marriage is enacted and new members are born. What is it to be born a member of a collective?

First, in our Western collectives (of which Jung was a member) we are not born free and equal before the law or before the eyes of our fellow human beings. Sex/gender, 'race' and religious type among other types, mark us for privilege or oppression depending on where we are born. Collectives of their very nature mean difference and inequality, since collectives both internally and interactively exemplify various power relations. Collectives mark us as their own through their practices of initiation, including the acquisition of language, through their relations with each other and through their value systems. We saw this in Plato's *Republic*, where a female body marks a woman as a potential possessor of a womanly, and thus an inferior, soul.

We belong to many collectives, some of which overlap and intersect. Sometimes we belong to collectives that reinforce who we are and the certainty of our being in the world. Sometimes we belong to collectives which are opposed to each other and which cause us strife because they undermine our identities, calling our being in the world into question. What we come to be through the project of individuation identifies us as the unique creatures we are: biological, social, symbolic. We need to recognise these three aspects of being human if we are to have a greater understanding of ourselves in the world because that conjunction crystallises our ethical relations and what follows from those, to the natural and built environments we inhabit.

How one becomes an individual is very clearly connected to the collectives to which one is exposed and to their customs, habits and dispositions. A collective is the source of value systems germane to its existence and survival, and is both the social origin and overseer of its members. The process of being born is not just the physical act of birth, but the passage into a collective or socio-cultural milieu *and* a natural environment: a nation, a land, a place. Being born physically pre-figures our psychological, ethical, social and aesthetic births, even though the conditions for these pre-exist our own existence. Young's sense of a collective's always having been captures this very nicely (Young 1990: 46). What we recognise as ourselves emerges through this birthing process: we see ourselves existing *now*, we know we were *then* and we will be in the *future*, even though our awareness of temporality is framed by knowledge of our mortality.

Attention to the social, the symbolic, and the biological which take account of the power relations among collectives and individuals, and the constitutive and appropriative role of the collective in making individuals, foreshadows the possibility of developing a rich conception of human being. We explain human being through the use of various discourses (the social, the biological, the symbolic) that we might think of as mythical. Indeed, one of the features of a collective is that it is concerned with the mythical, with myth making. Myths are stories that are the bedrock of the existence of a collective.[12] Myths bring with them archetypes of behaviour and ethical desirability, recognisable beyond the constraints of fashion and stereotype. These archetypes perdure. They remain within the horizons of a collective almost as markers of the solidity of its history, its debt to the past, its living memory. A collective will do its utmost to defend and protect its sacred archetypes since a collective, like Iris Marion Young's 'group', exists only in relation to other groups and that very relation may represent some threat to a collective's identity.

Structurally, collectives overlap and intersect in several different ways in varying degrees of complexity and simplicity. Equally, the truths each collective espouses can be complex or simple, and either opposed to or in agreement with those collectives with which it comes into contact. Some truths can be associated with a collective that has an identifiable set of discursive practices and ontological commitments specific to that collective. As well as claiming to be the unique 'possessor' of truth, the purpose of a collective's stories about itself is to establish allegiance to those truths. Mimesis, as we saw earlier, is strategically important from this point of view. Scientific, moral, biological, economic, aesthetic, religious and political discourses produce ways of orienting us as selves towards the world, towards each other and towards the collectives they represent. The truths that each discourse generates can be incommensurable or complementary: religious and scientific discourses (Christian fundamentalism and nuclear physics, for example) are often regarded as incommensurable, and economic and political discourses (capitalism and Western democracy) as complementary.

Myths, as bearers of symbol and meaning, tell stories that attempt to prescribe, explain and proscribe the dimensions of human being. The success or failure of each story is related to the constitution of the greater collective of which the discourse forms a part. The mythical face of a large collective such as a nation will be peppered by myths of greater or lesser dominance that contribute to the making of a national myth that in turn says something significant about a nation's character. For example, in Australia the myth of the Aussie battler who triumphs in the face of adversity against the forces of capitalism and consumerism is a myth derived from the working class and the post-Second World War refugee.[13] This suggests the varying degrees of homogeneity and heterogeneity that characterise a collective. In a smaller collective, such as birth family, cohesiveness is guaranteed by strong homogeneity. A larger collective like a kinship group, a basketball team, a national legal practitioners' society or a local country women's association will be homogeneous to a lesser degree than birth family, but more so than several generations of family from different parts of a country and other countries entirely (at, for example, a family reunion) which in turn may or may not be less homogeneous than a national basketball team, an international society of legal practitioners or a meeting of an international women's association for farm women.

Homogeneity and heterogeneity constitute powerful modes of overlapping and interlocking structures that reveal themselves in myth-laden relationships. The stories which each collective tells about itself, about its friends, about its enemies, allow for the possibility of quite nuanced myth telling and myth making the larger and more diverse the collective is or becomes. Largeness and diversity provoke strong relations of dominance over smaller collectives, especially those which are seen as contrary to the aims and existence of the larger collective. Larger collectives will attempt to appropriate, silence or ridicule the myths of smaller collectives in an attempt to be the sole arbiter of truth that is thought of as monolithic, singular, and timeless. Many members of the medical community, for example, label traditional health practices as 'alternative folk-medicine', a disparaging and trivialising labelling meant to convey the 'amateur' nature of the relevant practices. The mythical nature of the stories of the origins of modern medical science, developed through the overcoming of nature by reason and the male hand, is equalled by the telling of stories about the failure of natural remedies prepared and dispensed by 'witches' and 'witch doctors'. Even though each collective will be informed by the experiences of its members, all of whom will belong to other, different collectives of varying sizes and homogeneities, collective members will identify with one or several dominant collectives. Heterosexual, affluent, Anglophone, professional, white men and women embody several collectives which, in their intersecting multiplicity, produce a powerful, dominant collective. Indeed, it is at the structural intersection of the collectives that power is at its greatest.

Symbol and meaning are displayed in each collective in its language practices, its preferences in everyday customs and habits, how it works as a collective to promote and sustain its well-being. With promotion of its well-being as its primary focus, a collective will develop ways of protecting itself as a collective. This might be through the development of marriage rules, membership criteria, or the possession of native talent. Modes of protection are implicit in collective myths that tell members what is sanctioned by the group and what is not. Fairy tales, fables, songs, 'great literature', moral lessons from the lives of collective members (saints and sinners) all contribute to the perpetuation of the collective and to the image of itself that the collective fabricates. The heroes of a collective are remembered and honoured, their memories preserved in national holidays, avenues of honour, plaques and prizes.

The fleshiness that is our bodies finds itself woven into the fabric of these myths and the myths woven into the flesh of our bodies. Pierre Bourdieu acknowledges the dialectical relationship between body and structure of which myth is an integral part. He argues that:

> it is in the dialectical relationship between the body and a space structured according to mythico-ritual oppositions that one finds the form par excellence of the structural apprenticeship which leads to the embodying of the structures of the world, that is the appropriating by the world of a body thus enabled to appropriate the world.
>
> (Bourdieu 1977: 91)

Bourdieu is arguing that social structures prepare the body for its existence as a member of a collective and that it is because of that preparation that the body is actually able to accommodate the world. In other words, there is an implicitly social dimension to bodily existence: human bodies are social bodies. We saw this social dimension active in Jung's use of the persona as a response to social demands made of kinds of bodies. Jung explicitly accepts this social dimension which traverses the personal and collective psyche, and notes that 'equally, just as the individual is not merely a unique and separate being, but is also a social being, so the human psyche is a not self-contained and wholly individual phenomenon, but also a collective one' (Jung 1966: 147).

Compatibility of world structure and body through myth and ritual, through social practice and attitude sees the mutually interpenetrative effect of each upon the other. This mutuality draws us to recognise that it is not structure alone that so prepares the body: from a biological perspective the body is always already predisposed to exist as a collective member. Fitness of body for fleshy procreation is a condition of the survival of a collective. Without fertile, willing members, a collective is doomed.[14] On this basis, inter-sexed bodies, because of their sexual ambiguity, represent the possibility of failure of the collective, as does sexual desire for same-sex partners. A collective will advocate membership *under certain conditions* and will insist that certain *conventions* are maintained to ensure its survival. The dominance of hetero-normativity can thus be seen as a structural matter related to survival of a large, heterogeneous collective, such as a nation. For a same-sex collective, the obverse is the case: the intervention of heterosexuality would threaten its existence, its mode of being in the world. Conditions and conventions of membership limit who might be considered a member of a same-sex collective: the maintenance of this collective depends on sexual homogeneity with respect to partners.

At the level of a large heterogeneous collective, one's physical birth marks the completion of the annunciation of one's imminence; in pre-existing the individual's physical birth, the collective anticipates all membership, claiming the newly born as its own. The taboo against infanticide can be seen as symbolising this claim-in-anticipation. Even where infanticide has been permitted because the child fails to satisfy the *telos* of a collective (for example, the infant is a girl or has some 'deformity'), the prior ownership of the body by the collective can be deciphered. The collective evaluates its members and dispenses with what is not useful to it. This suggests that the body is never one's own, that the large heterogeneous collective will always have a prior claim to one's existence, and that teleologically, the purpose of one's existence is not individual and private but collective and social. Our lives, in other words, are not about our selves, they are about the collective and its persistence, its endurance through time and space as the social domain of human being. We do not live for ourselves; we live for the collective. Luce Irigaray's claim that little girls are initiated into the male symbolic, as we shall later see, is an example of this principle.

Overtly, the collective may not subscribe to these beliefs. Underlying assumptions about the ultimate importance of collective interests might be displaced in favour of pragmatic obfuscation of collective ends and ideals. Indeed, a collective might promote a contrary mythology of individualism, materialism and capitalism, constructing stories around ideals of personal achievement and perfection. We see this in literature and then film from the Greek hero Odysseus to Harry Potter. The successful construction of individuals might entail that they will take as natural and true the idea that they have choice, are free and responsible.

The origin of the individual as a choosing, free and responsible self is a critical consideration when the body as a living and lived-in organism becomes ontologically considerable as the fleshy site around which a collective centres its interests. What is this self and what is its origin? Is it Plato's tripartite soul which appears to be the life-spirit of a human being, a site of reason, judgement, desire and passion? What kind of site? Is it material or immaterial and what do these terms mean in relation to human identity? Is the self a myth or a fiction that the collective invents, an idea that we internalise and to which we attach properties such as persistence through time and identity with our bodies? If the self is the Platonic soul, what is its relation to the body? If, as Jung would have it, the self is the totality of psychic experiences, then what is the relation between psychic experience and body? Yes, what is this self? Unsurprisingly, the individual who emerges from its collective origin is, in the Jungian sense, a self. Yet the self, for Jung, is neither just the body, nor just the psyche, nor just the individual, nor all three 'elements' together. Rather, the collective, in appropriating the body as it does, represents itself in the psyche, the mental life of its members. And, broadly, this is how the collective works into the psyche.

In taking each body as its own, a collective marks and masks the body with identifiable signs of ownership. A collective clothes the body in sex/gender- and class-appropriate clothing, offers the body tokens of belonging such as birth certificates, records its existence as the offspring of other bodies for whom it has similarly performed. In acting as it does in relation to bodies that it schematises in specific ways as individuals, a collective contributes to the turning of a body into a self. This process is purely pragmatic from the perspective of a collective's survival, but it is a magical process of transformation in terms of the body that is being transformed. The collective can do this because its members are conscious, have an awareness that is exploited by language and other symbolic systems that intersect with the bodily senses.

The self lives its life immersed in webs of relations that signify the uniqueness of the developing self and testify to the potency of collective activity. Without that immersion, there would be no self identifiable as the self that one is. The self is, and continues to become, a specific cultural product, albeit an embodied, fleshy, sensuous existent. Its identity is in its becoming. Clearly, the self is not a mere entity wrought from the totality of relations. The gestalt that is a self, expressed in the use of 'I' and other transposable pronouns, is not reducible to a collection of social relations, no matter how detailed the descriptions and analyses of those relations might be. Of themselves, those relations are greater than any self, but the self exceeds their potential dominance. The materiality of the self, as a biological entity dependent on the materiality of the earth, demands recognition. The biological uniqueness of the body is seen in its uncontrollable wilfulness. No matter what we do, our bodies do not behave as we would always want them to, our bodies become ill and frail, and do not live for ever. Inevitably, neither the will of a collective, human ingenuity nor symbolic practice can sustain the self's desire for immortality. We are born as members of a collective and we die as an effect of multiple inscriptions of the various collectives to which we have belonged. Multiple inscriptions, depending on where and how we live, make us into the individual members of the collective whom we come to see ourselves as. We become individual selves, in other words, because of our experience and growth in various collectives.

So while the self as gestalt is an effect of membership of a collective and the self's fleshiness, the very being of the self does not seem to be explicable through mere elaboration of either collective or biology. The symbolic life in which anyone participates eludes the explanatory force that might be available through elaboration of both collective and biology. How is it that a collective produces individuals who can paint pictures, write poetry, make films, write music, who use symbolic forms to tell others about and to express themselves?

The complex relationship between self and collective is revealed in considering where a self begins and ends, where a collective begins and ends. For it is also clear that one can identify an apparently private and isolatable aspect or aspects of the self, which can take a moral and epistemic stand distinct from the hegemony of a collective. How is it that, although one might perform functions and roles within a collective, that what we might think of as the private world of oneself eludes the total scrutiny and surveillance of that collective? How can this be so? How a collective constitutes itself symbolically and how the self can be the possessor of a private world, inhabit a domain that seems irreducible to a collective, is mysterious given the collectivist origins of our being. The mystery is deepened rather than solved if we think of a collective as the source of the symbolic life that we live. For although collective members might all be exposed to similar cultural influences within a specific collective, it is not the case that each of those members will become exponents of its 'high' culture, for example. Not every member will be able to paint, write, compose, imagine, in a way that is lauded by a collective. The laudable is a category that is elusive to most of us. Excellence and genius seem to be beyond the social structures that nurture us through membership of a collective, into selfhood.

Not only is there a complex relation between member considered as an emerging self, and collective. Complexity is repeated in the emerging self's relation to its own fleshy body and its mortality; and to the consciousness that signals the possibility that this body is indeed a self or a potential self. The self is a matrix of relations, processes and enfleshed existence. Impossible to capture in the biases of any one mythical discourse, the self presents and represents itself in a variety of ways as an interior presence for consciousness and as an exterior presence for the collective. Its interiority is expressed in, for example, reflection, contemplation, rational calculation and dreaming. Its exteriority is expressed as it communicates with the collective through language, action and simple physical being in the world. The self is held together by the activity of consciousness as it mediates its own interiority and exteriority.

Although the consciousness that permeates the self is triggered by the interplay of collective and fleshy body, consciousness, like self, is a gestalt. Consciousness, indeed, is a condition of self. The biological origins of consciousness are a guarantee of potential satisfaction of the body's disposition towards being caught by the collective. While structures dispose the body towards membership of a collective, without the body as patient those structures are ineffective. The mutuality of body and collective in the production of self is thus mediated by the living nature of the body as represented in consciousness. The symbolic, the third aspect of human being, is seen in the intimacy of interiority and the exteriority of its public activity.

COLLECTIVISED CONSCIOUSNESS, THE BODY AND 'THE' UNCONSCIOUS

The effect of a member's existence in a collective and the constitutive role the collective plays in making that member a self inform Jung's and Luce Irigaray's work. Collectivist interpretation of the sexed body in ascribing roles to members who are seen to be of a particular kind manifests collectivist myth about sex and gender. In quite specific ways, both Jung and Luce Irigaray pinpoint these collectivist myths. Jung's identification of the myth surrounding women's bodies grounds his acceptance and valorisation of Western culture's orientation towards the female/feminine. Jung is mute in relation to the structuring effects of the collective on sexed body and self. Yet he acknowledges, even if subliminally, the importance of body in his overall identification of the embodied nature of consciousness and unconsciousness. In his seminars on Nietzsche's *Zarathustra*, for example, Jung proposes that 'the body is the guarantee of consciousness and consciousness is the instrument by which the meaning is created. There would be no meaning if there were no consciousness, and since there is no consciousness without body, there can be no meaning without body' (Jung 1998: 94). The significance of the body as the site, and possibly the genesis, of consciousness indicates Jung's commitment to an embodied conception of psychic life. But the *kind* of body that a body might be is not considered by Jung.

For Luce Irigaray, this is not the case and her critical identification of the collective's response to the feminine body can be seen in her attack on what she calls the masculine symbolic and which I think of as a critical analysis of a dominant myth. Rather than allude to the general category 'body' as Jung does, Luce Irigaray insists on the ontological difference between differently sex/gendered bodies. She points out that the dominance of purportedly neutral structures, myths and ways of being disguise the masculine nature of the most fundamental structures of collectives. Hence the above discussion of the relation between collective, individual and myth needs re-evaluation. Consequently, it is imperative that the mutuality of sex/gendered body, and the constraints and liberties manifested through collective myths and their attendant practices, be highlighted. Luce Irigaray highlights this and Spelman's reading of Plato, as we saw earlier, begins to do precisely this work, as does the work of many other feminist thinkers who attempt to re-vision the so-called neutrality of theory.[15] Such analyses demand that the notion of sex/gender bias in hegemonic structures of collectives first needs attention, secondly needs to be taken seriously and thirdly needs to be refigured in order to capture the ontological significance of sex/gender and how it is produced, reproduced and played out in the activities of collectives. Mimesis is a key notion in all of this.

Hence it is not simply a mutuality of collective and body, but a mutuality of collective and sex/gendered body and the effect of endemic power relations that need addressing. If structures are not neutrally involved with either collective or body and the body is sex/gendered, then the effects of mutuality and reciprocity between body and collective need radical reappraisal. Collectives, on this argument, are selectively disposed towards the body, depending on what is structurally dominant. Luce Irigaray's suggestion implies that any collective and its structures are dynamic rather than fixed. This raises the possibility that a sex/gendered body can be variously interpreted by a collective according to that body's membership of a number of collectives. And since the body is sex/gendered, it will not be fixed in its capacity to appropriate the structures of the world as expressed in collective aims and ambitions. The reciprocity of sex/gendered body and dynamically structured collective opens up the possibility for radical refiguring of relations that might have been thought of as fixed and determinate. On the face of it, the key to this possibility is consciousness. However, it is a particular reading of consciousness that holds the key, for collective attitudes are often found beyond consciousness. We see this in both Plato's and Jung's understandings of unconscious imitation. And certainly, Luce Irigaray's point is that the alleged sex/gender neutrality of symbolic structures and the interpretation of myth occur beyond conscious apprehension:

sex/gender neutrality is simply assumed. A specific reading of consciousness is therefore called for and this reading locates consciousness in unconsciousness or the unconscious.[16]

Jung argues that 'there can be no doubt that consciousness does originate in unconsciousness' (Jung 1990: 44). His twin commitment to the apparently causal role the body plays in establishing consciousness and meaning, and to the framing of consciousness by unconsciousness, makes it clear that for him the body plays a critical role as a site of unconscious as well as of conscious existence. If it is the case that consciousness is causally dependent on the body and that consciousness originates in unconsciousness, then there must also be a relation between the body and unconsciousness. Furthermore, if the body is born into a collective, the inference that consciousness and therefore unconsciousness must also be born into a collective is very clear. But what would it mean to say that consciousness and unconsciousness must also be born into a collective?

For Bourdieu the process of the body's being appropriated by the collective is to some extent an unconscious process. Bourdieu's idea is that unconsciousness is 'the forgetting of history'. The history of the collective is implicit in its actions but members of the collective, the *habitus*, as Bourdieu puts it, are never made epistemically aware of the social structuring that engenders them as a 'natural' product of the collective. Members of the *habitus* assume the naturalness of categories which contrive to reproduce themselves. It is in the interests of the *habitus* that its history be forgotten, remain unconscious. Regularity, predictability and abstruseness of its practices can thus be maintained without knowledge of what is happening, without epistemic awareness. An effect of restricting epistemic awareness is that collective members develop the illusion that they are authors of their own being, that they can anticipate the outcomes of their actions and will see themselves as agents. What agents are actually doing exceeds their conscious intentions because they are engaged in reproducing the objective ends of the *habitus*. They are part of a self-replicating network of relations and structures over which they have little control and the meaning of which depends on their lack of epistemic awareness. 'It is because subjects do not, strictly speaking, know what they are doing that what they do has more meaning than they know' (Bourdieu 1977: 79). We are not, on this basis, in control of the meaning of what we do: the meanings of our actions are in excess of our intentional attitudes expressed in what we think we believe and what we know. There is a subliminal aspect to semantics.

Such an account might imply that there is a deliberate loss of collective memory, that a collective either intentionally or unintentionally sets out to eliminate aspects of its own history. While it may be the case that collective memory is selective and fallible in what it remembers and reclaims as its own, it is also the case that the present comes into being and is lost immediately, so the present of its very nature is always more than itself. The impossibility of recording the whole history of a collective from the least to the most significant moments of its life is obvious. But there are times when a dominant group deliberately fails to remember its actions in relation to those, for example, whom it has subordinated, tortured and annihilated almost entirely. A collective's history might become hidden even as it happens, as has been the case with European invaders and the Indigenous peoples of Australia. Once uncovered, the heirs of fallible and/or false memory may find it difficult to accept their pasts, refusing to admit ownership of their politically charged histories. That said, there is an impossibility to the idea of perfect memory and the nature of memory is such that no collective can hope to be unforgetful of their pasts.

Yet the history of a collective moulds the present. A collective exists, in Bourdieu's terms, as not only a network of structured patterns and dispositions in this moment now, as a social presence, but also as an effect of a past, often unknown. The formation of a collective assumes a history to which a collective might give witness. A forgotten history means the existence of a collective unconscious. Hence a collective is born into unconsciousness and unconsciousness is born into collectivity because each is inalienably historical. Consciousness emerges out of this unconscious through its constant change, the dynamic nature of its membership and the myriad bodies to which the collective gives birth. Relations between the body, the unconscious and consciousness are mediated always by the collective in which they are found.

One of the functions of myth is as a preserver of a collective's history. Where a history is forgotten, elements of preserved myth may hint at stories of the subordinated which may also secretly exist in their own right. Together, the forgotten, the misremembered, the repressed and the remembered all inform the identity of a collective. And the most salient feature of all of this history *is* its collective nature. The collective brings itself and its members into being as conscious entities and the collective founds its own lost history. Unconsciousness is, on this story, *necessarily* a collective matter.[17] Enfleshed existence is the bearer of this collective unconscious insofar as a body is identified and marked by a collective. In each marking, a collective baptises a new body into its history, remembered and forgotten. Given that unconsciousness is a product of collective forgetfulness, it 'holds' origins of which a collective may no longer be aware but which now are silently passed into each generation. The consciousness of the collective, in its deliberate acts (naming, clothing, sex-appropriate habits) and its unconscious traces of the past, plays a formidable role in coaxing a body into a specific type of existence as either feminine or masculine. But it is not only *origins* that are held by unconsciousness. Thought of as the cumulative *structuring* of a collective, history is woven and re-woven into the fabric of each generation. Very clearly, the way in which the collective etches its memory of both body and consciousness into new bodies and new consciousness through both conscious and unconscious activity is ontologically significant for the selves who emerge in this process. The enfleshed body plays a formidable role as the vehicle for the *actuality* not just the *possibility* of consciousness. Responses from a collective to a *type* of body (female or male) permeate the actuality of each consciousness. But the *contingency* of all of these relations means that, although the relations and processes are to some extent determinative (some of them are causal), they *could have been otherwise*.

Responses to sex/gendered bodies reflect the existential biases and preoccupations of a collective. The self-expression of the collective in and through its members, together with the idiosyncratic nature of sex/gendered bodies (some of which might be biologically anomalous) that are the material condition of conscious existence, emphasise the dynamism of both collective and body. Reciprocity assures flexibility and the possibility of change and adaptation. The emergence of consciousness from *both* the collective and sex/gendered body is the emergence of a dynamic life force, the impetus for self-formation. This means that there is always an *a priori*, that there is always a given, but it does not mean that the *a priori* and the given are fixed, timeless, immutable. Rather, unconsciousness is itself a product of social structurings over many lifetimes and many instances of collectives. Unconsciousness is always already a collective unconscious; the collective unconscious is always already inscribed into each psyche within its domain; and individual consciousness is an effect of the sex/gendered nature of both body and collective.

The repetition of sex/gender roles, the underlying domination and subservience found within and across cultures are not attributable to timeless, unchanging essences in an equally timeless and unchanging collective unconscious. Instead, on this view, collective unconscious is traceable to history, memory and forgetfulness. The intersection of the collective and the individual at the point of consciousness is an intersection of possibilities and contingencies. From this perspective, Luce Irigaray's insistence on the importance of sex/gendered difference is an important intervention that grounds dynamic change. As an alternative to an ontology of sameness, based on the dominance of masculine orientation towards collectivity, the possibility of an ontology of difference, based on masculine *and* feminine orientations towards collectivity, surfaces. With that will come relations other than sex/gender roles such as class, 'race', ethnicity and sexual preference, all of which intersect in powerful networks that limit or liberate according to one's place in them, as Kimberle Crenshaw (1991) has also argued. That the starting point of critique is sex/gender formation does not by extension endorse that point as *the* origin of all oppression. One's own preoccupations and situation will be reflected in where one begins. The dynamism of relations illustrates this point quite nicely.

Given the ubiquity of the collective, its potency and its conformist-producing tendencies, one might argue that any notion of individual self is thin. On the other hand, aspects of consciousness such as deliberative capacity, rational thinking and decision making, regarded as intrinsic to notions of the self, might seem incongruous with the collective's pervasive, constitutive power. The questions about creativity, brilliance, non-conformity remain, even if one does argue for a dynamic relation between collective and sex/gendered body. While a collective might encourage the flourishing of the life of the mind, it is ultimately powerless to have complete control. Stories such as Philip K. Dick's 'We Can Remember it for You Wholesale' (2002) and films like *The Matrix* attempt to deal with the 'distinctively individual' in the face of collective ambition. Jung's contribution to this debate centres around his emphasis on the mid-life and beyond. Even as individuation, the becoming of an individual self, is a life-long process, one's embroilment in the collective is not totalising and irredeemable. What is at stake here are the modes of presentation of oneself to and in the world. Sex/gender, in terms of both identity and role, and as I have been intimating, is an important aspect of those modes of self-presentation. The mechanism of collectivising both sex/gendered body and consciousness requires careful deliberation. Put simply, mechanism is projection, but projection in concert with mimesis. Let us see how it works.

However, before doing that, we should note that the collectivist social ontology I have been advocating as so important to Jung's and Luce Irigaray's work is realist with respect to the body. In other words, the body for them is not a text or a performance but matter, flesh. I am arguing for the precedence neither of nature over nurture, nor of nurture over nature. The interpretative framework I employ does not deny the privileging of some concepts and ideas and flesh over others. The body for both Jung and Luce Irigaray is a condition of interpretation: bodies think, bodies come up with ideas and concepts and values. So, in a sense, the body is the *a priori* given of any theorising. The conjunction of the symbolic, the biological and the social is a recognition that in their work all three are taken seriously given that we are, as fundamentally biological creatures, animals that have a specific way of being in the world which is expressed through our symbolically mediated forms of collective 'habitus'.

Chapter 4

Projection

The mirror image

> Let me tell you why the creator made this world of generation. He was good, and the good can never have any jealousy of anything. And being free from jealousy, he desired that all things should be as like himself as they could be.
>
> (Plato 1970c: *Timaeus*: 29d–e)

> Then God said: 'Let us make man in our image, after our likeness. Let them have dominion over the fish of the sea, the birds of the air, and the cattle, and over all the wild animals and all the creatures that crawl on the ground.' God created man in his image; in the divine image he created him; male and female he created them.
>
> (*The New American Bible*: Genesis 1: 26–7)

> Unless we are possessed of an unusual degree of self-awareness we shall never see through our projections but must always succumb to them, because the mind in its natural state presupposes the existence of such projections. It is the natural and given thing for unconscious contents to be projected.
>
> (Jung 1969: 507)

In our everyday living in the world, an awareness of the way in which we are incorporated into collectives is important for us. Without such an awareness, we can become lost and remain unindividuated. Several mechanisms operate to facilitate the development of members of collectives into selves. If we can become familiar with those mechanisms, then our prospects for individuation and thus freedom are substantially increased. I have already outlined Plato's position with respect to mimesis or imitation and I have argued that Jung deploys mimesis in his discussion of identification. Jung endorses the positive psychic effects that imitation as identification can have but, as we saw, he realises that there are important limitations to its wholesale endorsement.

In Jung's discussion of identification we can detect that projection might also be operative and that, together, mimesis and projection play a major role in the psyche's representation of itself and the world, to itself. From the perspective of a collective, both mimesis and projection act in concert to ensure the reproduction of members adequate to the task of enabling a collective to flourish. Again, we saw this in Plato's desire to see boys imitate manly souls and so lay the foundations for the rational order so vital to a prosperous republic. Such a view is presupposed by Jung because to him the collectivist social ontology assumed in his idea of the collective unconscious represents a moral order which ultimately affirms the value of the masculine over the feminine. It is plain, then, that projection and mimesis take place at the level of the individual and also at the level of the collective. Before we begin to examine Luce Irigaray's response to mimesis and her characterisation of the symbolic which I read as a process of individuation, I first introduce the notion of projection and its connection to mimesis. I begin with a little thought experiment . . .

We are, all of us, mirrors . . .

Imagine yourself among a group of people in a house of mirrors. The walls, floors, ceilings, doors, architraves, cupboards, everything is made of mirrors. There are doors and windows leading into and out of the house. The house is gently lit by an unknown light source. You have been confined to the house for a few weeks, fed and looked after. During your time in this house, how would you feel? What would you be able to say you know and believe with respect to the multiple images that are produced by the mirrored reflections in which you are all produced and reproduced? If you were all to become separated, how would you find each other and how would you know whether you had found each other? Would it be possible to become separated in this house of infinity? What would you understand about the nature of the house, about infinity, about how the house of mirrors operates to generate and regenerate itself? What would you identify as you and what would be the false trappings of the not-you? Who would you be in such a house? And how would you know?

Whatever action you performed would be thrown back to you by the very nature of the reflecting medium that presents yourself to you. You would see reflections of yourself and your fellows everywhere. Those reflections would imitate your every action, your every movement. The radical possibilities for loss of self, loss of the other, finding of self and finding of the other, of radical unknowing and disillusion are contained by the walls of this house. Your immurement, highlighted by the infinity of images, would become almost insufferable. You would probably attempt to find a way out. After any initial panic, you might sit quietly and begin to figure out what you could do to help yourself. You might ask some of your fellows to help you out. The decisions you might come to, the choices you might make would, after all, be aimed at sorting out the existential crisis that you, and the others you are with, might be experiencing. For you, releasing yourself from the multiplicity of images reflected in the mirrors would become your most pressing concern. What is yourself? Who are you and who are your fellows? The you in the house of mirrors with other people, all of whom would be experiencing similar concerns, all of whom would be having to deal with the illusion, false moves, disquietude, is now a fragmented you, an intangible you, a you with no apparent centre, no unambiguous ground of ego-being.[1]

The trope of the mirror house exaggerates our existential situatedness even as it captures some of its fragmented nature. Just as our membership of various collectives and our lives within our collectives create multiple aspects of our selves, so in the house of mirrors one sees multiple images of oneself and others.[2] Often we do not know who we are as we change and adapt to the circumstances of our lives which offer us the prospect of freedom but also limit us in many ways. The house of mirrors keeps us within its walls and close to other inhabitants, yet distances us from an image which we can claim truly represents us. Are we one of these images, some of them, all of them? How are they connected if we are some or all? Does a principle of transcendence operate to connect the images and, if so, where does that principle come from? The house of mirrors is a house of deception and a house of uncertainty: nothing is certain but the multiple images we encounter. To discern our own image or an other's – the familiar is needed. Indeed, the familiar is an important interruptive trigger for the possibility of our becoming aware of ourselves as individuals.

Mirrors are two-dimensional surfaces with virtual depth. If you measure the distance between the virtual object behind a mirror surface and the mirror surface, then you will discover that the distance is exactly the same as the distance between the real object and the mirror surface. Mirror images are *in* the mirror, not confined in or by the mirror's surface. Let us imagine for the moment that the subject is alone in the house of mirrors. The gazing subject is contained by the mirror, has her/his existence imagistically captured, three-dimensionally, in a two-dimensional surface. The capture of the subject as an image in a mirror becomes the ground of her/his knowing what she/he *looks like*, how she/he *seems* to the world, even though that seeming is a seeming through her/his eyes given the impossibility of seeing as another sees. In that sense a mirror provides another eye through which a subject might see and be seen. The subject is turned in on her/himself as she/he sees that she/he exists in a world where she/he is similar to those with whom she/he has been communing and of which she/he is a part. She/he is enabled to move out from her/himself and is then thrown back to her/himself through the reflexive eye of the mirror. This eye meta-positions him/her as a subject: she/he can see her/himself as she/he has never before been able. Her/his gaze into the mirror allows her/him to see her/himself, but in the house of mirrors, a subject is returned to her/himself in multiple images. The gaze in itself is not responsible, however, for the subject's seeing her/himself and making the required identification that the image is her/him. Something else, the familiar, which she/he already recognises and knows assists in this process. While we might think of mirrors as passive surfaces, an object reflected is an object altered. This is the case not only because a mirror image is a reversal but because, crucially, the substance of a mirror, what the mirror is like, both contains and is contained in the image thrown back. Mirrors, as artefacts of humans, are imperfect and inconsistent, changeable, flattering or disconcerting in what they throw back to the viewer. Amy Hollywood suggests that before the Renaissance images produced by mirrors were thought of as deceptive, offering 'only the illusion of reality' as the 'reflection seen was deformed' (Hollywood 2001: 87). Read from this perspective, as Hollywood also points out, Narcissus, the Greek mythological character, would have fallen in love with an illusion, an imperfect and deformed reflection of himself. Importantly for my purposes, Narcissus does not comprehend that what he sees is a reflection of his very own being, a visual image or replica of him.

The appearance in the mirror of the familiar or the already known is a necessary condition of visual self-identification: the presence of others with whom one identifies without the aid of mirrors acts as ballast for the familiar. One sees what one already recognises and sees what one comes to understand as oneself in seeing the already recognisable. The familiar thereby grounds this capacity for meta-positioning, for seeing oneself as oneself. Underpinning the capacity to recognise oneself in a mirror is the capacity to perceive similarities in the objects of one's everyday surroundings and their images in a mirror. In other words, one can recognise oneself in a mirror because one can see and *already* recognise familiar others without the aid of a mirror or reflecting device. Merleau-Ponty argues that 'he who looks must not himself be foreign to the world he looks at' (1968: 134). As a foreigner to the world one looks at, one cannot recognise oneself: that is the position in which Narcissus finds himself, as does our gazer who is surrounded by so many images of herself that she cannot ascertain who *she* is amongst all of those images.

In the Narcissus story Narcissus is bewitched as much by ignorance of his surroundings as he is by the image before him. An isolated, apparently unfamiliar location sets the scene for this bewitchment. According to Thomas Bullfinch:

> There was a clear fountain with water like silver, to which the shepherds never drove any flocks, nor the mountain goats resorted, nor any of the beasts of the forest; neither was it defaced with fallen leaves or

> branches; but the grass grew fresh around it and the rocks sheltered it from the sun.
>
> (Bullfinch 1979: 101–3)

The conditions under which Narcissus might recognise himself, see himself, know himself in the fountain are not satisfied because the pristine situation in which Narcissus finds himself is not familiar to him. His gaze is constructed around a transparent surface in which it is arguable that there is no other reflection, nothing, it seems, to divert his attention away from the face before him. Without some already known object that becomes a reflected image, there is no point or focus of differentiating reference. He cannot bring his ordinary everyday understanding of rocks and trees to his situation, because his knowledge of the realities from which such understanding arises is not triggered by any appearance in the fountain that he recognises: the face in the fountain is the face of a stranger, a face he has not seen before.

For Narcissus, the necessity of a *recognisable other* as a condition of both self-reflection and self-knowledge is not met. Without the satisfaction of this condition, Narcissus is unable to identify the face gazing back at him as his own, is unable to re-position himself. He is unable to transcend his situation and is caught, instead, by his inability to recognise his identificatory state. In other words, he cannot meta-position himself, cannot extricate himself from the image before him. The other, whom Narcissus approaches as he moves his face close to the surface of the water, imitates him. Thus Narcissus is unable to either claim himself or discern the absence of an other. The copy and the copied are one: the copy mimes the copied, unaware of this original one-ness.

The potential for visual self-recognition is grounded in awareness of one's collective and its visually familiar paraphernalia. Success in making an appropriate self-identification is thus environmentally constituted but it has an interesting consequence. In the case of Narcissus, his failure to make the appropriate inference is environmentally constituted by virtue of an *absence*. Images that might tell him that he has an existence apart from this reflection in the fountain are lacking. He cannot mobilise his knowledge and his acquaintance with familiar *objects* and *people*, the presence of which will enable him to infer that the face he sees is *his* face. In other words, Narcissus needs to be able to represent himself to himself with the assistance of the recognised familiar. Our gazer in the house of mirrors also lacks the familiar. Multiple images, repeated, fractured, presented and re-presented, are not grounds for the familiar even when the images are of oneself. Seeing oneself as a specific individual is dependent upon self-conscious awareness within familiar surroundings from which one can extricate oneself. And this is what Jacques Lacan's mirror stage tells us.

Jacques Lacan, following Henri Wallon,[3] elucidated what he called 'the mirror stage' and asserted that 'the human child, at an age when he is for a short while, but for a while nevertheless, outdone by the chimpanzee in his instrumental intelligence, can already recognize his own image as such in a mirror' (Lacan 2002: 94). The precipitative force of this moment of recognition precedes the I/other dialectic symbolically and linguistically. The importance of the familiar or already known in this recognition is the leverage for image identification.[4]

Lacan argues that 'the function of the mirror stage thus turns out, in my view, to be a particular case of the function of imagos, which is to establish a relationship between an organism and its reality – or, as they say, between the *Innenweldt* and the *Umweldt*' (Lacan 2002: 97). He sees the imago functionally, as a kind of bridge mediating the child's inner world and its environment. Existentially, an image of the child, an image which returns the child to itself, outside the child, confirms its being in the world, its being among objects and its relationship to those objects. But it also can be read in terms of two external realities which are not the child, presented to the child for which she/he becomes a bridge. On this view, Lacan's child mediates the world as she/he experiences it, and that world reflected as images in the mirror. The child bridges the gap between an image and its origin, even when the image is an image of the child itself. As a bridge, the child is enabled perceptively to realise its own being through differentiation, and also to distinguish visually between the imago and the real. We can see this very clearly in Elizabeth Grosz's comment that in Wallon's study a child smiles at the image of its father in the mirror but is confused when the speaking voice of the father comes from the cause of the image, not the image itself: the child turns towards its father (Grosz 1990a: 36). The confusion experienced by the child becomes an opportunity for differentiation, for claiming the world as its own *because the turn towards the father's voice suggests the child can distinguish what is real and what is not.* Most critically, it is not the specular image that does that, it is the *auditory* impact of its father's voice.[5]

Such a view does not resonate with Jacqueline Rose's note that:

> Lacan is careful to stress, however, that his point is not restricted to the field of the visible alone: 'the idea of the mirror should be understood as an object which reflects – not just the visible, but also what is heard, touched and willed by the child'.
>
> (Lacan 1982: introduction, 30)[6]

In the turning of its head the child, very clearly, can distinguish between different sensory sources. The mirror does not deliver an auditory experience to the child but instead points to the existence of different modes of reality: images are reversed but somehow remain the same. As a particular case of the function of imagos, the mirror serves as a fulcrum around which different realities are enacted, but it does not contain all of those realities.

That the child can distinguish the source of an auditory sensation is a trigger for its own meta-positioning in relation to itself and its environment or the world in which it already situates itself. The interpolation of sound shifts the consciousness of the child from the gaze at the mirror image(s) to the world of objects which, together with the mirror, makes images possible. In other words, sound returns the child to the previously known and experienced, its familiar environment. In doing that, the sentience of the child is restored to its own flesh. The image remains in the mirror. It will be 'there' upon the child's return to the mirror, but the child *hearing, like the father speaking*, remains actually outside the mirror. The spatial depth of the mirror is not repeated in an auditory depth.[7] The visual admits of the virtual and of reversal, whereas the auditory does not.

In turning to the voice of the father, the child enacts what Jung regarded as central to projection: the need to dissolve identification with the object (the mirror image). The child cannot remain fixed on/in the image(s) in the mirror and, at the same time, fix itself on another sensory source: virtual sound is not emitted from the mirror as a virtual image is. The child, in other words, can relocate its focus by deploying a sense other than the visual, a sense whose duplication cannot occur in a mirror. No such event occurs for Narcissus: although it *sounds as if* Narcissus might be caught in projective identification, it is not the case that he is.[8] Narcissus remains fixed in the image before him, which suggests that Narcissus is, rather, trapped by his identifying with an object he believes to be distinct from himself. What is played out with the child, the image in the mirror, and the turn from the mirror, is the necessity for interruption of the identifying moment: consciousness emanating from itself uninterrupted entails identity with an other, without any return to itself; it entails a moribund loss in and to unconsciousness. The epiphanic moment, in which a child's other senses might come into play to return its consciousness to itself, slips away from her/him because of her/his immersion in the non-familiar.

The loss of consciousness to itself, indeed the collapse of consciousness into a potentially pernicious unconsciousness, enacts a child's progress into her/his environment, her/his absorption into her/his various collectives. Existentially, a child, if she/he is to become a self-conscious individual, cannot remain outside her/himself, thrown continuously by emanative consciousness into the world. To become an individual, to become individuated, a child needs the voice towards which she/he can turn her/his head. Who the child is to her/himself, and what she/he is in relation to the rest of the world, is generated through interruption which thus becomes a central question in individuation. Likewise, the who-ness and what-ness problematics of the house of mirrored infinity mimic the who-ness and what-ness of the process of individuation. The turn of the head away from the image is a first step in the individuation process. The house of mirrors becomes a trope for one's being in a collective above all because, unless we can turn our heads away from the images we see or can be rescued by something other than sight, we will be trapped in the house of mirrors, lost to ourselves. The imitative potential that our collectives offer to us becomes the matter of our being, but we need to step outside the moments, the patterns, to attend to the other who captures us. Interruption to identity and identification, and the loss represented therein, grounds this stepping out. We all live in houses of mirrors, our collectives, our worlds where we are made as intertwining images of each other, where we might lose ourselves if we did not eventually turn our heads away from those generative mirrors. This is an existential imperative. The infinity of images in the house of mirrors suggests the fragile nature of our certainty, our limited apprehension of our own being in the world, our being in our collectives, their being in the world and in us. But it also reveals our robust dependence on the visual and its constitutive nature.

One of the central issues emerging from this discussion is that the association between identity, as a form of mimesis, and projection, grounded in mimesis, involves the idea of dialectic as relationship. We might think of projection as a dialectical engagement of between-ness, an engagement *between* a subject and an object. The relata of this engagement, subject and object, need, however, to become *disengaged* if projection is to be recognised and then to cease. The visual can be seen as a predominant mode of engagement but the engagement itself is psychological. In other words, the sensual world of things and images, with which we engage and disengage, is fundamental to our psychic lives. Reflected images in their multiplicity can, metaphorically, result in the turning of the head. Spatio-temporal interruption becomes a saving moment for the gazer. How we deal with projected images, from ourselves, from the mirror of the collective, from the mirror of other selves, is thus a process of interruption, dissociation and return. These subtend the concept of individuation. The intimate relationship between mirroring, projection and individuation illustrates the dynamic nature of human being as many of us seek to comprehend our existential immersion in the cosmos. Our dependence on our senses is revealed and realised in the mirroring examples that I have been discussing. The reciprocal relations of subject and object say something about the processes involved in projection, so let us see what these processes are.

WAYS OF PROJECTION: CONSTITUTIVE AND APPROPRIATIVE PROJECTION

Early versions of projection theory can be found in Greek and Hebrew mythologies. In accounts of creation such as those of *Timaeus* and Genesis the Gods *intentionally* make humans, *consciously* bring humans into being.[9]

They are fully aware of their actions and we see them intending to create copies of themselves. They deliberately create images of themselves through imitating their own being *by making an other from their own substance.* Gods *consciously, actively, constitute or create an object, their image in human form, where before there was not one.* They concurrently produce the mirror and the image in it. These images are animated and capable of existence independent of their makers.

In these stories the Gods project their being, and importantly they know that they do. For them, projection is deliberate creation and is actively constitutive of something new. A world and its creatures come into existence and appear to persist independently of their makers post-creation. In *Timaeus* and Genesis the deliberate projecting by God results in a *human* copy that itself can deliberately project: it can intend, act deliberately and be aware of its intentions and its deliberateness. It can identify or disidentify with its origins. God's conscious projection creates a conscious object. The image of God is like God in two ways: first the image is good and secondly, it is conscious.

Symbolically, the original creation act of God is a prototypical model of the constitutive activity of the collective. Both God and the collective actively constitute the objects which they create. Their projection is constitutive of an object other than themselves even though that object is intended to be *like* themselves. Like the plurality of God, the plurality of collectives is humanly instantiated. 'In the divine image he created him; male and female he created them,' say the authors of Genesis. The Genesis account functions as a mythical pattern for human sociality. They, God, are collective, but they are also distinguishable as male and female. To the extent that the conscious collective deliberately attempts to produce images of itself, or unconsciously does so, it acts as if it were God. While humans are symbolically marked by their metaphoric divine origins, as male and female, as individual and as collective, they nevertheless have a capacity to exist independently of God. These differences are repeated in their relations with the collective. In *Timaeus* and Genesis we have, then, an instance of the symbolic origins of consciousness and unconsciousness as well as the symbolic origins of subject and object.

We can see in Jung's work, a continuation of the projection tropes in the above stories. But whereas the Gods seek to create through projective activity, their awareness of what they are doing is not echoed in Jung's understanding of projection. The difference is in the role that unconsciousness plays and for Jung unconsciousness is the source of projection. Jung claimed that '[p]rojection is a general psychological mechanism that carries over subjective contents of any kind into the object' (Jung 1998: 153). He saw this mechanism as either pathological or normal in the case of passive projection, and evaluative in the case of active projection (Jung 1971: 783). Jung argues that 'projection is usually an unconscious process not under conscious control' (Jung 1971: 486) and that it involves a subject's identifying with an object. A subject undergoes a psychological crisis that entails a subsequent need to dissolve the projected content. The subject must acknowledge her/his projective activity and then reclaim the projected content. The withdrawal of projection is a major factor in the individuation process. For Jung, recognition of projection is not simply a matter for the intellect (Jung 1971: 421). It requires a confrontation with unconsciousness through conscious engagement with its contents which are uncovered in active imagination, or in dream images (Jung 1966: 355–9). We can see then that Jungian projection has some of the elements of the early versions, but is significantly different in others. It is those significant differences that turn projection theory into a plausible way of accounting for psychological issues. It also helps us to understand how a collective can give an account of itself as the bearer and preserver of its perhaps forgotten historical past.

We should note, though, that Jung claims that projection is *usually* unconscious activity. This implies that some projection is not unconscious, that it is *conscious* activity and this is consistent with what we have just seen. Projection can, therefore, be either conscious or unconscious as well as active and passive. Consonant with his claim that projection is not usually under conscious control, Jung argues that passive projections 'are not intentional and are purely automatic occurrences' (Jung 1971: 784). Unconscious passive projection produces unconscious relocating of negative or positive emotion, characteristics or sentiments from one's own psyche to the person of another. We think another has the emotion, characteristics or sentiments which we ourselves actually have and refuse to acknowledge and maybe cannot even (temporarily) recognise. Falling in love, hating your former partner, or championing a cause with which you identify, are examples of this. The status of active projections is less clear. Are those projections conscious or unconscious?

Jung's two examples of active projection, empathy and judgement involve him in a discussion of two related concepts, introjection and introversion. Jung argues that empathy is really a form of introjection, 'a process of *assimilation*, while projection is a process of *dissimilation*. Introjection is an assimilation of object to subject, projection a dissimilation of object from subject through the expulsion of subjective content into the object' (Jung 1971: 768). Jung is here employing the tropes of inner and outer, of turning to and from a subject, to and from an object and the relevant properties each might or might not possess. As we shall see in Chapter 7, this is closely aligned to some of the questions associated with essentialism of which Jung has been accused. For now, let us accept Jung's claim that in introjection something about the object is internalised by the subject, taken as if it is the subject's own.[10] In projection, something about the subject is externalised, taken as if it belongs to an object. The two processes are the opposite of each other. If projection and introjection are opposites, then

Jung's inclusion of empathy as an exemplar of active projection is puzzling. He seems to be contradicting himself: how can empathy be *both* introjective and projective?

We might deal with this question by considering the dynamic complexity of the psyche. The trope of outward/inward movement recurs in Jung's discussion of introjection and projection. It echoes the going out of itself and then the return to itself of self-consciousness in Hegel's Master/Slave Dialectic. Empathy is both projection and introjection because these two processes are in dialectical engagement or in the kind of dialectical relationship I outlined in Chapter 1. From that perspective, one cannot empathise without moving out from one's psyche; one cannot empathise without returning to one's psyche. The psyche does not so much project an imagistic *content* in empathy but makes itself available to receive something from an object. In making itself available, the psyche exercises its structural capacity for reception of and receptiveness to an object. In other words, it engages in the work of Hegelian recognition. An object, in this case, can be thought of more broadly as that which is another to oneself. The psyche is called to respond, and it does so. In doing that, the psyche acknowledges the existence of the other. In responding to and acknowledging the other, the psyche is able to affirm its membership of a collective; able, that is, to realise that some of its origins are external to its own being and then to actively engage with aspects of those origins. Empathy is double-barrelled: it is a calling to the psyche from the world, and a subsequent return from the world. The making available of itself to another is tantamount to the psyche's moving out of itself.

The psyche does not, however, seek always to identify with the other. Active projection, what Jung calls 'subjective judgement', is a process of introversion and involves the psyche's distinguishing itself from the other: a 'differentiation and separation of subject from object' (Jung 1971: 784). We see this happening in the creation stories we looked at earlier in Chapter 2. Subjective judgement as a function of the psyche is teleological insofar as it has precisely this separation of subject from object as its aim. Jung argues that 'a subjective judgement is detached from the subject as a valid statement and lodged in the object; by this act the subject distinguishes himself from the object' (Jung 1971: 784). We saw this process of distinguishing oneself operating in Lacan's 'mirror stage'.

Jung's language is interesting because he seems to be thinking that a subject is able to form a judgement as a linguistic process. Subjective judgement is part of the content and linguistic expression of the human psyche and, as formulation in language, is an existentially constitutive activity of the psyche. Indeed, subjective judgement is a linguistic mode that helps me to form a view about, and conceive of, the ontologically separate from myself: I am not all that there is and I can judge this to be the case through language use.

Here, it might be claimed, subjective judgement acts as a guarantor against solipsism: the existence of the other determined through the formulation of a statement is a logical requirement for empathy to take place. Subjective judgement helps to reveal the other to the psyche. But the capacity of the psyche to return to itself in introversion means that the psyche can isolate itself as an entity distinct from the world on the one hand and the world as distinct from the psyche on the other. The distinction between world and psyche is clearly not a fixed and unmoving boundary. The role of the collective in contributing to the growth and development of its members attests to this. Although the line of separation is flexible and changeable, its motility functions as a porous membrane which allows an osmotic exchange between psyche and world. This capacity underlies the possibility of meta-positioning and, ultimately, the possibility of deliberate self-making and individuation.

Judgement and empathy turn out to be elements of the psyche's ability to manage itself in its collective world in either empathic identification or judicious withdrawal. Hence the dynamism of the psyche is such that projection operates differentially. The interplay between empathy, subjective judgement and the situatedness of the subject in her/his world exhibits the self-corrective potential of the psyche. We might, in other words, read Jung's elucidation of active projection as a model of how the psyche might work to achieve equanimity. The psyche's emanative orientation towards its collectives needs to be matched by the psyche's disposition to return to itself, to its introvert tendencies. The judgement function is missing from Narcissus' psyche, for example, and the possibility of achieving psychic equanimity eludes him. He cannot return to himself to form the judgement that he is the image he sees before him. The child's turn of its head as it responds to its father's voice, on the other hand, exhibits the activation of the judgement function together with a simultaneous de-activation of introjection. While the child can turn its head towards the father, the possibility of psychic equanimity remains. Psychic equanimity depends on the essential dynamism of the psyche, on the capacity of the psyche to be affected by change and to effect change. Jung's discussion of projection demonstrates this point. Whether or not active projection is conscious or unconscious remains a moot point. But it is an important question because we need to be clear about the status of the object, the other, in relation to the subject.

Accompanying the constitutive process of projection and before the moment of identification of subject with object, there is an attempt at appropriation of the object by the subject. Jung's claim that '[p]rojection . . . is properly so called when the need to dissolve the identity has already arisen' focuses on the idea that, in identifying with an object, the subject takes something to be the case that is not the case (Jung 1971: 783). Whether the subject invests the object with properties as in passive projection or whether the subject is involved in empathy or subjective judgement, the relation between subject and object is *appropriative*. In projecting, unconsciousness attempts to make an object its own by exercising control over the object towards which it projects or which it constructs. Characteristics that they may or may not have are attributed to objects. When such objects are actually constituted, when projection produces beings capable of existence independently of their projector, then the question of their being 'owned' by its originating source arises.

Thus God's instruction to Adam that he should not eat of the tree of knowledge of good and evil can be read as a test of obedience and loyalty. But it can also be read as an implicit affirmation of a paternalistic power relation between God and his creatures in which God exercises some measure of control. The rule of prohibition over eating the fruit of the tree of knowledge of good and evil that God imposes is couched in terms of death: 'the moment you eat from it you are surely doomed to die' (*The New American Bible* Genesis 3: 3). Adam's and the Woman's rejection of God's command makes the constitutive nature of projection ambiguous because it compromises God's ontological investment in their creation. Since Adam and the Woman reject the prohibition, they disentangle themselves from God's appropriating of their identities so that their potential full subjectivity can be realised. Indeed, unless Adam and the Woman *are able* to disentangle themselves, they can never be subjects, but will instead be incomplete selves incapable of moral engagement. When they eat of the fruit of the tree of knowledge of good and evil, Adam and the Woman turn their heads away from the voice of the father towards the voice and the promise of another (the snake). The snake represents the otherness, the individuated selves that potentially Adam and the Woman are. Unlike Lacan's interpretation, they are saved here by a turning away from the voice of the father, not a turning towards it. Adam and the Woman begin their own self-constitution or self-making once they have refused God. Perversely, they become more like God in this moment: they now have knowledge of good and evil, just as God before them did.

As a moment in the divine life, Adam's and the Woman's rejection of God's prohibition signals a transformation for the divine. Even God cannot be untouched by his own capacity and willingness to project. Appropriative projection is binding and limiting for both projector and recipient. Severance of appropriative projection is necessary for psychological emancipation. Without disobedience and betrayal, without interruption to the divine order, God is unable to withdraw his projecting activity. An inversion of the mirror stage takes place between God and God's creatures as Adam and the Woman force the father to turn his head towards them, to ask them who had told them they were naked. *That* is the profound moment of self-realisation for God and humans. The moment of release for Adam and the Woman becomes the moment at which the divine can return to himself, can separate himself from his own projections. God, Adam and the Woman cooperate in a dialectic of disentanglement and opportunity for release from the projection of the other.

This schematising of constitutive and appropriative projection and the drawing of a distinction between conscious and unconscious projection focuses once more on dialectic. The subject/object relation evident in unconsciousness' emanative activity is, very clearly, fundamental to Jung's discussion of projection and of the dialectic relation between individual psyche and collective. However, his discussion extends the Platonic conception of dialectic while remaining faithful to its fundamental structure. Given this, how can this relation be understood?

The collective unconscious pre-figures the essentially dynamic, dyadic, originary structure that we find between collective and member (Jung 1969: 134). The collective unconscious does not 'owe its existence to personal experience and consequently is not a personal acquisition' (Jung 1969: 88). It is a structuring network of 'mythological associations, motifs and images that can spring up anew anytime anywhere, independently of historical tradition or migration' (Jung 1971: 842), which sustains a dynamic rapport with consciousness. In resisting a self's or a collective's conscious efforts to disregard its wisdom, unconsciousness insists on its ordinary everydayness, which is nonetheless mysterious. The constitutive and appropriative effects of projection show themselves in the conscious choices a collective member makes as well as in the modes of being an individual comes to see as natural, as ordinary, as everyday, because of the collective entanglement she/he has experienced and continues to experience. Although she/he might be constituted through collective membership, consciously and unconsciously, and although a collective might appropriate her/his consciousness, a member is not totally constituted nor appropriated by her membership of a collective. Interruption, the turn of the head away from and to, expresses this.

JUNG, AND SUBJECT AND OBJECT

Jung's use of the terms 'subject' and 'object' and their cognates connotes a binary division between a perceiving/experiencing subject and a perceived/experienced object. From a methodological and a logical perspective, his use of the terms 'subject' and 'object' carries little ontological weight. They are technical terms employed to illustrate the dialectical, binary nature of subjectivity/objectivity, where, logically speaking, a subject requires an object and an object requires a subject, the position that we saw is argued by Hegel. A more sophisticated reading of the context of subject/object use would, however, take into account the considerable ontological weight borne by each term individually and together (Jung 1969: 134). Jung's reading of subject/object relations is specifically Hegelian in its orientation.[11]

Consonant with this orientation is the notion that objects are the furniture of the world: what we as subjects see, hear, smell, think about, bring into existence, destroy – the commonplace and familiar stuff of our existence. From this point of view, human beings are *at least* objects, *at least* part of the furniture of the world and, as such, objects that are recipients of projection. 'Human being objects' are receptive to their immersion or plunging, or being thrown into the world through their births into collectives. They have the capacity to be *and are* affected by these processes. They are 'picked out' as sites of collective projection and this implies that they are not *mere* objects. Significantly, the claim of the collective over the newly born, for example, is a claim that she/he does not exist in the realm of mere objecthood. What is important about a collective's members is that, although they might be viewed in some mundane or logical sense as objects, their objecthood exceeds those senses and their subjecthood is already implied before their birth into a collective. Nascent subject status is conferred on a new member by a collective before birth. The conferral of this status is a first active projection that begins the constitution of a collective member as both a subject *and* object of that collective.

Here we find our argument against Giegerich's original position. Because the collective is the origin of potential individuals who become subjects, subjects are always already in collective or social space which figures them as objects. Thus projection *and* subjectivity logically and existentially presuppose each as their otherness and are thus complementary. A subject can exist only because an other, an object, already exists. In projection, there is no distinction between subject and object until the projection is acknowledged; then and only then can a subject distinguish her/himself as something distinct from her/his projection as either the entirety of an object or some of its properties. Jung's subject who projects onto an object does so because her/his subjecthood is contingent on a collective where there are always already other subjects existing in and alongside the objects of the world; and where the ubiquity of the collective unconscious, sometimes silently, manifests itself. Indeed, the capacity to produce subjects out of fleshy sex/gendered bodies through the projection of norms, habits and customs, relies on the emanative nature of *collective consciousness and unconsciousness*. Subjects are always *inter*-subjects; and subjects are always potential objects for other subjects *and are always at the whim of the collective unconscious* (Jung 1969: 62).

In its potency, the collective unconscious renders impossible singular individual origin because the collective unconscious is the originary site of any projection. The centrality of the collective, either conscious or unconscious, to Jung's world view means that Jung foreshadows Maurice Merleau-Ponty's reminder of our place in the human world, the site of collectivity, 'the seat and as it were the "homeland" of our thoughts' (Merleau-Ponty 1962: 13–24). As a self produced by a conscious and unconscious collective with vested interests in reproducing itself, a subject will have internalised the membership requirements of the various collectives to which she/he belongs, through introjection and then introversion. The internalisation of those membership requirements for each specific kind of body represents a collective's constitutive activity but it also affects the formation of personal unconsciousness within a whole domain of collective constraints. The collective constitutes a self, and a self-as-a-subject through culturally reinforcing practices (baptisms, marriages, rites of passage, rules and regulations, ritualised feast days, systems of hierarchy, cultural prejudices) that reinscribe and normalise the central myths of a collective. A self cannot, on this reading, be a one-dimensional, purely conscious individual. Rather, she/he is multidimensional, conscious and unconscious, individual and collective, and intentionally self-directing only to the degree that she/he is conscious. She/he recognises, and is recognised by, her/his collective in a emanative and returning movement.

This is the root of Jung's commitment to individuation. Intersubjectivity, conscious and unconscious pervasiveness as well as multi-dimensionality are the foundation of psychic life and one's being in the world. Psychic life, however, exceeds its collective origins, exceeds any biological reductionism that one might be prompted to engage in and brings to the collective the richness of its personal and collective unconscious, the symbolic domain contingent on, but simultaneously autonomous of, consciousness and the collectivity.

The potential self appropriated by a collective at birth, the small mirror who mimics, sometimes unconsciously, the projected demands and norms of the collective, is only partially appropriated, partially constituted by any one collective. She/he is never *tabula rasa* (Jung 1969: 136). The fact of her/his multi-collective membership means that bodies (of which selves are a type) are the sites of intersecting attributions of social significance (Crenshaw 1991). However, attributions of social significance do not stand alone as the ontological force behind selfhood and enfleshment. Fleshy being with its biosocial origins guarantees an arcane individuality with the further potential to resist total identification with any collective. As an agent of projection itself, a collective fails to constitute any member as a perfect reflection of some ideal *desideratum*. Further, we must remember that a child pre-exists its appearance in the mirror. The collective through the fabric of its social networks and relations tells the child that it exists and, in the telling, both calls, and brings, the child into being. The collective has acted as if it were God's uttering the directive 'Let us . . .'.[12] What is special about the mirror is that it enables the child to refigure itself as someone *she/he* can recognise, ultimately, without props because she/he has become her/his own familiar, is an object for and of self-recognition, even though the appearance changes through time, although recognition of oneself as a fleshy body is only one facet of self-recognition and self-consciousness.

In the house of mirrors, the being of the self cannot be constituted through the visual alone. The orientation towards the eye, towards the visual, elevates the self away from the ground of its very own being by, paradoxically, threatening the potential loss of self-consciousness to a mirror image. The turn of the child towards the father's voice, a source of interruption, witnesses this. But the visual nature of the mirror and reliance on the visual aspect of the projection metaphor obscures the fleshiness of the embodied self. Touch, smell, sound and taste, even though culturally attuned, defy the absolutist tendencies of the visually orienting mirror metaphor. The touch of the flesh is the encounter that produces, ultimately, a self. In that touch the duality of human existence finds itself confirmed as the flesh redeems the self and redeems the collective. The simultaneity of constitution and appropriation through visual projection alone is eroded by the truth of the flesh. Immersion of the flesh in the fullness of its sensuality is demanded for the appearance of the self and its subjectivity.

The truth of the flesh guarantees the possibility of projection: the we-ness of the creator God in whose image *adam* is made, entails that *adam* and, consequently, *the creator* God*s*, be enfleshed *and plural.*[13] Men and women are *fleshy* images of an already existent dyadic configuration ('let us make man in *our* image, after *our* likeness'). The Genesis creation myth re-read from this perspective, endorses the flesh, endorses projection as ontologically constitutive, and logically presupposes human origins in a two-ness of image and mirror which replicate each other. Luce Irigaray's insistence on the originary significance of the two lips captures and almost caricatures this two-ness (Irigaray 1985b: 30–1). The two-ness of the lips symbolises the fundamental two-ness of difference and intersubjectivity: it is an oppositional alternative to the singularity of Lacan's primary signifier, the phallus. It is also a reaffirmation of the two-ness of the Hegelian insistence on a primary two-ness in his Dialectical, contrary to the singularity of the original position. The singularity of the penis cannot escape its dependent status shrouded in natality; correspondingly, the two lips reiterate theirs.

The metaphor of the two lips underlies Irigaray's quest for a divine for women, a feminine symbolic, and women's writing (*écriture feminine*). This trope sets Irigaray's conception of the feminine against dominant cultural Western ideals of femininity as she argues for the ontological singularity of the feminine. Jung's conception of the feminine embodied prevails in today's Western attitudes and values. His insistence, however, on a feminine aspect of the masculine psyche places him in an idiosyncratic position with respect to both the masculine and the feminine. Whether or not projection is conscious and why that matters becomes an issue for masculine-paternal-dominated collectives. The unravelling of these issues for Jung and Irigaray is the focal point around which the feminine becomes disputed, and I now turn to this debate.

Chapter 5

Divine reversal

> An inherited collective image of woman exists in a man's unconscious, with the help of which he apprehends the nature of woman.
>
> (Jung 1966: 301)

> In intellectual women the animus encourages a critical disputatious highbrowism, which, however, consists essentially in harping on some irrelevant weak point and nonsensically making it the main one.
>
> (Jung 1966: 335)

> Historically, we are guardians of the flesh; we do not have to abandon that guardianship, but identify it as ours by inviting men not to make us 'their bodies', guarantors of their bodies.
>
> (Luce Irigaray 1991b: 43)

What is the truth of the flesh? In Christian dogma, incarnational theology suggests that the person of Jesus as the enfleshed Son of God, and then the Son's sacrificial crucifixion, is the truth of the flesh. The flesh is made divine by the Father's incorporation into the world as a mortal through His Son. This Son triumphs over death in the salvific moment when He rises from the dead. Love, obedience, abandonment, filial devotion and faith are some of the key sentiments in this story. The truth of the flesh is found in sacrifice, death and deification of God-made-Man.

Luce Irigaray rejects this version of the truth of the flesh with its emphasis on the phallus (the symbolic/imaginary penis), the relationship between Father and Son and the marginalising of the mother whose *raison d'être* is precisely as mother to the Son of God. Of particular interest here is Lacan's 'The Meaning of the Phallus', in which he argues that 'the relation of the subject to the phallus is set up regardless of the anatomical differences between the sexes, which is what makes its interpretation particularly intractable in the case of the woman' (Lacan 1982: 76). The argument he develops about the symbolic/imaginary primacy of the phallus as signifier of desire for the Other in the case of both sexes as it mediates physical sexual relations, justifies, in his view, women's lack of sexual satisfaction as tolerable. But his closing endorsement of Freud's intuition 'that there is only one libido, his text clearly indicating that he conceives of it as masculine in nature' (Lacan 1982: 85) is the impetus for Luce Irigaray's insistence on the development of a feminine symbolic/imaginary.

In that symbolic/imaginary she proposes an appropriation and then refiguring of libido beyond the masculine symbolic/imaginary in a newly constituted feminine domain of meaning and desire. As we shall see in what follows, Luce Irigaray offers a version of the flesh as truth for women, which takes its inspiration from the flesh of woman, from the mother–daughter relationship and from mimicry or ironic imitation. But we begin with Jung and his rendering of the feminine.

Commenting on the 'nothing-but daughter', the 'woman who is so identified with her mother that her own instincts are paralysed through projection', Jung remarks that '[t]hese women remind me – if I may be forgiven the impolite comparison – of hefty great bitches who turn tail before the smallest cur simply because he is a terrible male and it never occurs to them to bite him' (Jung 1968a: 182).[1] This unsubtle characterisation of the woman trapped by the mother archetype, and who has not yet become conscious, brings together excessive identification or unconscious imitation, and the irrationality of the disordered soul. Such a woman cannot progress on the path of individuation unless she is able to confront her mother complex and resolve it in some appropriate manner. But what is appropriate to Jung's psychology is the analytical encounter which is circumscribed by order, by the conscious weighing of psychological options made available through the imagination as it engages with the unconscious (in word or drawing or dancing) and through dream analysis. Suppose, however, that the woman *does* bite the terrible male and that her *modus operandi* is *inappropriate*: instead of being lured by order, the woman embraces the anima feminine, the irrational which is not to be imitated. Suppose this . . .

ARCHETYPES, THE FEMININE AND THE COLLECTIVE

Jung's characterisation of archetypes is, unsurprisingly, influenced by both Plato and Immanuel Kant.[2] Kant, who lovingly calls Plato 'the philosopher', accepts a particular view of archetype as ideal, which we then see reproduced in Jung's notion of archetype. That a Platonic archetype is an ideal is controversial, so let us begin by looking briefly at Plato's treatment of Forms which gives rise to the idea of archetype. Again, we shall see the important role played by philosophy in the elaboration of psychological theory.

The Greek words 'Ιδέα and εἶδος are most closely translated as 'Form' and 'appearance' (Grube 1980: 1).[3] Forms are fundamental to Plato's ontology and epistemology, but what they *are* is controversial. Part of the trouble with interpreting 'Form' in Plato's work is that he says different things in different dialogues over different times. Most commentators agree that Forms are eternal, ahistorical entities, but their relation to material objects, that is, how they function in the empirical world, is disputed. Some scholars claim that we cannot even refer to Plato's *theory* of Forms. Julia Annas, for example, puts quotation marks around 'theory' in her chapter 'Plato's "Theory" of Forms' and maintains that 'Plato not only has no word for "theory"; he nowhere in the dialogues has an extended discussion of Forms in which he pulls together the different lines of thought about them and tries to assess the needs they meet and whether they succeed in meeting them' (Annas 1981: 217).

I. M. Crombie proposes several interpretations of Forms: as common structures present in all objects of the same kind (for example dogs); as meanings of sets of concepts, 'those namely which could be described as models or ideals', and as ordering principles which originate in mind (Crombie 1962: 50–1). He rejects the common structure and ideal model views and develops an argument to show that Plato treated Forms as 'independent substantial things . . . the originals of which the natures of physical things were images or reflections' (Crombie 1962: 51). That argument revolves around the idea that Forms are *a priori* ordering principles of a creative and intelligent divine mind. The physical world is chaotic and the divine mind endeavours to impose order on the chaos 'to reproduce in the physical realm a replica or embodiment of the system of rational order which it eternally comprehends' (Crombie 1962: 52). Timaeus, for example, explaining why the creator made the world, argues that:

> God desired that all things should be good and nothing bad, so far as this was attainable. Where also finding the whole visible sphere not at rest, but moving in an irregular and disorderly fashion, out of disorder he brought order, considering that this was in every way better than the other.
>
> (Plato 1970c: *Timaeus* 30a)

Things are created to satisfy a need or natural necessity: 'the need comes first, and the things devised to meet it are posterior to it' (Crombie 1962: 52). We can see this in Socrates' questions to Hermogenes:

> to what does the carpenter look in making the shuttle? Does he not look to the way in which the shuttle must, in the nature of things, operate? . . . And suppose the shuttle to be broken in making, will he make another looking to the broken one? Or will he look to the form to

> which he made the other? . . . Might that not justly be called the true or ideal shuttle?
>
> (Plato 1970c: 'Cratylus' 389a)

It is worth noting that Socrates is here referring to an ideal shuttle of which the broken shuttle was a copy. This seems to lend weight to the ideal model Crombie rejects, but I shall return to this point in a moment. Crombie argues that specific instances of the Forms never realise the perfection of the Forms themselves. Ideal or perfect specimens, if they were to exist, would always be after the fact of the prior existence of the Form in the divine mind. The principle of rational order, so important to Plato's conception of the soul itself, appears as the organising principle of the soul and the fundamental principle of the cosmos.

Jung is undisguised in his admiration for Plato and he invokes Plato as the inspiration behind his reading of archetypes. We see this in his introductory remarks to the mother archetype where he attributes the origin of the term 'archetype' to its synonymy 'with Idea in the Platonic usage' (Jung 1968a: 149). In that, he is close to Kant, who acknowledges Plato's influence in his understanding of 'idea' which we think of as analogous to Plato's 'Form' or *eidos*. Kant writes that:

> Plato made use of the expression '*idea*' in such a way as quite evidently to have meant by it something which not only can never be borrowed from the senses but far surpasses even the concepts of the understanding . . . inasmuch as in experience nothing is ever to be met with that is coincident with it. For Plato ideas are archetypes of the things themselves, and not in the manner of the categories, merely keys to possible experiences. In his view they have issued from highest reason.
>
> (Kant 1930: B370)

Crombie's reading of Plato is very similar to Kant's, emphasising as it does the eternal nature of the ideas (Forms) and the fact that ideas lie outside human experience and understanding. But Kant's reading is distinguished from Crombie's because Kant differentiates between 'idea' (*Urgrund*) and 'ideal' (*Urbild*), both of which are translated by 'archetype' in English. And although both idea and ideal are translated as 'archetype', Kant suggests that 'idea' is the meaning of Platonic idea whereas 'ideal' is 'the basis of the possible perfection of certain actions' (Kant 1930: A569/B597). Although the latter is in the domain of action, it is not difficult to translate the potential of 'ideal' into the domain of objects and to argue for the possibility of ideal Forms. That being the case, 'archetype' could mean either 'idea' or 'ideal', which would admit of construing (correctly or incorrectly) Forms as both ideal models and *a priori* ordering principles (of a divine mind). Crombie's rejection of the ideal model view can thus be seen to be unjustified. And it is worth while surmising that Kant's reading of Plato's Forms is what Jung has in mind when he embraces archetypes.

Without a doubt, Jung depends heavily on Kant as the inspiration behind analytical psychology. Jung says, for example, that:

> [i]f it be true that there can be no metaphysics transcending human reason, it is no less true that there can be no empirical knowledge that is not already caught and limited by the *a priori* structure of cognition . . . thinking, understanding, and reasoning cannot be regarded as independent processes subject only to the eternal laws of logic . . . they are *psychic functions* co-ordinated with the personality and subordinated to it.
>
> (Jung 1968a: 150)

The claim that there can be no metaphysics transcending reason is a central concern of Kant's *Critique of Pure Reason*. Likewise, Jung's commitment to the '*a priori* factor in all human activities, namely the inborn, preconscious and unconscious individual structure of the psyche' (Jung 1968a: 151), is a theoretical derivative of Kant. Even the idea that the collective unconscious is unknowable seems interpretable in terms of Kant's distinction between knowable phenomena and unknowable noumena to which the categories cannot apply. Archetypes are ineluctably intertwined as form and content: one infers the existence of the archetype, the Form, from its repeated and generalised occurrence in symbolic/imaginary content. And repetition and generalisation are explained, as Jung understands the issue, by what makes them possible in the first place: Forms or archetypes. In this, as Jung notes, he is a realist voice in a nominalist world and a Platonist over an Aristotelian (Jung 1968a: 149). He forgets to mention, at that point, that he is also a committed Kantian.

Jung's archetypes are always already *a priori* structural principles, but they are equally principles of order that simultaneously act as ideal models. Both of the views of archetypes embraced by Jung (the ideal model view and the principle of order view), together with their *a priori* status, cannot escape the very same problems that beset Platonic Forms. If, for example, Forms are fixed and definable whereas instances of the Forms are not, then we are faced with the problem of how to define a single individual. And how a Form can be both common nature and ideal model poses problems for instantiation: does an individual instance of the Form instantiate the ideal and, if so, how? If Forms are *a priori* and give individuals their identities, how do they do this? Is it because they are ideas in the mind of the divine being, so that the world and its objects mirror, imperfectly, the divine mind? If we use the language of participation ('an individual instance participates in a Form and that is what makes the individual what it is') what does 'participation' mean, especially when instances are always imperfect copies? If Forms are eternal and immutable, how do they become involved in the finite, changing matter that instances are? Is every individual an instance of a Form? For example, are goodness and tables and humans each of them instances of Forms? (Plato uses all of these as examples of Forms in various dialogues.) If being a table is an abstract 'property' of tables, then is there the property of being abstract as well as the property of being a table? I shall be looking at some of these questions when I explore essence in Chapter 7, but, as we shall see, the answers do not lie in Platonic philosophy.

As I have just now been suggesting, the Jungian archetype is not straightforwardly Platonic, given its apparently Kantian interpretation. But there is a further way in which we need to attend to the Kantian elements of Jung's analytical psychology. According to Kant, all objects of the senses are appearances which we represent to ourselves in space and time. Space and time are not absolute, but are instead subjective outer and inner forms of sensible intuition which represent objects spatio-temporally: we do not experience things as they are or directly, but as our minds constitute them. The mind organises and structures sensible input and produces spatio-temporal objects of knowledge (Kant 1930: B67). The mind, as in Schopenhauer, mediates consciousness and the world.[4] Jung endorses this view of the mind when he argues:

> It is my mind, with its store of images that gives the world colour and sound; and that supremely rational and real certainty which I call 'experience' is, in its most simple form, an exceedingly complicated structure of mental images. Thus there is, in a certain sense, nothing that is directly experienced except the mind itself. Everything is mediated through the mind, translated, filtered, allegorised, twisted, even falsified by it. We are so enveloped in a cloud of changing and endlessly shifting images that we might well exclaim with a known sceptic: 'Nothing is absolutely true and – and even that is not quite true'.
>
> (Jung 1969: 623)

The role of the mind as the constituter of objects of experience is clear here. That the mind's images are projected, constitutively, onto the world and its objects is also anticipated, as our minds are responsible for our sensory experiences of sight and sound. For Jung, the apparatus of projection includes the imposition of archetypes which structurally mediate *how* and *what* we apprehend. The mind represents the world to us. The feminine, the self, the masculine are effects of projective engagement with the world. We can see that Jung argues *against* a *tabula rasa* conception of the human psyche, and *for* a structuring of the psyche by *a priori* factors. Let us now turn to the anima, an archetype of the feminine, and see how the theory of forms or ideas plays itself out.

As *a priori* structures, some archetypes pattern the feminine, which is also grounded in the maternal body. The mother is the empirical or *a posteriori* site of exposure to the feminine; yet one's actual mother and other women with whom one eventually comes into contact are only partly implicated in one's construction of the feminine. Jung maintains that:

> In so far as the child is born with a differentiated brain that is predetermined by heredity and therefore individualized, it meets sensory stimuli coming from outside not with *any* aptitude but with *specific* ones, and this results in a particular, individual choice and pattern of apperception. These aptitudes can be shown to be inherited instincts and pre-formed patterns, the latter being the *a priori* and formal conditions of apperception that are based on instinct. Their presence gives the world of the child and the dreamer its anthropomorphic stamp.
>
> (Jung 1968a: 136)

This reading of the brain as a differentiated structure that, presumably at least, interacts with and/or is causally related to the psyche, which is itself an *a priori* structure,[5] could be read as a complement to the notion of a member's thrown-ness into a collective.[6] In this light, a new member's appropriation by its collective can be understood as the confluence of psychic structures and social collective structures which respond to each other. A new member can be appropriated by her/his collective because she/he has the psychic structural capacity and potential to be so appropriated. Thus not only would a collective grab a new member, the new member would be innately disposed to being grabbed by the collective as she/he is thrown. Archetypes or 'patterns of functioning' (Jung 1968a: 152) on this account would prepare the ground for and maintain the possibility of intercourse between collective and collective members in quite specific ways. The anima feminine archetype and the maternal feminine archetype would therefore be structural predispositions of the psyche that encounter and respond to the world or the social collective in a specific way. But archetypes are more insidious than this.

Jung argues that 'it is not, therefore a question of inherited *ideas* but of inherited *possibilities* of ideas' (Jung 1968a: 136). His elaboration of their inherited possibility resolves into a discussion of the structuring functions found in the psyche that are common to all humans. Jung remarks that although he has called archetypes 'images' his reference is not to their content but rather 'the term "image" is intended to express not only the form of the activity taking place, but the typical situation in which the activity is released' (Jung 1968a: 152).[7] This typical situation is the encounter between a collective member and the collective. However, the feminine must be always already interpreted through *a priori* structures that are projected and constitutive of their objects. *Archetypes are prior to their instantiation.* And since archetypes seem to have a causally structural role in the production of objects through their being constitutively projected, a typical situation would always be constituted by the activity of the projecting psyche.

According to Jung, '[t]he first bearer of the soul-image is always the mother' (Jung 1966: 314). How are we to understand the idea of the mother as bearer of the soul-image? Is Jung suggesting that the mother is the first recipient of the anima projection; or does he mean that the mother herself carries the soul-image within herself? Given the priority of archetypes, it seems that the former must be the case. If that is so, then one might wonder about the ontological integrity of the mother, or of any other object in the world. If archetypes are structural constituents that are projected, then the mother is clearly a *product* of an infant's projection. Not only that, since archetypes are also ideal forms, the projection is value-laden. It *carries* the ideal form with it. On this account archetypes constitute in a strong sense one's engagement with the world and also the cognitive nature of objects in that world. If that constituency is deterministic, then the reciprocity between self and object, individual and collective proposed in Chapter 3 is destabilised, and archetypes must be seen as pre-eminent *determinants* of being and of concepts of being. If objects have any properties or qualities of themselves, then the radical subjectivism, that the notion of *a priori* archetypes suggests, precludes their recognition as mutually constitutive in any subject/object dialectic. Indeed, this view of *a priori* archetypes reinforces the radical disjunction of subject and object which should, properly, be thought of more organically.

Perhaps one of the most important things of which we need to remind ourselves here is that archetypes are *a priori* structures of the collective unconscious expressed through members' psyches. Hence it is not only that archetypes function constitutively in relation to members' psyches; for at a collective level, archetypes are the unconscious constituents of the collective or community. This double figuring of archetypes reinforces the role of archetypes as bearers of ahistorical and atemporal structures that could be taken to be *natural* and *given*. Far from the plastic reciprocal relation I argued for earlier in my discussion of dialectic, subject and object, and collective member and collective, we are confronted, if *constituent* is read as *determinant*, with what seems to be a rather inflexible deterministic relation. Indeed, the collective unconscious on this view owes little to the historicity of collective memory. Jung's claim that subjects are always at the whim of the collective unconscious becomes a reminder that the collective unconscious, which transcends and pre-exists human consciousness, has the ultimate 'say' in how things are. For this reason it might seem as if ideas of choice, autonomy, and personal or collective freedom are part of a mythical consciousness constructed by collectives. If the collective unconscious can insert itself anywhere at any time, it is an illusion that we are free and self-governing for it is possible that the whim of the collective unconscious undermines any pretensions of that sort that we might have. The metaphysical and psychological issues raised by such a spectre are enormous, and the notion of individuation seems implausible.

Given this interpretation, we must conclude that problems raised by Jung's notion of archetypes mirror the problems that we find in the philosophy underlying them. Joint attention to the archetypes as psychic structures and as philosophical postulates is therefore necessary if such problems are to be solved. The case of the anima feminine is interesting from this perspective as calls to account for the feminine *in general* in feminist theory problematise innate structuring and/or dispositions and emphasise the role of collectives in its manufacture. But: *are women feminine by nature or by nurture*? Are women naturally irrational or made to be irrational as a result of their education and the expectations of their collectives? Can women and the feminine be thought of *beyond the boundaries of irrationality and physical disorderliness*? Some of these calls even dispute the existence of the feminine at all, claiming that the feminine is a social construction with political motivation and ends.[8]

Jung's analysis of the anima feminine as an originary site out of which grow other forms of the feminine tells us much about the weight he gives to the notion of the *a priori*. Yet even his comments here suggest the importance he attaches to lived experience. For example, he argues that 'the concept of the anima is a purely empirical concept, whose sole purpose is to give a name to a group of related or analogous psychic phenomena' (Jung 1968a: 114). Later, in discussing the nature of archetypes, Jung remarks that 'ideas in the Platonic sense . . . perform and continually influence our thoughts and feelings and actions' (Jung 1968a: 154), reiterating an apparently earlier view that the anima, as an archetype, is innate. Jung seems to be making a distinction between anima as *concept* and anima as *archetype*, given the empirical nature of the former and the *a priori* nature of the latter. That is to say, we develop our concept of the anima through our living in the world. The concept is dependent, though, on the prior structuring of the psyche by the anima archetype. The central issue here is not anima-specific, however; it is instead the issue of the relation between an *a priori* structure and its empirical expression as well as the concepts which arise from that expression. In my view, an important aspect of Luce Irigaray's work is that it tackles this very question. But her work also tackles the axiological questions that always accompany debates about the feminine. Jung's claim that the feminine ('primal darkness of the maternal womb') is unconsciousness and that unconsciousness is the 'primal sin, evil itself, for the Logos' (Jung 1968a: 178) captures very nicely some of these axiological issues, invoking as it does Plato's notion of the feminine as disorder, as irrational. Mimesis, in the work of Luce Irigaray, gives us a new strategy for dealing with such claims.

LUCE IRIGARAY, INDIVIDUATION AND MIMESIS

Luce Irigaray defies Plato's directive to mime only the good or what will bring about the good. The title of her essay 'Any Theory of the "Subject" Has Been Appropriated by the "Masculine"' (Irigaray 1985a: 133) discloses her contempt for standard academic methodology because here, as in her other work, she deliberately assumes the voice of the irrational feminine typical of Plato's rendering of the soul. In this regard, she can also be seen as a Slave challenging the Master (although not *straightforwardly*) to a struggle unto death; it is a struggle to death, nonetheless. She seeks an authentic life for women and her way of achieving her quest is through her insistence on the possibility of ontological difference. That is to say, she argues for the possibility of an ontologically different mode of being for women which is not derivative and, therefore, not secondary to a primary masculine.

On Luce Irigaray's account of feminine subjectivity that emerges in Plato's work (and, in my view, in Jung's), women cannot be considered to be good because they are the 'junk-yard' of men's projections: in women one finds the undesirable, unvalorised characteristics of men that they do not want to acknowledge in themselves. Since in the Platonic scheme disorder is undesirable and therefore unwanted, and women are always already considered to be inferior to men, they are the 'natural' repositories of men's projections. The disorder that allegedly marks women's souls as womanly potentially bears little resemblance to what women's souls actually might be like. Luce Irigaray attempts then to figure out what it might be like for women to say something not about women's souls, but the subjects they might be in the absence of men's projections.

Claiming that there is an existential impossibility in using the masculine voice to articulate a feminine that is not projected, Luce Irigaray imagines the possibility of a feminine subject initially issuing from the feminine voice currently couched in terms of disorder and therefore irrationality. Since writing is germane to theories of the subject, she deliberately subverts the discursive canons of philosophy and psychoanalysis by miming the feminine, the irrational disorder by which women are represented. This radical proposal entails a rethinking of the dimensions of imagination, ontology and individuation, boldly opening them to new possibilities. Simultaneously, it has the potential to re-imagine the feminine as more than an opposite derivative of the sameness of the masculine psyche. The feminine-feminine as distinct from the masculine-feminine constituted through and by the masculine symbolic/imaginary, which Luce Irigaray begins to articulate, is situated in a proposed *feminine-feminine symbolic/imaginary/ imaginary*.

Luce Irigaray concentrates on the idea that women have always been defined in terms of the Other of men. In this, she closely follows, but parodies, Lacan's analysis of feminine sexuality in 'God and the Jouissance of ~~the~~ Woman' (Lacan 1982: 138–48) as she appeals to, and then develops, her idea of primary two-ness and the two-lips metaphor. Lacan claims that

> whatever lines up under the banner of women it is by being constituted as not all that they are placed within the phallic function. It is this that defines the . . . the what? – the woman precisely, except that *The* woman can only be written with *The* crossed through. There is no such thing as *The* woman, where the definite article stands for the universal. There is no such thing as *The* woman since of her essence – having already risked the term, why think twice about it – of her essence she is not at all . . . There is woman only as excluded by the nature of things which is the nature of words, and it has to be said that if there is one thing they themselves are complaining about enough at the moment, it is well and truly that – only they don't know what they are saying, which is all the difference between them and me.
>
> (Lacan 1982: 144)

This claim, which precedes Lacan's identification of *jouissance* as feminine sexual excess comparable to the mystical, is an attempt to locate woman both within, and surplus to, the masculine symbolic/imaginary. His argument suggests that women do not exist because women are constructed through exclusion, through negation. One has essence or being only because one is included in the symbolic/imaginary (which requires possession of the penis, and thus the phallus). There are, then, anatomical prerequisites for inclusion in the symbolic/imaginary which women do not have. He argues that women are excluded from phallic *jouissance* (presumably the male orgasm) but that they have a supplementary *jouissance* (presumably the female orgasm) 'beyond the phallus . . . There is a *jouissance* proper to her, to this "her" which does not exist and which signifies nothing. There is a *jouissance* proper to her and of which she herself may know nothing, except that she experiences it – that much she does know' (Lacan 1982: 145). Lacan seem to be equivocating in his allusions to the ineffability of the mystical and the ineffability of feminine *jouissance*. His focus on the *jouissance* of the female body, and the mystical, is a fundamental but parodic aspect of Luce Irigaray's pursuit of a feminine-feminine symbolic/imaginary. We find in her parody of Lacan echoes of her mimetic challenge to both Plato and Freud. If Lacan is claiming the non-existence of ~~*The*~~ woman, Luce Irigaray is ensuring her retrieval from pre-oedipal, phallocentric Freudian and Lacanian theory.

Luce Irigaray accepts that women do not have the phallus. But she counters this with her claim that women in effect do not need the phallus: women have something else: the two lips. Women have essence or being by virtue of their anatomy[9] that has its own integrity, its two-ness which is always folding back on itself.

In her view women are passive recipients of men's projections through hegemonically masculine acculturation of girls. Hegemonically masculine cultures and the collectives which embody them are moulded around ideals of masculine perfection, of which the masculine divine is the exemplar *par excellence*. So projection operates at both constitutive and appropriative levels and Luce Irigaray adapts, quite deliberately, mimesis as a mode of contending with projection. Luce Irigaray's interest in mimesis embraces both Platonic and Feuerbachian projection theory. Her task is to investigate the possibility of a feminine-feminine symbolic/imaginary intertwined with a projected feminine divine. So she is not interested *only* in miming the feminine. Luce Irigaray appropriates, intentionally, some of the theoretical orientations of masculine theory and argues that the development of a feminine-feminine symbolic/imaginary requires the idea of a feminine divine. In other words, since ideals of masculine perfection are operative in the masculine symbolic/imaginary, so too, womanly ideals should be operative in both the production and activity of a feminine-feminine symbolic/imaginary.

Although Lacan and Freud are springboards for Luce Irigaray's work, she reads philosophy alongside and interwoven with psychoanalysis. But the nature of her radical proposal for an ontologically separate symbolic/imaginary as the foundation for women's being should be correctly figured as a great project of individuation for women. One cannot be individuated if one is unconscious; and my reading of Luce Irigaray suggests that, for women, becoming conscious involves 'escaping' the masculine symbolic/imaginary using the concept of a feminine divine as the keystone for the ensuing feminine-feminine symbolic/imaginary. Correspondingly, two-ness is privileged as the ontologically primitive number.

Hence Luce Irigaray's quest for a feminine divine is simultaneously the coming to be of a feminine-feminine, which displaces 'woman' as a persona-identity inside the masculine symbolic/imaginary, and a quest for women's individuation. Only with the creation of a feminine-feminine can an authentic individuated subject position become available to women. Feuerbach's analysis of the divine, as projected, incorporates some elements of Kantian philosophy which emerge transformed in Luce Irigaray's elucidation of a feminine divine. So let us trace the contours of Kant's and Feuerbach's arguments and then see how Luce Irigaray puts them to work.

THE SPECULAR DIVINE

> It's not simply a question of a mirror in which one sees oneself, but of the way in which it's possible to give an account of the world within a

> discourse: a mirror of the world. How I'm going to try to give an account of the world in my discourse. It's in this sense above all that I also played with the mirror, but not simply, because the mirror in a simple sense, in which I see myself, has served for the most part to constitute a masculine subject.
>
> (Hirsh and Olsen 1966: 13)

Feuerbach's idea that God is the mirror of man is anticipated by Kant's analysis of anthropomorphism in theology. We need to understand Kant's conception of 'God' in order to appreciate the significance of that analysis. In the *Critique of Pure Reason* Kant distinguishes between regulative principles of reason and constitutive principles of the understanding. Sebastian Gardner suggests that '[t]he legitimate use of reason is, according to Kant, regulative as opposed to constitutive: employment of concepts to *constitute objects* is the exclusive prerogative of the understanding. But reason is entitled to employ its ideas in order to direct or *regulate the understanding*' (Gardner 1999: 221). Kant argues that regulative principles of reason are ideas which 'we recognize as necessary, but whose source we do not know, and for which we assume a supreme ground merely with the intention of thinking the universality of the principle all the more determinately, as, e.g., when I think as existing a being that corresponds to a mere and indeed transcendental idea' (Kant 1930: B704). A regulative principle is a rule 'prescribing a regress in the series of conditions for given appearances, in which regress it is never allowed to stop with an absolutely unconditioned' (Kant 1930: B537). So although regulative principles of reason are not principles *of* the understanding, they are principles which direct the understanding. In other words they are supraordinate to understanding. The understanding and its principles are constitutive while reason and its principles are regulatory. The understanding does one thing and reason does another. In this sense a regulative principle is a formal idea of reason that does not give content to ideas (Kant 1930: B538). Kant argues that reason is employed hypothetically when we argue from particular instances to universals 'which are not themselves given' (Kant 1930: B675). He also says that the job of the hypothetical employment of reason is to unify and that 'the systematic unity (as a mere idea) is, however, only a *projected* unity, to be regarded not as given in itself, but as a problem only' (Kant 1930: B675). It is, in other words, a *pros hen* principle.

According to Gardner 'the concept of God is . . . not a basic given notion of the intellect, but a composite of several more primitive concepts, namely the concepts of highest being, absolutely necessary being and author of nature' (Gardner 1999: 238) and it is the hypothetical employment of reason as regulative principle which brings us to this concept. One's thinking 'as existing a being that corresponds to a mere and indeed transcendental idea' is one of the aspects of the composite 'God'. Kant argues that 'the contingent exists only under the existence of some other contingent that is its cause and from this we must infer yet another cause, until we are brought to a cause which is not contingent, and which is therefore unconditionally necessary' (Kant 1930: B612). Through a process of speculative reasoning, then, we get to the idea of a necessary being, a 'supreme being who remains an *ideal . . . an ideal without a flaw*, a concept that crowns the whole of human knowledge' (Kant 1930: B669). We cannot, however, *prove* the existence of this supreme being. Consequently, Kant argues that all proofs for the existence of God fail. Nevertheless, the notion of a supreme being functions as a moral guarantor. Luce Irigaray's idea that God functions as an ideal horizon *and* is a specifically male projection has its origins here.

Kant argues that 'for its own sake, morality does not need religion at all'. He maintains that '*[m]ankind* (rational earthly existence in general) *in its complete moral perfection* is that which alone can render a world the object of a divine decree and the end of creation' (Kant 1934: 3). The incarnation of God (the Christ), 'His only-begotten Son', models the perfection possible for human beings. He also argues that 'it is our universal moral duty as men to *elevate* ourselves to this idea of moral perfection, that is to this archetype of the moral disposition in all its purity'. However, we are not 'the authors of this idea, and because it has established itself in man without our comprehending how human nature could have been capable of receiving it, it is more appropriate to say that this archetype has *come down* to us from heaven and has assumed our humanity'. The idea of God 'as an archetype is already present in our reason' (Kant 1934: 54). Kant is here employing 'idea' in its sense as archetype that we saw earlier. Accordingly, we could not be authors of the idea of moral perfection as this idea lies outside human reason and understanding.

So Kant proposes a view of God that is simultaneously a postulate of reason and an idea implanted in the human mind by God, the archetype of moral perfection. Strangely enough, however, Kant takes an apparently opposite and altogether different view concurrent with these two complementary proposals. In criticising anthropomorphism in the 'theoretical representation' of God, Kant complains about its danger because '*we create a God for ourselves*, and we create Him in the form in which we believe we shall be able most easily to win Him over to our advantage' (Kant 1934: 157). Yet in a footnote he is clearly sympathetic to this view: 'Though it does indeed sound dangerous, it is in no way reprehensible to say that every man *creates a God* for himself nay, must make himself such a God according to moral concepts' (Kant 1934: 157). Kant refers to the God made by man as an 'ideal' – 'archetype' in its second sense – against which any representation one might have of the divine should be measured.[10] And this constructed moral ideal is just the inspiration behind Feuerbach's conception of God, which, contrary to Kant, however, is based on feeling rather than reason.

Notoriously, Feuerbach asserts that:

> Religion is human nature reflected, mirrored in itself. That which exists has necessarily a pleasure, a joy in itself, loves itself and loves itself justly; to blame it because it loves itself is to reproach it because it exists. To exist is to assert oneself, to affirm oneself, to love oneself; he to whom life is a burthen, rids himself of it. Where, therefore, feeling is not depreciated and repressed, as with the Stoics, where existence is awarded to it, there also is a religious power and significance already conceded to it, there also is it already exalted to that stage in which it can mirror and reflect itself, in which it can project its own image of God. God is the mirror of man.
>
> (Feuerbach 1989: 63)

This difficult passage identifies the relationship between human nature, religion and God. Human nature, argues Feuerbach, is a feeling nature, a nature which loves itself and it is this love which is projected and exalted as God. For Feuerbach, the possession of reflective consciousness distinguishes man [*sic*] from all other creatures. Feuerbach argues that religion is 'identical with the distinctive characteristic of man, is then identical with self-consciousness – with the consciousness man has of his nature' (Feuerbach 1989: 2). He claims that 'consciousness is essentially infinite in its nature. The consciousness of the infinite is nothing else than the infinity of the consciousness; or, in the consciousness of the infinite, the conscious subject has for his object the infinity of his own nature' (Feuerbach 1989: 2–3).

As the mirror of man, God is the mirror of man's infinity: hence God is the ultimate expression of human affirmative feeling and limitlessness. Man has conceived of God as a perfected mirror of himself, or an ideal in the same way that Kant's moral ideal is an anthropomorphised divine. In other words, man has reified his infinite consciousness: he has constitutively projected an ideal, perfect Being who embodies everything that man – he, himself – is not.

> Religion is the disuniting of man from himself: he sets God before him as the antithesis of himself. God is not what man is – man is not what God is. God is the infinite, man the finite being; God is perfect, man imperfect; God eternal, man temporal; God almighty, man weak; God holy, man sinful. God and man are extremes: God is the absolute positive, the sum of all realities; man the absolutely negative, comprehending all negations.
>
> (Feuerbach 1989: 32)[11]

This is an interesting twist when we remind ourselves that mirrors reverse the image in them. Feuerbach acknowledges this reversal when he claims that man constructs God as the antithesis of himself. The finitude, frailty and imperfection of man is contrasted with the perfection he is able to envisage and project. So there are two moments in the idea of God as the mirror of man: (1) God is the exalted, infinite feeling in man, and (2) God as the mirror of man reverses man's finitude and imperfection.

A consequence of Feuerbach's position is that 'man cannot get beyond his true nature' (Feuerbach 1989: 11). God subjectively exists as the idealised projection of human consciousness. Divine activity, Divine being, as comprehensible by consciousness, cannot be essentially different from human consciousness (Feuerbach 1989: 29). 'God' is not a necessary postulate at the end of a chain of backward inference as 'He' is in Kant's philosophy. God is identical with human consciousness in its most exalted state.

IRIGARAY AND FEUERBACH: SEXING THE DIVINE

If women were to have their own set of ideals towards which they could work, then freedom and autonomy would be a consequence of this: this is an underlying message of Luce Irigaray's work. Women cannot be free while they are subjugated by the master symbolic/imaginary. Thus her writing can be seen as a site of struggle in which a woman engages the master in mortal combat. This is not Hegel's original site of struggle: two equal self-consciousnesses do not face each other. Rather two self-consciousnesses re-engage after the initial battle, one knowing that she is constructed through the eyes of the victor, her master. Lacan's claim of woman's essence that 'she is not at all' cannot find closure unless the speaking voice of woman, albeit through the masculine symbolic/imaginary, is silenced. Luce Irigaray refuses this silence. Indeed, she denies that there is a silence at all given women's origins. This is where her appropriation of theology is particularly powerful.

Luce Irigaray appropriates Feuerbach's mirror trope and inverts it with a view to constructing a feminine aspirational ideal which offers to women the kind of divine guarantee offered to men by the masculine divine. Additionally, she deliberately distorts Lacan's concepts, the symbolic and imaginary and refigures them in tandem with the mirror trope. As masculine, the symbolic/imaginary cannot reflect feminine consciousness, a feminine subject, in part because there is not one. Subjects produced by the masculine symbolic/imaginary are effects of the metaphysics of the Same: that there is a single, masculine, hegemonic and common origin for all sexed/gendered positions.[12] Feminine subjects of the masculine symbolic/imaginary are *subject to* that symbolic/imaginary and not autonomous, self-directing subjects *of* the symbolic/imaginary. As such the feminine is a masculine construct, a masculine-feminine. Jung's anima-feminine – the feminine as 'she' exists in a man's unconscious – exemplifies this masculine-feminine. Hence Luce Irigaray's intuition that the symbolic and imaginary need interrogation – structure and content – gets right to the heart of women's lack of autonomy, integrity and subjectivity. The notions of woman/female/feminine are situated within, and arise from, a masculine but supposedly sex/gender-neutral symbolic/imaginary which lacks the capacity to abandon its own projective hegemony.[13]

Thus Luce Irigaray's most radical claim, in keeping with Lacan, is that there is only one sex and the feminine has been symbolised only as a masculine adjunct, the 'not' of the masculine, the Other of the Same.[14] But she is a woman working with the claim and a defiant and clever woman at that. The pursuit and development of a feminine symbolic/imaginary presupposes a philosophy of sexual difference which does not rest easily – nor is it intended to – with standard conceptions of secular and theological theorising that assume the neutrality of position and speaking voice. Luce Irigaray's two claims:

a that there is only one sex which represents itself as neutral (but which identifies the phallus as the primary symbol of a ubiquitous masculine libido); and
b that the feminine exists outside that sex but that it is yet to be

are profoundly disquieting especially when she satirises the masculine voices which produce one-ness or hom(m)osexuality (Irigaray 1985b: 171). The importance of *jouissance* is clear here: Irigaray takes up Lacan's idea that there is a '*jouissance* beyond the phallus'.

The masculinity and hom(m)osexuality of the symbolic/imaginary are the critical ground on which Luce Irigaray deliberately seeks to refigure the feminine, taking as her *telos* women's emancipation from the masculine symbolic/imaginary. In seeing woman as a product of the masculine symbolic/imaginary, Luce Irigaray identifies the condition under which she fails to be a subject: there is no feminine symbolic/imaginary that guarantees the authenticity of that subjectivity. And this is the context of her claim that '[d]ivinity is what we need to become free, autonomous, sovereign . . . If women have no God, they are unable to communicate or commune with one another' (Irigaray 1993a: 62). Feuerbach's contention that man projects his own God is foregrounded in this moment of realisation.

Quoting Feuerbach's 'God is the mirror of man', Luce Irigaray alleges that 'Woman has no mirror wherewith to become a woman. Having a God and becoming one's gender go hand in hand. God is the other which we absolutely cannot be without' (Irigaray 1993a: 67). She argues that the masculine-paternal God – the God of the Fathers and the God who is Father – has developed from a mirroring/projecting process in which men have engaged in order to displace their finitude: man as master constitutes woman as slave whose identity is contingent on the identity of the master. She maintains that there is a strong relationship between bodily experience and consciousness, and its symbolic/imaginary structures and contents. Sexed embodiment is primary in the constitution of sexed subjectivity and in the formation of consciousness.

Chronologically, however, there is an originary space in which the potential for a feminine divine can be located, the female body.

> [W]hen she sees the penis, the little girl is supposed to give up all her previous libidinal workings; her oral, sadistic-anal, and phallic instincts, her desire to bear the mother's child or give her a child, and her infantile masturbation. That whole economy would in some way be blotted out, forgotten, repressed . . . or 'converted' so that 'penis-envy' might thus be validated as the basis of female sexuality from now on.
>
> (Irigaray 1985a: 58)

'From now on' is the clue to her recognising two things: (a) that 'little' girls are always already different, a difference which needs affirmation, and (b), that the masculine symbolic/imaginary attempts to annihilate that difference. She asks:

> Why make the little girl, the woman, fear, envy, hope, hate, reject, etc. in more or less the *same terms* as the little boy, the man? And why does she comply so readily? Because she is suggestible? Hysterical? But now we begin to be aware of the vicious circle. How could she be otherwise, even in those perversities which she stoops to in order to 'please' and to live up to the 'femininity' expected of her? How could she be anything but suggestible and hysterical when her sexual instincts have been castrated, her sexual feelings, representatives, and representations forbidden?
>
> (Irigaray 1985a: 59–60)

Note that Luce Irigaray is not romanticising women: she is not saying that women are not fearful, envious or cannot hate. Rather, she is pointing out that the terms in which the emotional life of women can be enacted are an effect of masculine projection, *as if* there were no integrity and individuality to girls' and women's emotional lives. Even though anatomically girls and women are different from boys and men, that difference is simultaneously elided and confirmed.

Female embodiment is mediated by and represented through a symbolic/imaginary, which, in Freudian psychoanalytic terms, figures the female body as an atrophied male body (which lacks a penis in other words).

Women internalise this masculine orientation which is collectively valorised as if it were universally and 'naturally' true. We see this process at work in psychoanalytic theory: 'In the beginning . . . the little girl was (only) a little boy. In other words THERE NEVER IS (OR WILL BE) A LITTLE GIRL' (Irigaray 1985a: 48). Luce Irigaray contests the validity of this masculine symbolic/imaginary for women and challenges its hom(m)osexual economy with a view to raising the question of ontological difference. That is the fundamental issue: are girls and women the same as boys and men? And if that is the case, in respect of what is it true? Biologically there is a clear homogeneity between women and men: they procreate with fertile offspring. But anatomically there is a clear heterogeneity which, for girls and women, is symbolised as lack couched in terms of envy. Luce Irigaray is calling for an affirmation of female anatomical difference. Rejection of the Freudian/Lacanian psychoanalytic framework in which the female body is both schematised and symbolised is, for her, the beginning of a feminine-feminine symbolic/imaginary.

Now Feuerbach's philosophical framework appears also to rest on the notion of sameness and neutrality: 'man' includes 'woman' and the incarnational ideal is masculine (the Son of God), but supposedly an ideal for all, men and women. In Plato and in Kant the rational and ethical ideals are also figured in terms of male embodiment. If embodiment and the psyche are as intertwined as Luce Irigaray proposes, then it follows that they *must* influence each other. The potential full impact of that intertwining is, however, appropriated by the symbolic/imaginary, resulting in devastation for women. The feminine body is appropriated, interpreted and represented through the dominance that is the masculine symbolic/imaginary. The feminine is disengaged from its original embodiment and expropriated to become a masculine possession. Jung's reading of the anima feminine does precisely this: for example, the mother is constructed as a woman by the child because the child projects onto her, the mother archetype she/he has inherited *a priori*. Luce Irigaray, however, posits a sexed difference with symbolic/imaginary and ontological repercussions in which a potentially female-sexed subject informs a female-sexed consciousness.

The importance of the mirror as an existential medium returns at this point. Luce Irigaray argues that:

> [w]e look at ourselves in the mirror to *please someone*, rarely to interrogate the state of our body or our spirit, rarely for ourselves and in search of our own becoming. The mirror almost always serves to reduce us to a pure exteriority – of a particular kind. It functions as a possible way to constitute screens between the Other and myself . . . Although necessary at times as a separating tool, the mirror – and the gaze when it acts as a mirror – ought to remain a means and not an end

> that forces my obedience. The mirror should support, not undermine my incarnation.
>
> (Irigaray 1993a: 65)

Here, Luce Irigaray is contending that the mirror gaze by which women are (illegitimately) regulated as *objects* ('pure exteriority' and not subjects), needs to be discarded and replaced by another of their own making.[15] The mirror itself needs to become feminine. She reads Feuerbach's mirror trope literally and argues that if God is the *mirror* of *man*, and God is masculine, then the mirror of woman should be a feminine divine or god. Women, though, need not 'invent' just any old divine. As an ideal horizon, a feminine divine must be at once inspirational and faithful to the possibilities always already present *before* the little girl is appropriated by the masculine symbolic/imaginary. A little girl and thus a woman can never develop her birthright: her femininity potentialities are 'castrated'.

Hence Luce Irigaray's project to construct a feminine divine is a subversion of Feuerbach's (and Kant's) reassurances about anthropological theology insofar as it attempts to refigure the specular ideal in a sex/gender-specific manner. But her view retains the methodological inspiration evident in the projection trope. What we find, then, is an explicit critique of the dominant and constitutive sex/gender power relations in the trope, a critique which problematises the very notion of *anthropological* theology that might more properly be read as hom(m)ological theology. Luce Irigaray is postulating a gynological thealogy, a theory of divinity centred on the feminine/female body as it might ideally be experienced and theorised. Thus her reading of Feuerbach bears directly on her understanding of the always already sex/gendered nature of the Christian God and the creation of sexual difference through the masculine symbolic/imaginary. A mirror affects, projects and represents a body already pre-figured by the masculine symbolic/imaginary. From her perspective, embodiment is always already sexed/gendered *but feminine embodiment is corrupted.* It is imperative, therefore, that women's gaze into the mirror is refigured and re-represented. A symbolic/imaginary which is a feminine-feminine symbolic/imaginary and through which the mirror will alter its own gaze is what will engender feminine-feminine incarnation.

Luce Irigaray claims that women have no divine of their own and that they should develop their own sex-specific divine in relation to, and as a condition of, a feminine symbolic/imaginary. Her elucidation of the divine is thematically influenced by Christian traditions. For example, her discussion includes Christ's incarnation and the role of Mary, the Mother of God in the Christian religion, who, as Feuerbach indicates, is 'the keystone of theology' (Irigaray 1993a: 69). Her interest in these Christian themes is, however, concerned more with their symbolic/imaginary content than with their theological commitment. In her view, the idea of God as male, and

Mary as the Mother of the male incarnation of an already male Father God, offers a symbolic/imaginary account of masculine conceptions of the meanings of motherhood, fatherhood and divinity. Women mediate the possibility of a masculine-paternal incarnation. Women are to be mothers of sons for fathers and a male God is the perfect projected ideal for masculine being.[16] Interestingly, in 'Divine Women' Luce Irigaray argues that Feuerbach, although aware that 'without the woman-mother there can be no God', conflates 'woman' and 'mother'. '[H]ence', as she puts it, 'there can be no correspondence with a possible state of identity for the woman as woman' (Irigaray 1993: 69). Indeed, we find Feuerbach's realisation about the importance of the Mother to Christian theology later in Jung's discussion of iconoclasm in the Reformation and the loss to Protestantism of the meaning of the Virgin Birth.[17]

Luce Irigaray maintains that 'God' has played a critical role in the development of the masculine symbolic/imaginary and she mines the symbolic/imaginary for its value as an ideal horizon. An horizon is perceptible, locatable, but shifts and is never achievable. The term 'horizon' is a metaphor for the unattainability of perfection, a *telos* emanating from consciousness. If 'God' can be shown to be an ideal horizon for men, an horizon which informs their symbolic/imaginary, then the development of an ideal horizon for women, a feminine divine, is possible for women as the basis of a feminine symbolic/imaginary. The deliberately imitative or mimetic gesturing of Luce Irigaray's thinking here self-consciously takes on board some postulates of both metaphysics and theological anthropology from two interrelated sources: Immanuel Kant and Ludwig Feuerbach. Luce Irigaray mimes the feminine imposed on women, but she also mimics the substantive issue of the status of the divine found in Feuerbach's analysis of theology.

We can see then that her claim about the ontological primitiveness of two-ness disrupts the monology of the masculine symbolic/imaginary through her insistence on the ontological primacy of the feminine body and its *jouissance*. She accepts and endorses the idea of sexed identity in terms of a radical ontological distinction between men and women. If we return to her assertion that theories of the 'subject' have been appropriated by the 'masculine' we can see that Irigaray's insertion of quotation marks around 'subject' and 'masculine' indicates her ironic use of those terms and what they might signify, while simultaneously affirming the importance of what is contained within the quotation marks. 'Subjectivity is denied to woman' (Irigaray 1985a: 133). Thus she pinpoints the highly contested territory of the self and the subject on the one hand and of sex/gender distinctions on the other.

There are two ways of interpreting her argument. The first interpretation suggests that women have not yet attained subjecthood, have not been subjects or selves ontologically distinct from men: what subjecthood they do have is derivative of projection from men. This is not so much a case of projection from individual men but rather a collective projection in which attitudes and values, inherited intergenerationally and supportive of the *telos* of a particular collective, produce women as subjects within that collective. The second account of creation in Genesis, in which woman is made from the rib of man, is an early version of this interpretation. The woman is an image of the man (adam) in the sense that in his body, his flesh and bones, her origins lie. Her being is derived from the being of the man.[18] The second interpretation revolves not around the idea of derivativeness, but instead problematises woman's having a soul and therefore being a self at all. The question *habet mulier animum?* ('has woman a soul?') illustrates this view and it is a question which Jung mentions in his discussion of anima and animus (Jung 1966: 298). Regardless of whether he takes it seriously, the question illustrates a Western cultural orientation towards woman as a category of human being. The having of a soul was what distinguished 'man' from other creatures. The relation between having a soul and being a self or a subject is connected to the question of worth. If woman does not have a soul, then she is not of the same ontological order as man: she is not quite human. If she has being, it is not to the same degree as man. Either way, the question of woman's subjectivity is raised within the context of theorising subjectivity and women's lack of agency because it is precluded by the potency and action of the masculine symbolic/imaginary. So how does Luce Irigaray understand 'woman' and where does she stand in relation to the question of women's subjectivity?

THE PRESENT AND FUTURE WOMAN

Luce Irigaray recognises that women's position in relation to the masculine-feminine symbolic/imaginary is not irrevocable. For her, the symbolic/imaginary is mutable and is historically produced and situated (Irigaray 1991b: 38). That the symbolic/imaginary is masculine is, therefore, a contingent matter, and open to change. But a *change* in the symbolic/imaginary order is *not* what Luce Irigaray wants: she wants difference and ontological difference at that. Without a speaking voice, without being a gender or a specific sexuate-ontological kind, ontological difference is not possible. So Luce Irigaray does not want to introduce sexual difference into the masculine symbolic/imaginary at all, but she wants to use the masculine symbolic/imaginary to create an *alternative* feminine-feminine symbolic/imaginary, *a symbolic/imaginary other than, different from the masculine symbolic/imaginary*. She wants women to have a *genre*. She argues that there is no neutral symbolic/imaginary which could be ruptured by the introduction of feminine difference.

Luce Irigaray's use of 'woman', 'the feminine' and 'the female' is always already interpreted within the double context of biology (the material) and culture (discursive and social practices). Because of her emphasis on female morphology, her critics read her as assuming an underlying commitment to 'woman' as a natural kind and it is here that her alleged essentialism is located. Luce Irigaray, however, does not suggest that 'woman' is a *natural kind* term, a term like 'tree' or 'acorn' or 'cloud', a term that names a culturally unmediated object, property or thing in the world. Rather she claims that 'woman' is already a *genre*. She uses the terms 'the feminine' and 'the female' deliberately in a mimetic strategy contrived to acknowledge the pervasiveness of the male symbolic/imaginary and its structures. The masculine symbolic/imaginary renders women as other, the remainder, the excess of men.[19] Employing the notions of projection and mirroring, their critique and re-mobilisation, Luce Irigaray brings the notion of woman as other to man under the spotlight. She argues that womanly otherness is an effect of men's commitment to mono-ontology (signified in/by the phallus). The point that Luce Irigaray makes is metaphysical: *the pros hen* principle that says that everything is related to one central sense (in this case, the phallus and the maleness of libido) manifests itself in the principle of sameness implicit in ontology. In seeing woman as his other, man attributes one-ness of being to himself and her as they have a joint origin; however, woman is derivative of man (just as the Woman is made from Adam's rib in the second Genesis account). But in this ontological reduction that produces woman as his other, Luce Irigaray sees a space for escaping from the very condition of woman's production. The argument is two-pronged:

a 'Woman' and its instantiations are an effect of the ubiquity of the male symbolic/imaginary. The term 'women' is culturally and biologically mediated through the symbolic/imaginary. The symbolic/imaginary/imaginary is masculine.
b In spite of this, *women* are in excess of the male symbolic/imaginary; paradoxically, their excess lies, in part, in the femaleness of women's bodies. In excess lies the source of retrieving women's being from the reduction of the masculine symbolic/imaginary/imaginary.

'Woman', on this argument, looks as if she is an effect of the masculine symbolic/imaginary. Women, on the other hand, are enfleshed bodies in which the biological and the cultural converge to produce a sex-specific *genre*, an other to man which is not derivative and not reductionist. In truth, though, according to Luce Irigaray, the genre 'woman' universally connotes a complex socio-cultural-biological type broadly conceived through anatomical specificities. The feminine that emerges with the *genre* 'woman' is at once ontologically irreducible and materially different from the masculine, the *genre* 'man' and 'woman' as constituted through the masculine symbolic/

imaginary. The starting point for her argument is in the masculine symbolic/imaginary and her treatment of the masculine symbolic/imaginary through irreverent parody. The reverse image in the mirror becomes the means by which Luce Irigaray resituates women and the feminine and helps, potentially, to achieve their ontological separatism.

In an interview in 1996, Luce Irigaray remarked:

> Some years ago, out of discouragement, I decided that I would begin again every moment of the day with the relation of two. This didn't go so badly – it's interesting. Obviously, this two is always potentially a sexuate two. It's difficult to explain, but interesting, because between man and woman there's a negative, a type of irreducibility that doesn't exist between a woman and a woman. Let's say between a man and a woman the negativity [*la négativité*] is, dare I say it, of an ontological, irreducible type. Between a woman and another woman it's of a much more empirical type and, furthermore, can only be understood and can only live in the ontological difference between man and woman. It's complicated.
>
> (Hirsh and Olsen 1996: 8)

Several points are noteworthy in this set of remarks. First, Luce Irigaray, following in the tradition of René Descartes, is confessing to practising philosophy as meditative awareness: for her comment is about the self-aware doing or practice of philosophy rather than a statement of mere philosophical theory in which she is open to an ontological alternative ('I decided I would begin again every moment of the day with the relation of two'). Secondly, the remarks identify difference in terms of the negative and the irreducible ('between man and woman there's a negative, a type of irreducibility that doesn't exist between a woman and a woman'). And thirdly, Luce Irigaray distinguishes between the ontological and the empirical ('Let's say between a man and a woman the negativity [*la négativité*] is, I dare say, of an ontological, irreducible type. Between a woman and another woman, it's of a much more empirical type'). I take the 'it' of 'it's of a much more empirical type' to be a reference to negativity, thought of as negation or not-ness. Women and men are not one, women and women are not one (the latter is perhaps a reference to the two lips, to the 'sex which is not one') (Irigaray: 1985b). For Luce Irigaray, the negative-irreducible – the not-ness of woman and man, and the not-ness of woman and woman – decipherable in terms of the ontological and the empirical is the foundation for difference between woman and man on the one hand, and woman and woman on the other: woman and man are ontologically different, and woman and woman are empirically different. Two-ness can thus be read either ontologically in the case of woman and man; or empirically in the case of woman and woman. Hence to begin again every moment of the day with – to carry forward the awareness of – the relation of two is to remember the fundamental two-ness of being, a primeval not-ness or otherness. This can be characterised through identification of the origin of human being in the mother (who has coupled with the father) whose two lips have seen the birth of either ontological or empirical difference. Two-ness is thus the origin of being in its multiplicity and in its own bearing of duality, the primary site of which is the body in its sexuate being.

We see in these remarks Luce Irigaray's commitment to the importance of the body as a sexed entity and the significance, from a symbolic/imaginary perspective and biologically to the sexed body. She echoes Jung's recognition of body-type as an important ontological contribution to psychic identity, even though the implications of this recognition are continents apart for each of them. While Jung, like Plato, sees body-type as a marker of inferiority, Luce Irigaray valorises the sexed body of the woman as a site of origin and debt. It is the femaleness of the female body, its ontological difference from the male body, that becomes the ground for the prospect of a feminine symbolic/imaginary through the assistance of feminine writing (*écriture féminine*) and the constitution of a feminine divine. The potential for making a feminine symbolic/imaginary emerges out of the reappropriation of the feminine body for women. Refiguring or modifying the symbolic/imaginary, which Luce Irigaray understands as irretrievably a masculine symbolic/imaginary, is out of the question for Luce Irigaray. No longer are women's bodies to be conceptualised within allegedly neutral symbolic and imaginary orders, but are instead to be retrieved as an affirming site of being and lived experience for women. Recognition of the ontological difference between bodies as sexed entities, as sexed materialities, is, for Luce Irigaray, fundamental to the project of women's 'escaping' the male symbolic/imaginary order. One of the consequences of her focus on woman's body, the female or feminine body, is the accusation that she is essentialist. The idea that because she is talking about female anatomy, she must be talking about fixed and unchanging characteristics of a shared biological essence of all women, is an important element in these essentialist accusations.

From both a philosophical and a psychoanalytical perspective, Luce Irigaray's early work concentrates on the idea that women have always been defined in terms of the other of men. Her works, *Speculum of the Other Woman* (1985a) and *This Sex Which Is Not One* (1985b), explore the theories of Plato, Freud and Descartes, and attack what, she argues, is their profound androcentrism. As we have already seen, she takes exception to Freud's and Lacan's inclusion of women in the symbolic/imaginary as inauthentic other, a different mode of being who is nonetheless the same and other (Irigaray 1985a: 260). By that, Luce Irigaray means that women and the feminine are the disowned aspects of masculine being. In her view, woman is the displaced recognition by man of what he does not want to admit about himself to himself. Woman is thus an aspect of man's false consciousness. The projected irrationality, the spontaneity, the weakness of feminine being is the rejected otherness of masculine being.

Luce Irigaray's idea that the feminine is both the same and other is found in Jung's idea of the anima. Jung's anima concept is doubly figured as an other that is an internal relation and as an other that is an external relation. Such a construction is reminiscent of Sartre's being-in-itself and being-for-itself and being for another.[20] For Jung the otherness of the feminine is an otherness of value-laden negativity: the feminine in men is an internalised other, the devalued, the inferior, the unwanted, the disorder of the anima feminine. But it is also an externalised other projected onto women, a sorceress that causes men to lose their identity in love. The marking of the feminine in this way carries the burden which is captured in the *pros hen* principle of masculine metaphysics and which Luce Irigaray plays on: man and woman are one, but the one which they are is enveloped by the masculine which projects its unwanted aspects from man's internal divisibility. If we apply this to Jungian theory, we can see that the extent to which the anima feminine is tied up in the anima projection appears to leave little if any room for the development of an authentic feminine other, ontologically distinct from the masculine othering of men's projected psychic properties. From Luce Irigaray's perspective, woman is a figment of the masculine imaginary, caricatured in the masculine symbolic/imaginary as an other of the same. And women to varying degrees internalise that projection through cultural immersion and construction.

Her critique of the masculine symbolic/imaginary, as I suggested above, is methodologically unconventional, deliberately contrived to capture the way women have expressed themselves 'artistically rather than simply, coolly, logically' in masculine modes of expression and argument (Hirsh and Olsen 1996: 2). She says that she does not 'want to participate in the repression' of women's mode of expression. Hence her poeticised critical responses to Plato and Freud do not take the form of clear, succinct, logical argument. Instead, these responses contrive to evoke the madness of the unconscious, the territory of the feminine (Irigaray 1985a: 141). Luce Irigaray's approach is a deliberately subversive methodological imitation of the role assigned to the feminine in the masculine symbolic/imaginary. That subversive methodological imitation, or mimesis, is a return to the Lacanian mirror of reflection and representation. Grasping the identity projected onto her from the masculine symbolic/imaginary, Luce Irigaray willingly appropriates that identity to invert it and to destabilise the stereotypical woman it reproduces. Her early texts pre-empt the configurations of a feminine and of a woman that are not contained by the rules of logic, by fixed boundaries or by rational austerity, but which are the fulfilment of man's projection onto woman. Her texts embody the restless movement of thought and intuition that condemn their origins in the texts from which they arise.

Luce Irigaray's work challenges both the assumptions and the rational methods of philosophy as she seeks to articulate a feminine voice, a voice that will authorise itself through feminine writing. Her challenge has been the source of accusations that she is essentialist, because, it is argued, she merely reinscribes conceptions of women that have dominated masculine thinking about women, the feminine and the female. Not only that, her focus on the female body draws attention to the biological specificities of the female body from which springs the issue of biological determinism. Among Francophone feminist thinkers, however, essentialism has not been an issue as it has been for Anglophone feminist thinkers. This may be due to the different historical circumstances that have been the occasion of feminist practice and theory; and it may also be because of the misunderstanding of essentialist issues prevalent in Anglophone literature. Luce Irigaray herself complains that she is misread because:

> in the United States my books are read mainly in literature departments. But they are philosophical books and I think that there is a great deal of misunderstanding about them because the heart of my argument is philosophical, and literary scholars are not always prepared to understand this philosophical core.
>
> (Hirsh and Olsen 1996: 2)

The misunderstanding Luce Irigaray attributes to readers in the United States is not, of course, entirely the cause of essentialist accusations, nor would the United States be the only place in which her work is misunderstood as she sees it. However, as I shall argue, the understanding of essentialism is not itself deeply informed by the philosophical tradition in which Luce Irigaray locates herself. Essentialist accusations about her work are founded in a double misunderstanding of the nature and origin of essentialism, in a misunderstanding of her work because it is taken out of the philosophical context of its origins.

The woman's voice in which Luce Irigaray speaks is a voice, then, which is philosophically modulated and imitative. From an ontological perspective, this voice is different from what she interprets as the voice of masculine rationality. From an empirical perspective this voice may not capture the understanding that many women have of their own voices. But her use of the feminine voice deliberately engages the feminine of the masculine symbolic/imaginary, and from that perspective she universalises what is already universalised through the masculine symbolic/imaginary. In other words, the ironic inflection of that voice is meant to destabilise the feminine as it is constructed through the masculine symbolic/imaginary. It is the embryonic authorising voice of difference and doubly so. Difference will, in other words, distinguish this voice in its commitment to two-ness and irreducible difference. The importance of the authorising voice of God in men takes its place in Luce Irigaray's proposal for a feminine authorising voice. Just as God functions as an *a priori* principle and ideal horizon for the masculine symbolic/imaginary, so too a feminine divine will function as a feminine symbolic/imaginary. But this requires an 'escape' from the masculine symbolic/imaginary, the complexities of which Luce Irigaray is well aware. She shows this awareness in her discussion of the divine and its importance as an aspirational ideal.

Chapter 6

Mimesis revisited

Demeter and Persephone

> All men (especially according to Feuerbach) and all women, except when they remain submitted to the logic of the essence of man, should imagine a God for themselves, an objective and subjective place or path for the possible assemblage of the self in space and time: a unity of instinct, heart and knowledge, a unity of nature and spirit, a condition of the homeland and of sainthood. Only a God can save us and guard over us. The feeling or experience of a positive, objective and glorious existence for our subjectivity is necessary for us. Such as a God who helps and guides us in our becoming, who holds the measure of our limits – women – and our relation to the infinite, which inspires our endeavours. Not only as *an opposition to or critique of but as a position consisting of new values*, 'essentially' Divine ones.
>
> (Irigaray 1993a [her emphasis])

We have already seen that Plato's directive that women should not be imitated and that Lacan's assertion that there ~~*The*~~ woman does not exist, are each challenged by Luce Irigaray; and that she uses the prospect of a feminine divine as her way of making the challenge. The making of a feminine divine involves the concurrent development of a feminine-feminine symbolic/imaginary, but we need to pause here to see precisely what that might involve. Morny Joy has pointed out that Luce Irigaray's mimesis is a productive reconfiguring (Joy, 1990). Luce Irigaray's is not imitation *simpliciter*, as we have already seen in the way she poses the question of a feminine divine: the divine which will emerge together with a feminine-feminine symbolic/imaginary offers an aspirational ideal for women, which is focused around affirming the female body. So I shall begin this chapter by taking a brief but closer look at Luce Irigaray's practice of mimesis as both the productive and de(con)structive project that it is.

Luce Irigaray transforms Plato's understanding of mimesis as simple and imitative narration. She says that in Plato 'there is mimesis as production which would lie more in the realm of music and there is the mimesis that would be already caught up in the process of *imitation, specularization, adequation* and *reproduction*' (Irigaray 1985b: 131).[1] She explicitly acknowledges that mimesis assists in the reproduction of the symbolic/imaginary and women's embodiments, but also suggests that women, who are voiceless as subjects, are diminished by the relation which purportedly holds between women and mimesis. If women are to 'solve the problem of the articulation of the female sex in discourse' then a 'direct feminine challenge' would not work. If women were to 'speak as a masculine "subject" . . . to postulate a relation to the intelligible' then 'that would maintain sexual indifference'. She argues that mimesis or mimicry has been historically assigned to the feminine in the masculine symbolic and that 'one must assume the feminine role deliberately. Which means already to convert a form of subordination into an affirmation, and thus to begin to thwart it' (Irigaray 1985b: 76). The 'one' to whom Luce Irigaray refers is woman: for men to assume the feminine role in this context would be for men to diminish even further the appended identity that women have.

What does it mean to speak as a masculine 'subject'? How does one assume the feminine role deliberately? The answers to these two questions lie in destabilising the certainty of 'the codes theory has set up for itself' (Irigaray 1985a: 365). These codes are at once: (a) apparently structurally necessary if meaning is to be made and gleaned in the way a masculine subject rationally and logically orders the world with words; and (b) vulnerable to corruption. Luce Irigaray focuses on their vulnerability, and deliberately ignores the apparent necessity of their rational ordering. In her deliberate corruption she assumes ironically the role of the masculine-feminine. She by-passes 'high theory', the domain of the intelligible, and turns instead to the female body and its relations to other female bodies, as moral, ontological and epistemic inspiration for women. What is said by men about the female body, women and the feminine becomes the site of an encounter between the feminine of the masculine symbolic and its ironic appropriation. *What* Luce Irigaray says and *how* she says it imitates a feminine role that women have not chosen. Women are characterised as irrational or disordered and Luce Irigaray's writing endorses this lack of order. In other words, Luce Irigaray suggests that women should use the masculine-feminine strategically[2] to mime and to exploit women's specification within phallocratic, masculine discourse.[3] She takes a risk in not only arguing this point but in *doing it*. We are *meant* to be shocked, upset, disturbed by Luce Irigaray's method which delivers a feminine-feminine subject to the pages we read. The shock, the disturbance, will produce a reaction and in that reaction is, partly, the potential for change. This is her polemics of difference.

Two related traditions in the polemic over difference converge: the psychoanalytic and the metaphysical. The psychoanalytic tradition is found in Freud's discussion of and hypotheses about feminine sexuality. In this context, difference is sexual difference – woman is different from man because she is anatomically different because she lacks The Most Significant Organ – and it involves interpretation of the castration and Oedipus complexes, penis envy and the construction of feminine sexuality in terms of lack. As we saw earlier, Luce Irigaray maintains that Freudian sexual difference is a matter of treating little girls and their aberrant anatomy as little boys. The metaphysical tradition has its origins in the debate about universals, which has a direct bearing on the question of essentialism, as we shall see in Chapter 7, and on the accommodation of difference under terms of identity, a long-standing debate in Western philosophy.[4] There we find an emphasis on how to account for difference within an overarching metaphysic of the Same, what we can think of as the search for identity and unity. This metaphysic is indeed apparent in both the formulation and activity of the masculine symbolic and its tendency towards one-ness, the very function of Kant's regulative principle of reason.

Luce Irigaray courts both traditions, albeit critically, as she re-claims difference's ontological dimensions by affirming the dereliction of the feminine. First, the sexual difference which originates in Freud's and Lacan's works depends upon an already prejudiced negative assessment of the role of the phallus in the development of feminine sexuality and, as we have seen, she disavows this view. In the second place, it is an internal difference contained by the masculine symbolic, a difference resulting from the dialectic between positive masculine and negative masculine (or feminine). We might read Luce Irigaray's interpretation of Plato's cave analogy in this light (Irigaray 1985a: 243–365). We might also reflect on the similarity between sexual difference within the masculine symbolic and Jung's sexual difference within the psyche, the play of positive and negative, characterised, for example, in the dialectic between masculine persona and anima feminine.

Luce Irigaray's proposal that women should mime the feminine is a proposal for onto-symbolic ungrounding (Vattimo 1993: 4). To unground is to subvert the assumptions of the metaphysics of the Same, that everything is one, seen already in *pros hen* and Kant's reason as regulative. The possibility of opening a gap in, and getting outside, the masculine symbolic arises through subverting the very matter of the symbolic: its structure and the images to which it gives value. Structure and value are embedded in internal difference: without difference there is nothing. The masculine symbolic needs internal difference. Paradoxically, 'internal' difference is the key to the possibility of 'external' otherness. The production of 'external' otherness problematises the uniqueness of the masculine symbolic as the sole horizon in which the feminine could be understood. Ideally, an alternative feminine-feminine symbolic/imaginary will be the direct effect of ungrounding. If the masculine symbolic can be ungrounded, destabilised by the assertion of feminine difference, its hold on the feminine will crumble.

Ungrounding through mimesis should, therefore, be thought of as an avenue to 'external otherness'. Mind you, dialectic as relationship would continue to play its role in the resultant configuring of masculine and feminine. Luce Irigaray's later works are testimony to this (Irigaray: 1992, 1993c, 2000, 2002). And like the feminine-feminine, ungrounding is itself dependent upon the contents and structure of the masculine symbolic. *One must start somewhere*. So the explicit relationship between internal and external otherness – difference found within and surrounding the masculine symbolic – provides the impetus for ungrounding. That particular relationship is task-specific because ungrounding will eventually dissolve the appropriative power of the symbolic from which it has arisen in the first place. Ungrounding, therefore, undermines but creatively uses inside difference, by challenging the ontological assumptions implicit in the masculine symbolic.[5] The point is that there is a possibility of moving beyond masculine construction by insisting that difference itself can be re-formed, by acting from within the masculine symbolic (through mimesis). Ontological independence for the feminine, as feminine-feminine, comes about through this process.

Having seen the role that mimesis plays in the potential formation of an ontologically distinguishable feminine, let us now return to Luce Irigaray's claim that women are without a genre. Luce Irigaray argues that women are in a state of dereliction (Irigaray 1993b: 126). Women are derelict *not* because women lose identity within a patriarchal system but because women have never had any identity except within the masculine symbolic and imaginary. So Luce Irigaray is not arguing that women are automata, robotic vehicles through which the masculine speaks. She is, instead, arguing that women's being is circumscribed by symbols and images that are assumed to be equally relevant to girls/women as they are to boys/men. The appropriation of girls/women and their bodies means that women have no essence *and that there is no ethics of sexual difference*. Mimesis is the preliminary step for the creation of a feminine or womanly essence and the symbolic/imaginary, the domain of unconscious phantasy and its structuring, can be refigured to provide the images necessary for the projected feminine-feminine. Luce Irigaray deploys the notion of 'forgotten ancestry', female genealogy, to develop her project further (Irigaray 1994).

MORAL IDEALS, EXISTENTIAL LESSONS AND THE SYMBOLIC/IMAGINARY

> But the Demeter-Kore myth is far too feminine to have been merely the result of an anima-projection . . . Demeter-Kore exists on the plane of mother–daughter experience, which is alien to man and shuts him out.
>
> (Jung 1968a: 383)

> To make an ethics of sexual difference possible once again, the bond of female ancestry must be renewed. Many people think we know nothing

> about mother–daughter relationships. That is Freud's position. He asserts that we must look beyond Greek civilization to examine another erased civilization. Historically, this is true, but this truth does not prevent Freud from theorizing on and imposing, in psychoanalytic practice, the need for the daughter to turn away from the mother, the need for hatred between them, without sublimation or female identity being an issue, so that the daughter can enter into the realm of desire and the law of the father.
>
> (Irigaray 1994: 109)

Luce Irigaray explores and condemns the banishment of female genealogy from Western mythic narratives. She points out that both the mother–daughter relationship and the primal mother do not exist in Western cultural/mythic consciousness and/or they have been obscured. This does not mean that they are not mentioned at all. Rather, it means that these relationships do not feature as ideal horizons that found a moral and pedagogical perspective. Women's appearance in the canon is atrophied and secondary to men's domination of the ontological and moral spheres. For Luce Irigaray this represents the destruction of female ancestry 'especially in its Divine aspect' (Irigaray 1994: 91–113). The 'Divine aspect' of female ancestry, if recovered, can inform the producing of a feminine divine such as we have discussed in Chapter 5. The Demeter and Persephone (Kore) myth provides Luce Irigaray with an avenue for exploring the mother–daughter relation and the primal mother. Jung also discusses this myth and is interestingly ambivalent in the conclusions he draws. On the one hand, he seems to hold the mother–daughter relation in high esteem, acknowledging the specificity of its sex-genderedness. But on the other, he speaks of the mother–daughter relation as something to be overcome, and implies that its persistence is pathological to both mother and daughter. That is a surface reading, at any rate. Apropos of the discussion in Chapter 3, we should also note Jung's admission that there are aspects of the anima feminine that are not projected (that clearly belong to the woman herself).

Luce Irigaray relates two versions of the myth of Demeter and Persephone. In the earlier Homeric version[6] Persephone is picking flowers and is abducted and raped by Hades, the god of the underworld; in the other, Persephone is a temptress and seduces Hades. Luce Irigaray argues that the latter is an attempt to make Persephone responsible for her own abduction ('blame the victim') because the abduction and rape is such a terrible crime that patriarchy cannot accommodate it (Irigaray 1994: 102). Even if that is the case, a tacit admission of its monstrous nature is missing from later Freudian and Jungian accounts of the myth. There is no agreement or consensual sex between Persephone and Hades, and Persephone is not responsible for something to which she never agrees. Persephone is betrayed by the masculine-paternal. *Hades abducts and rapes her.* Persephone's father either does not hear, or refuses to help his daughter, as she is dragged off by Hades. Yet Homer's account accentuates the unwillingness of Persephone and the complicity of her father in her abduction and rape:

> He caught her up reluctant on his golden car and bare her away lamenting. Then she cried out shrilly with her voice, calling upon her father, the Son of Cronos, who is most high and excellent. But no one, either of the deathless gods or of mortal men, heard her voice, nor yet the olive-trees bearing rich fruit: only tenderhearted Hecate, bright-coiffed, the daughter of Persaeus, heard the girl from her cave, and the lord Helios, Hyperion's bright son, as she cried to her father, the Son of Cronos. But he was sitting aloof, apart from the gods, in his temple where many pray, and receiving sweet offerings from mortal men. So he, that Son of Cronos, of many names, who is Ruler of Many and Host of Many, was bearing her away by leave of Zeus on his immortal chariot – his own brother's child and all unwilling . . . And so long as she, the goddess, yet beheld earth and starry heaven and the strong-flowing sea where fishes shoal, and the rays of the sun, and still hoped to see her dear mother and the tribes of the eternal gods, so long hope calmed her great heart for all her trouble . . . and the heights of the mountains and the depths of the sea rang with her immortal voice: and her queenly mother heard her. Bitter pain seized her heart, and she rent the covering upon her divine hair with her dear hands: her dark cloak she cast down from both her shoulders and sped, like a wild-bird, over the firm land and yielding sea, seeking her child. But no one would tell her the truth, neither god nor mortal man; and of the birds of omen none came with true news for her. Then for nine days queenly Deo wandered over the earth with flaming torches in her hands, so grieved that she never tasted ambrosia and the sweet draught of nectar, nor sprinkled her body with water.
>
> (Homer 2006)

Homer's compassion for Persephone and his clear sympathy for Demeter are eloquently expressed. And if what Luce Irigaray suggests is true, then it seems as if Freud and Jung disregard Homer's condemnation of Zeus' and Hades' complicity. Doubtless, Freud's and Jung's responses fail to see the abduction and rape as the heinous crime that it is. Instead, their focus on the mother–daughter relationship displaces the reason for Demeter's anguish: *her daughter has been abducted and raped and she cannot find her.*

Bani Shorter's interpretation is probably even more disturbing since she interprets the myth as exemplary of an initiation rite, an 'archetypal metaphor for personal human experience' (Shorter 1987: 74). Her explanation of the myth in the context of the Eleusian Mystery Rites implies a justification of rape as a symbol of 'a girl's being wrenched out of childhood by something that radically changes her condition and status whether it be sudden onset of menstruation, or initial intercourse or marriage' (Shorter 1987: 76).[7] The reading of rape in this way is extremely disquieting. The violence and lack of consent that is Persephone's experience cannot be justified or valorised, even in the name of sacred archetypes. Such a reading displays an unwelcome masculine figuring of appalling horror. The fact that in the Eleusian Rites '*men as well as women* were initiated by identical rites' (Shorter 1987: 74) does nothing to elide the moral reprehensibility of the events in the myth. As either explanation or justification, the initiation scenario fails to account for the clear endorsement of abduction and rape which are normalised within a dominant masculine-paternal symbolic/ imaginary. Shorter's account sanctions the entry of Persephone 'into the realm of desire and the law of the father' as if there is nothing problematic about it.

Jung's interpretation of Demeter–Persephone illustrates, in a very precise manner, his inability to comprehend the mother–daughter relation as he overlooks the rape at the centre of the story (one can hardly say that it is peripheral). For him, Demeter is exemplary of the perversion of maternal instinct in which the whole of a woman's identity is consumed by her 'more or less complete identification with all the objects of her care'. Jung sees Demeter as compelling 'the Gods by her stubborn persistence to grant her the right of possession over her daughter. Her Eros develops exclusively as a personal relationship while remaining unconscious as a personal one. An unconscious Eros always expresses itself as will to power' (Jung 1968a: 167). In other words, the central issue for Demeter, according to Jung, is one of control. Really, she should accept what the gods have done and accede to their wishes and simply hand over her daughter and stop all of her fussing and pestering and carry-on. The nobility of Demeter's rage, the depth of her anxiety and anguish seem to be incomprehensible to Jung (and he as much as admits that). Demeter's is not furore over the theft of a cow or a bale of hay or any other possession. Rather, it is the agony of paternal betrayal, of loss of innocence and of sexual violation.

Both Jung's and Shorter's readings assume a lack of womanly autonomy in which a woman can determine for herself where and with whom she wants to be. Indeed, woman's autonomy as an issue in the Demeter–Persephone myth is not even a question for Jung or Shorter: the rule of the father symbolically structures even this tender story of mother–daughter relations, appropriating its images for the ends of the masculine paternal. Jung's and Shorter's readings of the myth are uncompromising in their valorisation of the masculine-paternal. Jung interprets Demeter's maternal solicitude as an aspect of the emotional and personal maturity that needs to be *overcome* in order to advance along the path of individuation. For him, walking that path entails negotiation of masculine-paternal initiatory ritualised practices in which there is no place for the implicitly pathological characteristics of the mother–daughter relationship. Hence that relationship needs to be reconfigured. And Shorter dilutes the moral economy of the myth to the extent that rape is always an already symbolically charged act.

Unsurprisingly, Luce Irigaray's reading of this myth focuses on Persephone's father's betrayal as he colludes with his brother, and on the exchange arrangements in which Persephone's virginity is the prize. Like Persephone, little girls are 'caught up in the dealings, contractual or otherwise, between men, between men and male gods'. Luce Irigaray recommends that little girls should keep away from such arrangements until their virginity can no longer be the subject of exchange between men and male gods. She goes on to say that a girl should 'remember virginity signifies her relationship to her physical and moral integrity, and not the price of a deal between men' (Irigaray 1994: 108). Because a girl has been torn away from 'her mother and the earth, from her gods and her order', a girl becomes desolate, lacking in identity, and the empty subject of masculine desire (Irigaray 1994: 109). She becomes a woman without feminine-feminine identity.

The Demeter–Persephone myth further elaborates Luce Irigaray's ongoing commitment to the disruption of women's embodiment as the site of originary identity which is subsequently corrupted by masculine symbolic appropriation. By attending to stories such as this, and taking seriously the distortion of a potentially feminine-feminine imaginary that we find in accounts like Jung's and Shorter's, women can retrieve not only a sense of physical integrity, but of women's psychic integrity as well. Such stories need to do two things, however: they need to be disruptive in the sense that they valorise the unvalorised feminine by uncovering, for example, the morally praiseworthy acts of women that stand outside and against the masculine paternal law.[8] And they need to promote those actions as morally desirable, even when such actions are regarded as mad or bad because they do not conform to standards of rationality that embody a manly notion of order. Demeter's loyalty to her daughter's welfare is not self-interested vanity, but a profoundly genuine other-regarding ethic. The mother–daughter relation here embodies a tenderness and love completely absent from the father–son story of the Christian testament. Demeter is not willing that her daughter be sacrificed; Yahweh offers his son as a blood sacrifice which reinforces the masculine-paternal law and the Hellenic virtue of manly courage. Jesus is no cowardly man with a womanly soul!

So Luce Irigaray, through finding and then reorienting ways of looking at mother–daughter relations, is attempting to salvage aspirational ideals that can become a divine horizon for women. The Demeter–Persephone myth becomes exemplary of such an aspirational ideal. Furthermore, in reclaiming the story and refocusing its core problematics, Luce Irigaray reinvests the female body with its own dignity: virginity is not a 'commodity' to be bartered and the maternal body is esteemed as the ground of ethical origin. For her, female genealogy, the honouring of the mother–daughter relationship and the honouring of the mother *per se* are essential to the development of a feminine-feminine symbolic/imaginary,[9] but they also have redemptive potential, for through them, Luce Irigaray believes, awareness of the importance of social justice and ecology can evolve (Irigaray 1994: 112). In other words, Luce Irigaray sees a clear relation between the symbolising of the maternal body and the mother–daughter relation, and the symbolising of the environment and human–environment relations. Difference will emanate as an effect of the ungrounding of the masculine symbolic, but it is a difference that affirms and is not based on lack or dominance of a set of prejudicial values. Female genealogy is retrieved and re-created and re-reading women's mythic traditions is integral to this process.[10] The re-reading, retrieval and refiguring of that tradition will be part of the process of making a feminine Divine.[11]

In this light, we might also consider briefly Luce Irigaray's reflections on the Greek goddess Aphrodite who is not known for her mothering qualities. Indeed, Aphrodite is usually acknowledged for her beauty and as the goddess of love. But she is a rebel and shows remarkable devotion to her followers. According to her, Aphrodite is the embodiment of a deity 'who manifests the possible spiritualization of blind drives or instincts through tenderness and affection . . . In Greek, Aphrodite's specific attribute is called *philotes*: tenderness' (Irigaray 1994: 94). The dialectical relation Luce Irigaray proposes here sets up the potential for an ideal relation between *agape* and *eros*, a combining in love of the carnal and spiritual. She argues that women are predominantly seen through maternity, through being mothers and that women are women *before* being mothers. *Women are not made into women by the maternal experience*. A feminine-feminine symbolic/imaginary will recognise this when myths such as the myth of Aphrodite is re-read to acknowledge and affirm the sexual being of woman without the negative figuring of the masculine symbolic.

It should be very clear by now that mimesis is not a vacuous and mindless process of mere copying. Certainly, one of its aspects is ironic, but the genuine ontological possibilities it offers to women who are dis-figured and mis-figured by the masculine imaginary/symbolic are far-reaching and emancipatory. Mimetic praxis is a self-conscious choice towards the ideal of feminine-feminine, of sexual difference, of manifesting a Divine feminine and of creating a feminine sexed subject. There is a direct relation between mimesis and the projection of a female divinity. What is projected is an ideal, and this is why a feminine Divine is the condition for the development of a feminine-feminine symbolic/imaginary.

One of the consequences of Luce Irigaray's view is that she seems to be making a set of claims about women, the female and the feminine that she universalises. To whom and for whom does she speak? All women, some women, herself? If 'all women', how is one to characterise the class of all women and its members? Is there anything which can be said of all women? If so, has not one fallen into the essentialist trap of positing an ahistorical, universal essence which defines women? Even with the mimetic strategy, it might be argued, Luce Irigaray does not go beyond the bondage of women within the masculine symbolic. On one view mimesis simply revalorises and reinscribes the feminine and traditional conceptions of woman. I think that such complaints miss the point of the subversive nature of mimesis and its appeal to multiplicity and difference which diffuses universality and sameness.

It might be argued, however, that Luce Irigaray's project essentialises women: this has been a standard Anglophone response to much of her work. I think such responses are groundless, partly because they do not acknowledge the structural level at which Luce Irigaray is dealing with the problems as she sees them. And when it comes to discussing Jung and his views and statements about women, the same criticism might apply in relation to the anima-feminine.

Chapter 7

Jung, Luce Irigaray and essentialism

A new look at an old problem

> The system of dualism in Western philosophy as a method of organising ideas has produced numerous theories attempting to describe and validate separate and opposing sexual characteristics. The distinctions of mind/body, good/evil, Logos/Eros have all at times been utilised in the spurious quest to give male supremacy a philosophical justification. By defining women as separate and as radically different (not just in a biological capacity but, as theorists as diverse as Nietzsche and Jung have argued, in essence from man) the realities of power and exploitation and cultural apartheid have been obscured or even justified.
>
> (Summers 1994: 80)

At the beginning of Chapter 3, I asked the question, 'And what is a woman, and what is a man, anyway?' We have been exploring how the 'what is?' question in relation to women and the feminine can be approached through the notions of projection and the possibility of a feminine-feminine symbolic/imaginary. Each of these ideas is intertwined with the recursive flow of the Master/Slave Dialectic. But I now want to turn to another way that this question has been interpreted in and by philosophical literature. My reasons for turning to philosophy are the same as those I invoked in my Introduction: philosophy has been the source, and inspiration behind the analysis of, many ideas about power, sex/gender relations and psychology. Indeed, we all make philosophical assumptions even though we may not be aware that we do.

One of the fundamental ways in which answers to the 'what is?' question have been dealt with is by looking at properties or attributes. We say, for example, that a dog is a hairy, barking, tail-wagging, carnivorous quadruped that can be kept as a domestic pet. We say that material objects have extension – they occupy space, are measurable – and they endure through time; but that mental objects like thoughts do not – at least that is what Descartes thought, and there are many who still think so. When we say these things about objects, we are talking about what they are like in terms of their composition, what they look or appear to be like, or what is commonly believed about them (some materialists would argue that thoughts are a special kind of brain state and as such are really material and therefore they do have extension because they can be located in space, in someone's brain).

The same kind of discussion about women and the feminine and their properties and what they are, or appear to be like, pre-existed the current social-constructionist ideology (that social and discursive practices are the origin of our categories and their members) we have been exploring. Some of the discussion revolves around the female body and its properties, as we have already seen, as well as around the idea of the soul and its order or inner harmony (or lack thereof). But it is important for us to be aware that for a very long time individual instances of things were seen not as products of social and discursive practices but as effects of their internal makeup. And the importance of this view is realised when we consider the kinds of views that prevented women from taking up various occupations. Women were seen to be fit for motherhood and the caring services like teaching and nursing by virtue of the fact that they have the kinds of bodies that fit them for specific professions. Recall Plato's argument that one should do the one thing for which one has a particular kind of nature. Women's nature, on this argument, meant that there is a limited number of careers which they, as women, could do well (unless of course they had manly souls, in which case we could become rulers or guardians).

Contrary to the position taken up by Lacan in his allegation that there is no essence to woman, women were held to have a nature or an essence that was fixed and immutable. Lacan's position is not, however, to do with what we shall see as the question of essential properties, but with the simple notion of *being*: on his view women have no essence because women have no being. Women are subsidiary to, and derivative of, men and their symbolic.

'Essentialism', as the view about essential properties has been called, posed philosophical quandaries long before women began to raise questions about their identity and how they became those identities. Because the debate has been central in feminist theory, and because essentialism is not well understood from a philosophical perspective, we shall now carefully explore this important debate.[1] Our examination will show why social constructionist ideology has been seen as an alternative to the questions essentialism raises.

ESSENTIALISM: A PHILOSOPHICAL VIEW

Part of the dialectical process in Plato's Dialogues, as I have already suggested, is aimed at definition of abstract ideas or universals like justice, truth and knowledge. Following Socrates and Plato, this focus on definition in a general sense has become a central preoccupation of Western philosophy. If a definition can be given, then it acts as a clarification, reference point and measure of whether or not something is an instance of the definition. In spite of his protests that he was not a philosopher, Jung follows the philosophers' stead in numerous places, and his 'Definitions' in *Psychological Types* is a good example of philosophers' attempts at precision of thought and reference *and definition.* Jung's explanation for why he includes a list of definitions of the psychological terms he uses in the way he uses them highlights the very problems that Plato saw in the use of terms: to give the investigator 'some fixity and precision, and this can best be done by discussing the meaning of the concepts he employs so everyone is in a position to see what he means by them' (Jung 1971: 674). The provision of fixity, precision and meaning in definitions captures the 'essential and fundamental phenomena' that characterise concepts and terms (1971: 673). In turn, this reveals Jung's place among theorists who *in general* seemed to be committed to the idea of essential and fundamental phenomena as the marker of any concept, idea or, indeed, any thing. What makes something what it is, in other words, is revealed in definition and definition therefore serves to point to the essence or the essential properties of any concept, idea or thing. An essence is what is necessary to something in order that it be what it is.

Beyond Jung's definitions for his key concepts and their potentially essentialist connotation lies, however, a more pernicious issue. His uncritical adoption of stereotypical characterisations of women and men, couched in terms of collective unconscious pre-figuring, opens the door to reading him as ahistorical and apparently essentialising when it comes to women and the feminine. Because of the ethical and political implications which ensue, this latter is not a simple matter of outmoded theorisation.

From a philosophical perspective, the questions of definition, universalisation and essence, all of which are interwoven, occupied an important place in debate and scholarship during the twentieth century.[2] Much of this scholarship was a further elaboration of the philosophical conversation begun by the Greek philosophers, and in many ways still addressed the question of definition that had been so central to their work. We can find this even today in the debates about 'race' and class as well as in the feminist canon. However, the contextualising of terms and the development of theories of power, in conjunction with the raising of political minority voices, brought up issues about the value-laden nature of some language practices. On this basis, both the ontological and epistemological assumptions that are embedded in language have become the focus of critique. Feminist and 'race' theorists and practitioners have been at the forefront of much of this debate. We need to bear in mind that essentialism as a *political* issue post-dates essentialism as a philosophical issue. The accusation that is implicit in the recent use of the term 'essentialist' often, in my view, fails to acknowledge the long history of essence in Western philosophical thinking. Such an accusation is meant to be grounds for dismissing the scholarship and commitments of thinkers because, the theory goes, the socio-political implications are dire. Thus 'being essentialist' connotes problematic socio-political loyalties which fail to take account of the world as it really is: as hierarchically divided along 'race', class, colonial, postcolonial, and sex/gender lines. The addressing of essentialist assumptions has, therefore, become central to addressing socio-political inequalities.

The accusation that Jung and Luce Irigaray are essentialist in their coverage of woman and the feminine is canvassed among their commentators. Susan Rowland, Christopher Hauke and Roger Brooke are all recent writers who deal with Jung's alleged essentialism.[3] In the context of feminist debate specifically around Luce Irigaray, Naomi Schor, in *The essential difference* locates the first 'salvos' in the essence debate 'between Beauvoir and Beauvoirean "equality feminists"' (Schor 1994: viii–ix). She argues that Monique Plaza was the first of Luce Irigaray's critics to accuse her of essentialism; but Schor also points out that Teresa Brennan locates the debate in Britain in the work of Marxists. Whatever the case, as Schor also notes, Toril Moi's *Sexual Textual Politics* brought the issue of essentialism and anti-essentialism to a much wider audience.[4]

In my view, much of the debate, even as it is articulated by Moi and by the various authors in *The essential difference* collection, is a debate about stereotypes rather than essence, and towards the end of this chapter I return to this idea. *The essential difference* collection reveals some shared conceptions about essence which are not philosophically sophisticated and which tend to ignore the vigorous debate that has taken place over essence for many centuries in philosophy.[5] Gayatri Spivak, for example, says that 'essentialism is a loose tongue. In the house of philosophy it's not taken seriously. You know it's used by non-philosophers simply to mean all kinds of things when they don't know what other word to use . . . within analytic philosophy, people like Hilary Putnam seem to be much more astutely coping with the problem of the irreducibility of essences without any fanfare; but they don't look, they don't sound like post-structuralist feminists or anything like that . . . The question of anti-essentialism and essentialism is not a philosophical question; that's why there isn't any rebuttal from the house of philosophy' (Spivak 1994: 159–60). What Spivak is suggesting here is not at all clear as she seems to be claiming first that philosophers do not take essence seriously, but that the philosopher Hilary Putnam does even though he does not sound like a post-structural feminist; that non-philosophers do not actually know what they mean when they use the term; and that essentialism is not a philosophical issue, anyway. On this basis, we should not be too concerned with Spivak's comments if hers are an assessment of the state of play in philosophy regarding essence or, it seems, even in non-philosophical circles. Putnam, for instance, argues about clear and borderline cases and the fuzziness of the line between them, and his arguments, to my knowledge, have not been used by any feminist accounts of women's essence and its problems.[6]

Saul Kripke's treatment of essence and the ensuing debate, which predates and prevails Spivak's remarks, is ignored by Spivak. Charlotte Witt's work on essence on Aristotle and Kripke and her later work on feminism and essence, and Elizabeth Spelman's, to whose work we have already been introduced, are contemporaneous with the 1989 publication of Spivak's interview in *The essential difference*. This suggests that, indeed, some inhabitants of the house of philosophy have been very concerned with the problem of essence, after all. So Spivak's assessment of the house of philosophy betrays an unfamiliarity with the inhabitants, the rooms and furnishings, and even where that house is.

Luce Irigaray's work has been susceptible to complaints by some feminist scholars that mirror complaints made about Jung: that she reinscribes notions of a universal feminine with scant regard for differences in culture, 'race' and sexual orientation and that she is, therefore, essentialist. The debate around her work has more or less been settled by appealing to the politically important notion of strategic essentialism, but for many, there are still issues with her focus on heterosexuality and universality.[7] But what *is* essentialism and why is it so contentious? What are the philosophical issues and how do they intersect with socio-political concerns?

I shall begin my discussion with the question of definition and essentialism. Garth L. Hallett comments that a 'critique of essentialism ought not to be essentialist' (Hallett 1991: 3). In principle, I am sympathetic to Hallett's view, even if it begs the question. But that all depends on what is meant by 'essentialism' and 'essentialist'. The key to this revolves around how 'definition' is to be understood, and so what follows is an elaboration of the idea of 'definition' as it relates to essence.

PROPERTY ESSENCE

The debate about essence addresses questions fundamental to ontology or the study of being and, by implication, epistemology or theory of knowledge. Definition has been central to many of these questions with a focus on language and linguistic practices. Hence we should note at the outset that the question of essence involves two overlapping concerns:

1 the definition of terms: this may involve developing concepts, ideas or notions, and
2 the uncovering of essential features of whatever is to be defined: language, in other words, both reveals and points to the 'real being of' or what lies behind, the concept, idea, notion.

In feminist theory, in particular, constructions and critiques of essentialism focus on problematising (i), with (ii) being absorbed into the all-embracing epistemological range of (1). The epistemological problem can be stated in at least two ways :

a If a definition gives the essence or the essential properties of an object, then anything that does not have those essential properties falls outside the definition and hence cannot be counted amongst the population[8] of objects to which the definition applies. Borderline or marginal instances, on this account, could not be included in the definition. If, for example, having an XX chromosome is an essential property of women, and an XY is an essential property of men, then any entity that does not have an XX chromosome, but does not have an XY either, is neither a man nor a woman. If being human means being either a woman or a man, then anything that does not have either an XX chromosome or an XY chromosome is not human.
b There are two strands to this argument:

    i Definition is a linguistic activity. Because definition is a linguistic activity, definition is socially embedded. Because definition is socially embedded, then any definition is going to be historically situated; so definition is open to revision over time.
    ii The other is that definition is both predicative and descriptive. In predicating and describing, a definition points to an object which is the source of the predication and description. Predication and description, in other words, uncover the properties of an object. Thus definition is about 'translating' into linguistic form the properties of an object. Some properties of an object are essential to its definition. If an object is defined, then its essence (or its essential properties) is defined. If giving the definition of an object changes over time and definition gives essence, then the essence of an object must change. Hence objects, if they have essence, do not have fixed, immutable ahistorical essence. But essence is fixed and immutable, so objects do not have essences.

John Locke's notorious distinction between nominal and real essence is precisely the concern of (1) and (2).[9] Locke argued that 'essence may be taken for the being of anything, whereby it is what it is' (Locke 1947: 234) and that '[t]he measure and boundary of each sort or species whereby it is constituted that particular sort and distinguished from others, is that we call its essence, which is nothing but that abstract idea to which the name is annexed' (Locke 1947: 242). For him, the abstract idea of a substance is its nominal essence, and the 'real constitution' of a substance is its real essence:

> It is true that I have often mentioned a real essence, distinct in substance from those abstract ideas of them, which I call their nominal essence. By this real essence I mean that real constitution of anything which is the foundation of all those properties that are combined in, and are constantly found to co-exist with the nominal essence; that particular constitution which everything has within itself, without any relation to anything without.
>
> (Locke 1947: 245)

Locke's understanding of essence is in terms of the coexistence of both real and nominal properties of anything. The 'thing' (in 'anything' and 'everything') is a reference to particulars. For Locke species, universal categories, general terms, are ontologically dependent upon the existence of individual things or simple substances. Real essences are concerned with real particulars (like lumps of gold or instances of triangles). Abstract general ideas are formed out of acquaintance with particulars. Nominal essences are contingent upon the existence of real essences and sometimes, as in the case of the triangle, they coincide:

> Thus a figure including a space between three lines is the real as well as the nominal essence of a triangle; it being not only the abstract idea to which the general name is annexed, but the very essentia, or being of the thing itself, that foundation from which all its properties flow, and to which they are all inseparably annexed.
>
> (Locke 1947: 236)[10]

Locke's view, which I shall call the Internal Property Essence View (internal properties like colour, shape, line, angle, solidity are, in combination, the essence of a thing), relies on the idea of properties or characteristics that constitute essence.

The Internal Property Essence View in various formulations has been influential in the recent development of metaphysical theories of identity in analytic philosophy.[11] Some feminist thinkers, not so much concerned with metaphysics or analytic philosophy but with the politics of identity, have seized on Locke's focus on properties and his distinction, and have argued that nominal essence can be seen as a forerunner of social constructionist views of language because nominal essence is a constructed essence, a product of naming practices. On this basis, nominal essence has been touted as a potential explanatory tool for developing an understanding of feminists' concerns with essence.[12] Teresa de Lauretis, for example, employs the distinction in her argument that 'essence' should be taken seriously by feminists as a means of identifying, albeit from an historically locatable perspective, the historically specifiable difference that marks feminist thinking as a distinctive mode of intellectual (and political) endeavour (de

Lauretis 1994: 4). de Lauretis' intuition that most feminists are talking about nominal rather than real essence is borne out in an examination of feminist theory.[13] That is largely because their focus on various forms of constructionism operates as a politically motivated remedy for addressing issues raised by questions of identity. I shall return to this point shortly.

On the other hand, Diana Fuss is less sympathetic to the possibilities that nominal essence might offer feminists. She asserts that real essence connotes 'the Aristotelian understanding of essence as that which is most irreducible and unchanging about a thing; nominal essence signifies for Locke a view of essence as merely a linguistic convenience, a classificatory fiction we need to categorise and to label' (Fuss 1989: 5). Fuss uses Locke's distinction partly to point out that it roughly corresponds to the 'oppositional categories of essentialism and constructionism'; partly as an analytic device to distinguish between the ontological and linguistic aspects of essentialism; and partly to suggest that 'it is equally important to investigate their complicities as types of essentialisms, members of the same semantic family' (Fuss 1989: 5). Her recognition of ontological and linguistic aspects of essentialism is a recognition of real and nominal essences. But, she claims, an appeal to nominal essence as a means of escaping the essentialist trap is bound to fail as constructionism is itself essentialist.

The issues identified by de Lauretis and Fuss focus on the question of properties and how they are to be understood in relation to identity and difference. Specifically, the property question in feminism is a political question: if identities are formed by virtue of possession of properties, then what will count as a member of a group will be determined by certain properties that might be thought of as essential in the sense of necessary properties. Properties thus become a defining feature of a member and her/his group. But which properties? And what if a potential member does not have an essential or necessary property or cluster of properties required for membership of a group? Are the relevant properties in question real or nominal in Locke's sense? The numerous problems perpetrated by the Internal Property Essence View are far beyond the scope of this book. But two things are worth noting:

1. Locke's view takes up some of the issues in Aristotle's views on substance and essence, and
2. the Internal Property Essence View has enjoyed enormous currency (and debate) through the work of Saul Kripke in recent metaphysics and versions of this, however crude, are often at the basis of feminist criticisms of essence.

I leave aside the Internal Property Essence View except to say that a link between Locke and Aristotle is not difficult to find; for instance, Aristotle also uses the triangle in his discussion of essence and one can imagine that this is the inspiration for Locke's use of the example (Aristotle 1941: 'Posterior Analytics' I 73a), especially since Locke holds that we get the idea of a triangle from our acquaintance with many instances. Since Aristotle has been cited as the origin of recent essentialisms, it is arguable that he held a version of the Property Essence View.[14] However, it is doubtful that he held the view which Fuss ascribes to him. She says that '[e]ssentialism is classically defined as a belief in true essence – that which is most irreducible, unchanging and therefore constitutive of a person or thing. This tradition represents the traditional Aristotelian understanding of essence (Fuss 1989: 2). In what sense the tradition characterises Aristotle's view is moot, especially since one view of Aristotle's notion of essence has it connected to individuals' membership of a species, of which Fuss does not take account. Aristotle himself says that essence is a thing's 'substantial reality' (Aristotle 1941: *Metaphysics* I 88a) which does not imply Fuss' interpretation at all, but it *does* give grist to Witt's way of reading and re-reading Aristotle.

Witt does take account of species membership and has argued that the classical view, that she calls the 'standard view', is a misreading of Aristotle; and this because the question with which he is concerned is not the question presupposed by the Internal Property Essence View. Hence Witt's alternative view of Aristotle suggests a way of re-reading the idea of essence that does not involve a version of the Internal Property Essence View. And if that is the case, then it is possible that the notion of essence might be more useful to the critics of Jung and Luce Irigaray than has been thought. But let me begin with some of the complexity that is Aristotle's view of essence.

ORIGINARY ESSENCE

In the *Metaphysics*, Aristotle's discussion of essence occurs as part of his discussion of substance. He tell us that essence is one of the four things commonly held to be substantial (along with the universal, the genus and the substratum) (Aristotle 1941: *Metaphysics* VII). Aristotle says that 'substance is commonly thought to belong most obviously to bodies; and so we say that not only animals and plants are substances, but also natural bodies such as fire and water and earth and everything of the sort, and all things that are either parts of these or composed of these (either of parts or of whole bodies) e.g. the physical universe and its parts, stars, moon and sun' (Aristotle 1941: *Metaphysics* VII 1028b 2–13). He goes on to say that others have posited the existence of eternal substances like the Forms and objects of mathematics, so his task in the *Metaphysics* is to figure out which of the common statements are right, what substances are, whether there are any non-sensible substances, how sensible substances exist and whether sensible substances are capable of independent existence.

These are some of the things he says about essence:

a 'the essence of each thing is what it is said to be *propter se* or what something is of itself. For being you is not being musical, since you are not by your very nature musical . . . What, then, you are, you are by your very nature' (Aristotle 1941: *Metaphysics* VII 1029b).

b 'And all essences alike exist or none of them does; so if the essence of reality is not real, neither is any of the others . . . The good, then, must be one with the essence of good and beauty one with the essence of beauty and so with all things which do not depend on something else but are self-subsistent and primary' (Aristotle 1941: *Metaphysics* VII 1031).

c 'Essence is precisely what something *is*' (Aristotle 1941: *Metaphysics* VII 1029b2–1030a).

d 'Since we have the existence of the thing as something given, clearly the question is *why* the matter is some definite thing; e.g. why are these materials a house? Because that which was the essence of a house is present . . . Therefore what we seek is the cause, i.e. the form, by reason of which the matter is some definite thing and this is the substance of the thing' (Aristotle 1941: *Metaphysics* VII 1041b).

e 'A definition is a phrase signifying a thing's essence. It is rendered in the form either of a phrase in lieu of a term, or in lieu of another phrase; for it is sometimes possible to define the meaning of a phrase as well' (Aristotle 1941: 'Topics' 101b–102a).

All of the above points emerge in Witt's analysis of substance and essence where Books VII–IX of the *Metaphysics* are her focus. She makes out a case for understanding essence as *cause*, thus refiguring some generally held views about Aristotle and essence. Essentialists, argues Witt, 'believe that some constituents or properties of objects are essential to those objects, while other constituents or properties are not essential to them. There is an inner "core" or essence that constitutes the object and that cannot change so long as the object exists; the object might differ with respect to many of its features but not with respect to its "core" or essence. Or so the story goes' (Witt 1989: 1). Witt sets out to dismantle this view of essence, 'the standard view' as she calls it. She argues that the standard view which focuses on properties and species essence is a misreading of Aristotle and she defends a view of Aristotelian essence which re-reads Aristotle's notion of 'definition'. There are two elements to the standard view: core properties and membership of a species.

Before moving to Witt's account of Aristotelian essence, we should note that she argues that the standard view attempts to answer a different question from the one with which Aristotle was concerned. She asks:

> if the basic function of essence is to place individual substances into species, then what could serve the purpose better than an essence that is a universal property, shared by individuals of the same kind? If this were the role of essence in Aristotle's theory of substance, then the idea that essences are universal properties of substances would seem extremely plausible.
>
> (Witt 1989: 4 and 125)

The standard view presents a view of essential properties that tells us what 'an individual object must have in order to be that very object' (Witt 1989: 125). Give the essence and you give the conditions for membership of a species and thus the conditions for individual identity. In other words, the standard view is an account that gives the conditions of an object's being what it is. But, as we shall see, Witt argues that Aristotle's concern was not with this question but with 'What is it?' Beginning with her analysis of the standard view, Witt goes on to argue the case for the cause of being of a substance as its essence.

'The standard interpretation holds that Aristotelian essences are species essence', which means that one's membership of a *species* gives one an essence that makes one into the kind of thing that one is. One is born with an essence because one is born a human being, so essence is innate. Further, giving a definition involves talking about something's membership of a species: essence is shared, a collective rather than an individual matter. And the principle of individuation: what makes an individual what it is, is matter (Witt 1989: 2–3). From this we can see that, according to Witt, there are five aspects of essence that we need to be aware of here:

1 the giving of a definition of an entity is the giving of an entity's essence,
2 essence is non-linguistic,
3 essence is innate,
4 essence is collective, to do with natural kinds or species,
5 individuation is accounted for by appeal to the notion of matter.

These five aspects are not individually mistaken but, read together, Witt argues they produce an interpretation that is mistaken in three ways:

a the idea that 'the most important function of essence is to explain species membership',
b 'the essence of an individual, composite substance is universal rather than individual', and
c 'an essence is not a property (or a cluster of properties) of the substance whose essence it is' (Witt 1989: 3).

She points out that Aristotle's use of definition as a methodological procedure to get at what something is is inspired by Plato. In 'Euthyphro', for example, Socrates asks Euthyphro 'for that special feature through which all holy things are holy' and also to 'explain to me what this standard itself is, so that when I observe it and use it as a means of comparison, I may affirm that whatsoever actions are like it' (Plato 2003: 'Euthyphro' 6d–e). Plato's answer, as we have already seen in Chapter 4, would be couched in terms of Forms. Participation in a Form is what gives something its identity as the very identity it is: things are instances (albeit imperfect ones) of forms. Aristotle does not follow Plato here, even though Socrates, like Aristotle, is after what makes something X and is also seeking a measure of correct linguistic use.

Methodologically, then, Aristotle is influenced by Plato, and in *Metaphysics* Aristotle examines four common understandings of substance: the essence, the universal, the genus and the substratum. He focuses on essence as 'one of the four possible definitional responses to the question, "What is substance?"', which concerns principles and causes (Witt 1989: 101). So the giving of a definition involves the giving of principles and causes which in turn involves the giving of an essence which in turn answers the question of what a substance is rather than appealing to the idea of a Form. Instead of a definition being related to language (the giving of a meaning of a word), definition for Aristotle is the giving of the cause of something's being what it is. If we use the example from 'Euthyphro', Aristotle would hold that the practice of holiness by making offerings and having due reverence for the Gods is what causes holy things to be holy, just as the practice of virtue causes us to be virtuous.

Witt argues that for Aristotle, the definitional question, 'What is it?' (What is substance? What is Socrates? What is a woman?) is not the question 'How do we define this word?' nor is it 'What are the properties of this thing?' nor 'What properties must this thing have in order to be this thing?' It is the question, 'What is the cause of being of this thing?' Since Aristotle's notion of cause is very rich, to give the cause of something's being will ultimately be to give a very rich account of its origin.[15] She maintains that the cause of something cannot be a property of that something, because that would mean that a property would be both prior and posterior to that something (Witt 1989: 122–3). So while the material out of which something is made does indeed pre-exist that something, it has no form as that something until all the causal conditions are met: leather for shoes might pre-exist a pair of shoes, but the idea and the implementation of the idea of the shoes so that they can be used as footwear, need to all come together in the substance that is the shoe.

This brings us to Witt's claim that essences are not to be thought of as species-essence. The idea of species-essence engages the idea of essence as shared and universal by virtue of a core of properties that are common to all members of a natural kind or species. On Witt's view, Aristotle's essences are neither properties nor universals but are, instead, 'substances and particulars, or individuals' (Witt 1989: 144). She maintains that Aristotle also held that no universal is a substance (Witt 1989: 153). She points out that at 1038b 15–16, Aristotle argues that:

1 Substance is said to be that which is not predicable of a subject.
2 The universal is always said to be predicated of a subject.
  Therefore,
3 The universal is not a substance.

Witt argues that there is a puzzle about the causes or principles of substances which suggests that 'there are good reasons for holding that they are universal and not particular, and also good reasons for holding that they are particular and not universal' (Witt 1989: 163). According to Witt, this issue is resolved in Aristotle's account of potential and actual knowledge in which he argues that we can have actual knowledge of particulars, and also through understanding what Aristotle means by the notion of an individual essence. Witt reads Kripke against Aristotle in her final chapter to deal with the question of individual essence. She argues that Aristotle and Kripke are engaged in fundamentally different projects. Kripke offers an account of essences in terms of necessary properties and trans-world identity, with which Aristotle is not concerned. I am arguing that the mis-reading of Aristotle such as occurs in feminist interpretations of Aristotelian essence is the attribution of a Kripkean-type position which Aristotle does not hold.

Discussing material substances, Witt notes that:

> Aristotle acknowledges the importance of its source or origin in the causal history of the substance. Where an object actually 'comes from' seems to be central to our understanding of it. Hence the importance of genealogies for humans, pedigrees for animals, and so on. On a more abstract level, material substances are such that there must be some origin for their generation; they do not pop into existence from nothing, nor do they generate themselves, they are not eternal. So, Aristotle thinks we should always look for the origin or source of the generation.
>
> (Witt 1989: 190)

This view of Aristotle, let us dub it the Originary Essence View, can prove to be liberating rather than oppressive to feminist theory. Luce Irigaray's call for the reclaiming of a female genealogy is compatible with, and potentially enhanced by, the Originary Essence View. Additionally, one's membership of a collective becomes an important contributor to the development of one's causal history.

Undoubtedly, this view moves us a long way from the Property View of Essence. Essence is refigured as an explanatory mechanism that can incorporate social, symbolic and biological factors in the production of individual identity. This theory provides the means for understanding the uniqueness of each collective member while simultaneously allowing for the possibility that group identity and affiliations can be explained and understood and, as we shall see, this is enhanced by an elucidation of 'stereotype'. Individual women have essence but this is by virtue of their membership of their various collectives. Let us see how this plays out in accounts of the feminine.

RETHINKING FEMINIST THEORY AND ESSENCE

Irrespective of re-readings of Aristotle's metaphysical views, many feminists think of Aristotle as a villain. In relation to natural kinds, Aristotle argues that some members of the species are more perfect forms of that species than others. Even if 'male and female are appropriate affections of animal', the male is the more perfect specimen of the species (Aristotle 1941: 'Politics' 1253b, 1254a, 1254b). For Aristotle, an imperfect embodiment of the species lacks something, so that the female should be understood as the privative of the male. (One cannot pass this by without, of course, remarking on Freud's and Lacan's view of women in terms of lack of a penis and control over the phallus.) Not only that, she is passive in the reproduction of the species (she provides the matter while he provides the form, and form is superior to matter). His discussion of the role of semen in intercourse and generation (between female and male, not woman and man), which Aristotle uses in the opening chapters of the *Metaphysics*, has been interpreted by many as one of the most influential texts in creating the binary female/male (Aristotle 1941: 'De Generatione Animalium' 715a–731b). That binary, they argue, privileges the male and aligns him with the good and dis-privileges the female and aligns her with the bad (Aristotle 1991: 986a).[16] Aristotle's views are reiterated in his discussion of the inferiority of women compared with men (Agonito 1977; Aristotle 1941: 1254b, 1260a). His work, it is argued, has influenced the concept 'woman' and thus how women have been both perceived and constituted: as illogical, natural mothers, care givers, whores, virgins, emotional, irrational.

I claimed earlier that feminist readings of Aristotelian essence do not take account of species-essence (which, as we have seen, Witt thinks is a mistaken interpretation at any rate) and few engage in debate in any full-blown way, with the Internal Property View.[17] As far as I know, no one has countenanced Witt's Originary Essence View. So it is interesting to contemplate precisely what feminists *are* rejecting when they reject essentialism as I have articulated it. Because the relevant meanings of 'essence' are unclear, we are left in the position of assuming that some interpretation of the Internal Property View is their target. My hunch is that the charge of ahistoricity is linked to the idea of essential properties which are taken to be necessary properties, with (ii) (p. 134) above resulting. Elizabeth Grosz has maintained that essentialism 'refers to the existence of fixed characteristics, given attributes, and ahistorical functions which limit the possibilities of change and thus of social reorganisation' (Grosz 1990b: 334). A Kripkean interpretation of the Internal Property View, since it would entail the concept of necessary properties, would be disqualified as an account of womanly or feminine or female essence; however, it is plausible that Grosz has a version of the Internal Property Essence View, very like Kripke's, in mind.[18]

On the other hand, the Originary Essence View does not depend on, nor lead to the idea of, necessary properties. Given the notion of cause at play in the Originary Essence View we can see that woman's essence could potentially be thought of in very productive ways. Such an account gives us every reason to think that women do have essence and that, in part, women's origins are beyond their control: but that is the same for every human being.

What, then, of the more generally held views about essence in feminist literature? What can we say of them? Feminists who are critical of, and dismiss, essence are making, it seems to me, legitimate claims about the use and abuse of certain ways of figuring and understanding the use of the terms 'woman', 'feminine' and 'female'. Such uses do, indeed often, fail, to attend to socio-cultural and historical differences in women and can, indeed, universalise the experience of a dominant and articulate group of women. On the other hand, that women give birth and are mothers (to both daughters and sons), have specific forms of exclusive and exclusionary sociality, are objects of exchange and victims of rape and exploitation cross-culturally and universally, is undeniable.[19] The oppression of women *as a class* cannot be gainsaid, *even when some of the oppressors are women themselves*.

It seems to me that the attribution of characteristics to woman, the feminine, the female, is, in effect, the attribution of stereotypical properties or sets of properties. Feminist thinkers react, then, not to *essence* but to the deployment of womanly, feminine or female *stereotypes* as they appear in Plato, Aristotle, Kant and Jung and which are reproduced in the academic and the social imaginaries *as if* what is said is unquestionably the case. The work of early second-wave feminist scholars like Simone de Beauvoir, Betty Friedan and Mary Daly is testament to this perspective. The problem is, however, that the assumptions which underpin the use of stereotypes (the assumption that woman is of a specific inferior kind, for example) have been problematised by most feminist thinkers, but not as stereotypes. And, paradoxically, in the elaboration of 'stereotype' we can find both the cause of the problem and part of its solution. This may seem like a strange claim:

after all, stereotypes, I am claiming, are the issue here, so how can stereotypes possibly be helpful to a constructive view of women's being, and the potential for women to be subjects? The answer to this question has to do with the explanatory potential of stereotypes; and this is how.

Hilary Putnam's account of stereotypes is illuminating. He notes that 'a "stereotype" is a conventional (frequently malicious) idea (which may be wildly inaccurate) of what an *X* looks like or acts like or is . . . I am not concerned with malicious stereotypes (save where the language itself is malicious); but I am concerned with conventional ideas which may be inaccurate' (Putnam 1975: 249). Putnam argues that there are certain things a speaker is required to know in order to know what a word means. Meaning comes about through implicit acknowledgement of stereotypes. Hence someone who knows what 'tiger' means 'is required to know that *stereotypical* tigers are striped. More precisely, there is one stereotype of tigers (he may have others) which is required by the linguistic community as such; he is required to have this stereotype and to know (implicitly) that it is obligatory'. Importantly for our purposes, Putnam insists that features included in a stereotype do not make it 'an analytic truth that all *X*s have the same feature, nor that most *X*s have that feature, nor that all normal *X*s have that feature, nor that some *X*s have that feature. Three-legged tigers and albino tigers are not logically contradictory' and even if an *X* ceased to have the relevant feature, then that does not mean that they ceased to be an *X* (Putnam 1975: 250). Putnam notes that stereotypes can contain mistaken information, but that they nonetheless 'capture features possessed by the paradigmatic members of the class in question', so even given mistaken content they still have value for linguistic communities (Putnam 1975: 250). Stereotypes facilitate the communication of meaning, with or without agreement between speakers and with or without agreement with the world. He concludes that 'the fact that our language has *some* stereotypes which impede rather than facilitate our dealings with the world and each other only points to the fact that we aren't infallible beings, and how could we be?' (Putnam 1975: 51).

The characterisation of women that feminists find objectionable is exemplary of what Putnam is talking about here. First, women are presented both maliciously and inaccurately: indeed it is part of the stereotype that women are thus characterised. Secondly, one of the complaints of feminists has been that some women will be excluded from the class of women because they do not possess the properties necessary for membership of that class. And thirdly, language practices and their potency in linguistic communities, with their power to construct and destruct, persuade and belittle, can be understood within the meaning framework of stereotypes.

Plato's and Aristotle's philosophy and Jung's analytical psychology are instances of the first point. In Plato's case, a woman's 'railing at her husband, or striving or vaunting herself against the gods, thinking she is happy, or overcome by misfortune, or grief, or tears' embodies the stereotype 'woman' specific to his world (and with overflow to the present time). On Putnam's reading of 'stereotype' there are no properties necessary or essential to membership of the class to which the stereotype is applied, even though there are specific things someone needs to know in order to know the meaning of a term. So, for example, to use the term 'woman' one might need to know that, stereotypically, women have sexual relations with men, bear children, suckle them and then nurture them through childhood. It does not follow from this that all women will have to be or do these things, nor does it follow from this that men, for example, cannot nurture children (even though this may be contrary to *their* stereotype). So just as tigers may be albinos or three-legged, so women may be lesbian, childless (and by choice) bottle-feed babies and have their children raised by a nanny. There is nothing self-contradictory about a woman who does not fit the stereotype. The meaning of 'woman' is contingent on the stereotype, and ironically, that feminists criticise the stereotype in the first place is possible only because of the stereotype. In other words, we need the stereotype 'woman' in order to give meaning and make sense of the world in which we use the term. That does not, however, commit us to any determinate ontological presuppositions.

Linguistic communities, then, through language practices need to invoke stereotypes for meaningful discourses and communication. When white middle-class feminists speak about women or woman's experience or even the feminine, they certainly are, on this story, employing stereotypes. But they speak only for all women if they subscribe to a view of stereotype which would yield self-contradiction were they to be using some notion of essential or necessary property. But if Putnam's account is correct (and I think it is), then language use can be liberated from the narrow confines we see invoked in both talk of stereotypes *and essence*.

An interesting consequence of this theory is that Plato and Jung in their use of the term 'woman' are indeed invoking the stereotype 'woman' and that is why we can understand them, know what they *mean in the first place*. Unfortunately, however, their use not only harnesses what needs to be implicitly acknowledged but reiterates some pejorative, devalorising and divisive opinions about women. My contention is that the *content* of such stereotypes is neither essential nor necessary to woman-ness.

So let us put this all together with Originary Essence in relation to Jung and Luce Irigaray and go back to the question of their alleged essentialism.

ESSENCE, STEREOTYPE, JUNG AND LUCE IRIGARAY

Witt's account of essence as cause gives us an opportunity to re-think the triple influences on the making of a collective member: the symbolic, the social and the biological and Putnam's reading of stereotype gives us the meaning framework in which to think the relation between essence and collective. Witt's and Putnam's accounts also give us pause to rethink the essentialist charges against Jung and Luce Irigaray. Let us take Jung's case first.

I argued that Jung's notion of the archetypes as *a priori* structures of the collective unconscious are constitutive but that they also look as if they might be deterministic. The origin or source of generation for a collective member is her/his material, social and symbolic existence in her/his collective(s). Given this, it is unclear how archetypes, as just one aspect of the essence of someone and as interactive with other aspects of a collective member's being, can be deterministic. Indeed, Jung is very clear that one's experiences have a great impact on how one apprehends one's world. Archetypes structure that experience as they are re-presented in active imagination and in dream images. That one understands those images means that they must engage with stereotypes. Putnam's point that there is no meaning unless there are stereotypes is well taken here. Indeed, we can posit a strong connection between an archetype as structure and a stereotype as its cultural manifestation given his view. What makes our dreams understandable is the presence in them of stereotypical presentations that are culturally embedded and which we encounter as a matter of fact as we go about our lives. We know meanings of words (and pictorial images) because we use stereotypes; and the stereotypes themselves are in a structural chain that emanates from the collective psyche, the collective unconscious. Archetypes and stereotypes are the already given of psychic constitution but how they work together is contingent on their specific manifestation in collectives and their cultures.

So, to return to the anima feminine: how is she to be understood now that we have travelled into some foreign terrain? How are we also to understand the carping disagreeable tyrant of a mother from whom one needs to escape? First, we might say that there are multiple factors that contribute to the feminine and to the idea of woman, as Jung himself admits. All language users in specific collectives are vulnerable to exposure to the stereotypes that sit behind their language use. Particular individuals more or less instantiate the stereotype (or else we would not meaningfully be able to use terms like 'anima', 'mother', lover', 'father' or even 'god'). 'Anima' picks out a set of stereotypical properties implicit in which is either an ideal or its opposite. The anima feminine who 'intensifies, exaggerates, falsifies and mythologizes all emotional relations' embodies a stereotype which indeed no woman has to satisfy even though some women may and certainly not all women will. And the actual women onto whom such an image is projected will bear the soul image because they are always already understood to be women; 'woman', recall, requires stereotypical content in order to be understood. Furthermore, the misappropriation of a stereotype involving malice and wild inaccuracy is possible; for perhaps the psyche will tend to continue structuring, through its archetypes, the material it receives as if it were the case. And the same kind of argument might apply in the case of the mother archetype.

What we can see here, too, is that stereotypes are conveyors of value and potentially conveyors of what seem like timeless truths and apparent neutrality. Meaning, indeed, is tied up with value ('mother' means overweight, nagging, manipulative hag, for example). The pedagogical transference of such stereotypes through praise or blame (the good/bad woman dichotomy for instance) occurs by promotion of images which we are meant to imitate (or not) as the case may be. Again, we saw this in Plato's plea that boys should not imitate women. So Jung is not guilty of essentialism, but he is guilty of propagating malicious and inaccurate conceptions of the feminine through thoughtless imitation of cultural stereotypes. In Jung's case, we might take a lesson from Charlotte Witt's wisdom about Aristotle in relation to women. We might hold that, like Aristotle, Jung simply held mistaken views about women and the feminine. Then we could get on with the business of attending to Jung's theories, knowing that we can ignore his statements about women and the feminine, since they are false. Such an admission and the move beyond that are appealing in their simplicity. Yet Jung's statements about women form part of the foundations of his theorising, and for this reason, they cannot be ignored. And that is precisely why we need to look so carefully at them.

As for Luce Irigaray, we can now see that her insistence on a feminine-feminine symbolic/imaginary self-consciously yet ironically mimics the stereotypical image of woman found in the Western canon. Likewise, her appropriation of 'god', even as she values Feuerbach's rewriting of the concept, deploys stereotypical elements of the Christian symbolic/imaginary. She is very aware of the integral importance of history in the production of a feminine-feminine subject. Her acknowledgement of genealogy is two-fold: (a) with the masculine-feminine symbolic/imaginary, and (b) how that imaginary can be creatively manipulated to restore women's genealogies from lost or masculine-paternal interpretations and projections. Women's essence is derivative *in part* from the masculine-paternal symbolic/imaginary, yet its propulsion towards and engagement with a *telos*, implicit in Aristotle's notion of cause, which is embraced as woman's own ideal horizon, is the framework for a feminine-feminine symbolic/imaginary. To that extent, the forward-looking-ness towards the ideal horizon accompanies the masculine-feminine which is simultaneously accompanied by a newly mined genealogy. The positive refiguring of that genealogy, itself an aspect of women's essence (as we saw in the Demeter–Persephone case), can be seen as the formal cause of woman. Her essence is thus fluid and mobile, unconstricted by the negative demands and limitations of the masculine symbolic. Luce Irigaray's task, then, implicitly endorses important aspects of

Aristotle's notion of essence as cause. Essence is originary, not in terms of what properties something must have, but in terms of its manner of coming into the world, its origin and why it is here. In the case of woman, the feminine and the female, the story told becomes a story re-told and reconfigured. The stereotype 'woman', which subtends Luce Irigaray's project itself, is fluid and mobile. Its plasticity is an element of the possibility of a feminine-feminine. The concept 'woman' and her instantiations are nonetheless centred on mutable properties, heterosexuality, maternity and succour expected of women. To sum up the essence and the stereotype arguments, the being and the characterisation of woman can be elucidated without dependence on either essential properties or notions of necessity.[20]

The alternative to using terms like 'woman' seems to me to be the death of a thousand qualifications. Once we begin to ask 'which women?' when we begin to theorise woman and the feminine, we have immediately failed to grasp how language works: not all women are white or middle-class or Protestant; predominantly, that is not the case. Nor are all women black and poor and fast runners; predominantly that is not the case. But this does not mean that we cannot talk about women as a group or class, the understanding of which is set by the stereotype 'woman' as I outlined above. Putnam's interpretation of 'stereotype' operates as a common-sense notion around which meaningful generalisations can be made; and also around which malicious and false claims can be made. The protests of feminist writers such as de Lauretis and Fuss are justified; but the object of their analysis is misdirected in that the metaphysical culprit is not essence but a negative deployment of stereotypes.

What, then, is it to be a woman? What is woman-ness? What makes a woman a woman? This is the question that founds and informs feminist debate and it is a version of the 'What is it?' question at the basis of the Originary Essence View. We can see that, aided by Putnam's notion of stereotype, an answer with much potential for the making of a feminine-feminine subject lies in the direction I have been outlining. And at this point, I cannot decide whether Hallett's imperative has been met or not.

So now, having done much theoretical archaeology in this and the preceding chapters, let us return our focus to the question of individuation.

Chapter 8

Conclusion

Speaking of the collective unconscious . . .

In Chapter 1, I raised some questions about the *knowability* of the unconscious. I argued that the claim that the unconscious is unknown is incoherent given that it seems to be *knowable* through archetypal images and our experiences. I want now to return to this claim and to reflect on it in light of the arguments I have made in this book. In particular, I shall examine the possible connection between Lacan's symbolic/imaginary and Jung's notion of the collective unconscious in relation to Luce Irigaray's call for a feminine-feminine symbolic/imaginary. Andrew Samuels argues, as I noted earlier, that 'Lacan's Symbolic and Imaginary may be aligned with Jung's archetypal theory (collective unconscious) and personal unconscious respectively' (Samuels 1985: 40). Symbolically, there is an obvious alignment between the phallus as the principal signifier in Lacan's symbolic and the Logos as the masculine principle in the collective unconscious. And if Samuels is correct, and this will depend on what is meant by 'aligned', then Luce Irigaray, because she insists on a feminine-feminine symbolic/imaginary, appears to be arguing, in part, for a *feminine* collective unconscious; and this, it seems to me, is incoherent, if we accept that the collective unconscious is unknown. As an unknown, sex/gender predications (or any predication) cannot be made of the collective unconscious.

But the claim that the unconscious is sex/gendered already appears in Jung's work, or, at least, it seems to. We saw earlier that Jung figures *unconsciousness* as feminine, when he discusses the necessity for the Logos (the masculine principle) 'to extricate itself from the primal warmth and primal darkness of the maternal womb; in a word from unconsciousness'. He then claims that '[n]othing can exist without its opposite; the two were one in the beginning and will be one again in the end. Consciousness can only exist through continual recognition of *the unconscious*' (Jung 1968a: 178). There are several things to be said here:

1 Jung appears to conflate an original (maternal and thus feminine) unconsciousness with *the* unconscious.

2 On his argument, the unconscious does not have an opposing force (the conscious) *simpliciter*. If there is a maternal-feminine unconsciousness, then there must be a paternal-masculine unconsciousness, given the principle of opposition that Jung invokes. Hence the ideas of a feminine consciousness and a masculine consciousness would also need to be invoked.
3 If (1) is the case, then the origin of all unconscious matter is in the feminine. And if (2) is the case, then (1) cannot be the case. The two propositions are inconsistent with each other.

This is a logical mess! And it is made worse by Samuels' aligning the Symbolic with the collective unconscious and the Imaginary with the personal unconscious. In support of Samuels, we might consider Lacan's remark that:

> a psychoanalyst should find assurance in the obvious fact that man is, prior to his birth and beyond his death, caught up in the symbolic chain, a chain that founded his lineage before his history was embroidered upon it. He must work at the idea that it is in his very being – in his 'total personality,' as it is comically put – that man is in fact considered to be a whole, but like a pawn, in the play of the signifier, and this is so even before its rules are transmitted to him, insofar as he ends up discovering them; this order of priorities must be understood as a logical order, that is, forever current.
>
> (Lacan 2002: 392)

The Jungian dimensions of this quotation are not hard to detect. Locating humans in a pre-personal unconscious is analogous to locating humans in the always already existing collective unconscious. The logical order of priorities, forever current, readily translates into Jung's archetypal psychology. Jung's archetypes as structuring mechanisms of the unconscious logically order the psychic world of the subject, even if the meaning of the order and its logic are not clear to the subject. (One also might wonder whether Lacan is engaged in the kind of unconscious imitation and identification we have seen in Jung's notions of imitation and projection.)

Freud's claim that there is only one symbolic/imaginary, and then Lacan's and Luce Irigaray's claims that the symbolic/imaginary is masculine, have some distinctive epistemological implications for the collective unconscious if Samuels' assertions about Lacan's symbolic chain are true. Yet an account of an alleged sex/gendered nature of the unconscious is worrisome when we consider Jung's assertion that we cannot know the unconscious. If we cannot know the unconscious, how can we claim that it is either masculine or feminine and what would that mean, anyway? On the other hand, Samuels' aligning of the symbolic with the collective unconscious and the imaginary with the personal unconscious looks as if it ought to be correct. However, when we consider what the stable and ubiquitous signifier of the symbolic is, it is difficult to see how it can be aligned with the collective unconscious: it's a phallus and the phallus is irretrievably connected with male anatomy, with male function and with masculine libido. We name the phallus and we can figure out how the phallus works in the symbolic order, so in a sense we can know the symbolic. An alignment seems to suggest that there is a sharing of some properties.

But alignment does not mean identity, and it could be argued that any alignment is purely from a functional perspective. On this view, the collective unconscious and the symbolic *function* in similar ways, as do the personal unconscious and the imaginary. But what does that mean? It can mean nothing more, I would suggest, than recognition of the psychic transpersonal origins of any member of the collective, in the mother. And that this should be seen at several levels.

1 We need to distinguish between the collective unconscious and the symbolic on the one hand; and the personal unconscious and the imaginary on the other. Let us think of Jung's archetypes as constituting the unconscious matrix, the collective unconscious or the ancient structure in which the symbolic is embedded. On this view. Lacan's symbolic can be considered as an *effect* of the collective unconscious. But it is an effect that is a *reaction against* the maternal-feminine, an effect aimed at *overcoming dependency on the maternal-feminine*. What we witness here is a struggle unto death which is carried across from an unconscious to a conscious level.
2 And this effect turns back on itself: it is reflexive. It is an effect not only of the collective *unconscious*, it is also an effect of the *collective conscious* where masculine-paternal relations of domination and oppression obtain in response to the recognition of the original dependency relation. That the phallus is the principal signifier is an effect of the dual contributions of the collective conscious and unconscious, a reflexive, dialectical relation. The expression of these relations is in the masculine-paternal imaginary: for example, stories tell of the victorious reign of the phallus and of the Logos (heroism, conquering the feminine, rational detachment from the emotions).
3 Jung's talk of the necessity to escape an original maternal-feminine unconsciousness requires more than the archetypes: it also requires for men a symbolic system that is capable of mediating the man's relationship to the maternal-feminine. And that symbolic can be found in the phallus as primary signifier in the Lacanian symbolic *for men* as well as in Jung's idea that Logos is the masculine principle. The two support and complement each other.

4 The belittling of women and the feminine as an aspect of the power of the phallus does indeed constitute a projection of masculine insecurity about never escaping the maternal-feminine: in this scenario, women cannot be 'granted' autonomy and the prospect of independence, freedom and thus individuation, unless they are identifiable as negating extensions of the masculine symbolic.

Points (1)–(4) bring together Jung and Lacan (and the mediating influence of Freud). But taking the principle of opposition that Jung invokes requires that there be both unconscious maternal-feminine *and* an unconscious paternal-masculine. How do we deal with the unknown-ness of the unconscious? One way in which this might be addressed is to argue that the symbolic/imaginary is so structured that our *perceptions and interpretations and thus our understandings of the symbolic are sex/gendered.* We bring to bear the prejudices and biases of the masculine symbolic/imaginary. In other words, we invoke a system of representation which we take to be descriptive of the unconscious, but which is actually self-referential. What we might think of as a sex/gender status of the unconscious is a consequence of how we understand and employ the symbolic and the Logos principle. The latter colonises, through projective engagement and appropriation, a domain to which it has no entitlement. What we *think* we know in the collective unconscious is a mirror image of phallic self-importance. We cannot make any *direct* epistemological claims about the unconscious. Yet we can continue to refer to the feminine (and the masculine) unconscious *as if* it is the genuine referent of symbolic attributions. The symbolic/imaginary represents the psychic terrain, but only insofar as it understands itself as an extension of its own limited self-understanding.

We can make *indirect* epistemological claims: by inference, we can say that the unconscious acts in certain ways to influence us (through dreaming perhaps), that the unconscious can remind, alert and relate things to us which we may not want to acknowledge. The role of the unconscious in this case is to help us to recognise ourselves in our unconscious ineptitude. That is part of the process of individuation. So, from a relational perspective we can come to know (*connaître*) the unconscious; but we cannot know (*savoir*) that it has this set (rather than that) of internal properties or relations in the sense of internal property I invoked in Chapter 7. Currently, this schematic is more clearly spelt out for men, largely because of the power relations that work to privilege them. The story for women has yet to be told, and this is where Luce Irigaray's work is so important.

Charles Shepherdson points out that Lacan had made a radical break with Freud in 1972 when he declared that there are two ways of relating to the symbolic (Shepherdson 2003: 136ff; Lacan 1999). For Lacan that is partly what the appeal to *jouissance* is about. Perhaps Lacan thinks that women can have no relation to the unconscious, that it can only be imputed because woman is the origin of men (and the Logos and, indeed, the phallus (and, bless us, women)), who fear that they cannot escape the original unconsciousness from which we all emerge, maternal-feminine unconsciousness. Lacan seems to ridicule women and their attempts to know; yet he, at the same time, asserts his own epistemological privilege (Lacan 1982). But, we might argue, Luce Irigaray has 'got his number'. She wants to make sure that there *are* two ways of relating to the symbolic. And the second way entails making another symbolic from materials extant but obfuscated by the arrogance of the symbolic which sees itself as all. Hence there *will* be two ontologically distinct ways of relating to the symbolic, but furthermore there will be *two symbolics* to which both men and women will relate. Just as women are currently outside but constructed from within the masculine symbolic, so men will be outside a feminine-feminine symbolic/imaginary. (And it remains to be seen whether women will then construct men as men have constructed women.) So the upshot of Lacan's claim is not to differentiate merely between two different ways of relating to the symbolic. More radically, there are two different symbolics with two different ways of relating to each and they, in turn, relate to sex/gendered perceptions of the unconscious.

In her essay 'The Poverty of Psychoanalysis' Luce Irigaray quotes Lacan's 'premise' that '[i]t is to that extent I say that the imputation of the unconscious is an incredible act of charity' (Irigaray 1991b: 98). Lacan is arguing that there is no certainty that women have or are in relation to the unconscious, that if men attribute the unconscious to women, then it is out of charity rather than because it is demonstrably the case, as it would be for men. The emptiness of ~~*The*~~ woman: she is the negation of the man and does not actually exist and her lack precludes giving affirmative content to the idea of woman, located outside, but nonetheless caught in, the symbolic chain. Luce Irigaray asks whether or not the unconscious would protect women or take desire away from them, arguing that many women feel 'shut in', 'closed up', 'withdrawn', that 'something inside them has become inaccessible', that they 'don't know how to get back in touch with it' after they have experienced analysis. She argues that *post factum* women feel a sense of powerlessness and suffer from depression and asks whether this is 'from the "imputation" of a *jouissance* which is not theirs?' (Irigaray 1991b: 99).

Jouissance, we noted, is the feminine excess Lacan identifies that is beyond the phallus, the pleasure in feminine desire that actually and symbolically exceeds the male experience of orgasm (or so Lacan believes). The notion of the unconscious is, then, for Luce Irigaray deeply problematic in relation to women, if it means that experience of a *jouissance* constructed as an aspect of the masculine symbolic/imaginary about women signals that women are in the unconscious yet outside the chain of signifiers. And that is why she is so determined to construct a feminine-feminine symbolic/imaginary: a feminine-feminine symbolic/imaginary can link up with the feminine forcibly abandoned at the little girl's entry into the masculine symbolic. It will give woman access to her own unconscious: the maternal-feminine origin, unmediated by the demands of male narcissism (Irigaray 1991b: 99ff).

And what is to become of the idea of the masculine unconscious in all of this? Even if we argue for a figurative feminine unconsciousness, known through symbolic/imaginary processes of identification, we still need an account that will allow for the effective 'doubling' of the unconscious at a collective level.

The epigram from Genesis with which I prefaced Chapter 4 has a plurality of origins not a singularity: 'Then God said: "Let us make man in our image, after our likeness." . . . God created man in his image; in the divine image he created him; male and female he created them.' The masculine archetype of creation implicit is this story is forgotten, erased by the threat of the feminine. If Luce Irigaray's efforts to initiate a feminine-feminine symbolic are successful, then a spin-off from that will be a recovery and restoration of the *masculine* unconscious. At least that would be my wager. If this were the case, the idea of individuation would involve an immense shift, a turn away from the domination of the unconscious, the conscious, the symbolic and the imaginary, by the phallus. The phallus would need to re-identify with the unconscious Logos. And the emerging feminine-feminine symbolic would eventually need to engage this paternal origin. The upshot of each of these moves would mean the abandoning of Giegerich's commitment to an original position presently so typical of male theory (and practice).

That said, there are two remaining issues with which to grapple. I am optimistic about the potential for a transformation of the Master/Slave Dialectic. So I turn to some thoughts on this matter in relation to individuation, the clinical and the social.

CLINICAL AND SOCIAL IMPLICATIONS

Acknowledgement of different modes of access to the symbolic/imaginary, a reclamation of the feminine unconscious in a feminine-feminine symbolic imaginary and the recognition of a masculine unconsciousness entails certain transformations of our thinking and of how we practise our thinking. Luce Irigaray identifies the sense of loss and the powerlessness some women feel in the psychoanalytic process, a loss and powerlessness which is experienced by many women outside as well as inside the consulting room. Bani Shorter, who is a Jungian analyst, seems to endorse a masculine-paternal reading of the Demeter–Persephone myth, as I argued in Chapter 6. Jung's construction of women and the feminine is less than laudable. Each of these three cases pinpoints various aspects of hegemonic masculine-paternal praxis that assumes the otherness of women and absent men from masculine unconsciousness (exhibited, for example, in their devotion to war and violence). But it is Luce Irigaray who speaks out and she refuses to speak for men and argues that men must sort out their men's business for themselves (Irigaray 1992).

She argues, as we saw, that in analysis there is a transference of masculinist privileging assumptions about the psyche in which women are colonised by men's projections. Not only that, she, following Lacan, is arguing that there is no authentic speaking position for women. So her gamble, to imitate, deliberately, the voice of the other (the feminine of the masculine symbolic/imaginary), to find a feminine divine horizon and a feminine-feminine symbolic imaginary, has the potential, if it works, to refigure the way in which women understand themselves, and men, and men understand themselves, and women.

Andrea Nye points out that '[a]ccording to Lacan, women have no stable place in a language that is structured around a phallic presence' (Nye 1986: 45). The speaking position of women in analysis is unstable just as it is in any other situation dominated by phallic presence. But the problem is that there is no other place, so the speaking position of women is forever frustrated. Luce Irigaray's work gestures towards a stable place from which women can speak in, and out of, analysis. She is attempting a feminine-feminine subjective position, as do Hélène Cixous and Catherine Clément among other Francophone theorists (Cixous and Clément 1996).

In my view, women can be individuated only if they are able to establish a speaking position that is genuinely their own. The instability of the subject position offered to women through the masculine symbolic is such that it forces women to remain always as Hegel's Slave at the moment of his conquering by the Master. There is no liberating site from which they can bargain with a conscientised male audience that is prepared to listen and to act. The action required is recognition of the subjugation of women by men, the genuine-ness of this as an issue and then an abandoning of some of the power which the phallus authorises.[1] This is a collective matter for women and also for men and then ultimately for women and men together. But there can be no together until there is a profound recognition of two-ness. An angry Luce Irigaray's message to analysts is this:

> Let me tell you, gentlemen psychoanalysts, you are pitiful exploiters. You don't even have the daring, the inspiration, the joy, the energy, or the pride of your own phallocratic assertions and positions . . . And before you set yourself up as judges of the desire that animates a woman, bear in mind that it might be time – if we are to re-evaluate the ethics of psychoanalysis – to think about a new ethics of the passions.
> (Irigaray 1991b: 103)

Her diagnosis is not confined to the psychoanalytic situation, as we have seen when we explored Jung's unexamined notions of the feminine (and the masculine) and Bani Shorter's response to the Demeter–Persephone myth. Jung and Shorter are tokens of a type: they iterate and reiterate commonly held assumptions about women and their place in a masculine world. As exemplars, they go some way to explaining why it was men as keynote speakers (on the whole) and why women are seen as secondary and not (really) to be listened to. The Master does not really have to listen to the Slave; and one Slave is easily replaceable by another.

Philosophical analysis of the assumptions and ideals behind analytical psychology is called for, but not only because Jung was so influenced by philosophical argument. His philosophical commitments are obvious. If we were all to reflect on our own philosophical assumptions and ideals, our personal and professional lives would be enhanced because we would be forced to recognise our deepest being and to consider matters of the greatest gravity. Socrates says this of himself:

> If on the other hand I tell you that to let no day pass without discussing goodness and all the other subjects about which you hear me talking and examining both myself and others is really the very best thing a man can do, and that life without this sort of examination is not worth living, you will be less inclined to believe me.
>
> (Plato 2003 'Apology' 38a)

Socrates' comment can be taken as an endorsement of clinical analysis. But it can also be applied to the actual method itself: to the structures and institutions that support examination of the psyche. Like all other structures and institutions, as Young (1990) points out, these contain their own assumptions and biases. My work here has been to show that from a philosophical perspective, and through taking Luce Irigaray's critique of the masculine-paternal and patriarchy, seriously, we can uncover assumptions and biases that are detrimental to developing the full potential of women.

POSTSCRIPT

An assumption that I have made throughout this book is that there is a clear division between female and male bodies. In this conclusion I have followed Jung's schematising the two sexes and Luce Irigaray's masculine and feminine, as apparent opposites. Yet, as I noted in Chapter 3, Foucault's analysis of Adéläide-Herculine Barbin, a hermaphrodite in the nineteenth century, is an analysis of a body and life that were profoundly influenced by the fact of her/his inter-sexed and clearly sexually ambiguous being. The implications for my analysis of an embodiment that does not conform and is seen as anomalous highlight the kind of ethics to which we need to address ourselves in the individuating process. I have claimed, after all, that this is a book about the ethics of individuation.

The central issue here is that of difference. Recognition of difference and an ensuing openness to the value of difference is difficult to achieve, above all because projective and appropriative mechanisms seem to operate at the 'natural' levels I described earlier. A neat ordering of the world into categories that are stable from one perspective (the perspective of the Master) and unstable from another, or several others (the perspective(s) of the Slave), cannot predispose towards the best conditions for human flourishing. Much can be learned from Luce Irigaray's moral and professional courage. Respect for difference and learning to understand difference as a value must surely suggest a renewed interest in our moral characters as individuals involved with one another personally and professionally. Ultimately, we do travel alone. Even with others.

Notes

Introduction

1 Hegel 1977: 178–96.
2 See, for example, Jung 1968a, *passim*; 1968b: 429–33; 1970: 719.
3 The singularity of the original position depends on the possibility of a third, a point of view external to the two subjects who face each other. But this would require an 'outside' to the two self-consciousnesses, which assumes the existence always already of another (to the two self-consciousnesses). But because this third, this point of view, is an observer of an other (the two-self consciousnesses thought of as an original position), the position entails an original two-ness, an observer and an observed.
4 Lacan 2002: 810–11.
5 Rockmore 2003: 104, 106.
6 See, for example, Butler 1999b: *passim* – see especially 242 note 18; Kojève 1996; Taylor 1975; Fox 2005.
7 For a discussion of 'modern inwardness' and the inner/outer metaphor see Taylor (1989: 127–98). The separation of inner and outer is also central to Lacan's mirror stage. See Lacan (2002: 97). I discuss the mirror stage in Chapter 4.
8 Jung 1968a: 525–626. See, for example, Miss X's being stuck to the earth (identification with the other) (527); the complementariness of inferior and superior functions (interdependence of self-consciousness and the other) (541); 'letting go gives the unconscious the opportunity it has been waiting for' (the life/death struggle begins) (563).
9 See, for example, Jung 1969: 828ff; 1968a: 229ff; 1967: 195–7.
10 See, for example, Jung 1968a: 1, 259, 489ff; 1969: 351ff; 358ff; 1977: 1069.
11 Ellenberger's account (Ellenberger 1970) of the discovery and history of the unconscious is very good on this score, as is Nagy's account of Jung's relationship to nineteenth-century philosophy and early psychology (1991).
12 Luce Irigaray's two essays 'Le Genre féminin' and 'Les Trois Genres' (in Irigaray 1987) are later translated as 'The Female Gender' and 'The Three Genders' (in Irigaray 1993a). 'The Three Genders' also appears in Irigaray 1991b). Luce Irigaray says that she has a 'project in working on *genre* in discourse: *Genre* as index and mark of the *subjectivity* and ethical responsibility of the speaker. *Genre* is not in fact merely something to do with physiology, biology or private life, with the mores of animals or the fertility of plants. It constitutes the irreducible differentiation *internal to the human race* ['*genre humain*']. *Genre* represents the site of the nonsubstitutable positioning of the *I* and the *you* and of their modalities of expression. Should the differences between

the *I* and the *you* disappear, so do demand, thanks, appeals, questions.' Of course, one of Luce Irigaray's claims is that there is no feminine *genre* as things currently stand: there really is no I (feminine) and no you (masculine) since I (feminine) is an absence in the only existing symbolic, the masculine symbolic. So there is no demand or thanks or appeal, or questions, not *really*. So, for women to have *genre* would be for women to take up a subject position as women, and this necessitates the making of a new symbolic/imaginary. Also, as Carolyn Burke points out in her essay 'Translation Modified', 'genre' in French means both 'gender' and 'genre' (or philosophical 'kind'). See Burke, Schor and Whitford (1994).

13 Margaret Whitford claims that the introduction of a feminine divinity into the symbolic is one of Luce Irigaray's aims. But this misses the point about 'a feminine Divine' and fails to articulate what I see as a peculiarity of Luce Irigarayean difference. See Whitford (1991: 141).

14 This is significant because, as I shall argue in Chapter 7, the sex/gendered nature of the symbolic/imaginary has profound implications for the collective unconscious which we take to be sex/gender-neutral. But Lacan's symbolic and imaginary are a rewriting of Jung's archetypes as structure and content, of which the collective unconscious is constructed.

15 See, for example, Jung 1971: 305 (the supreme power of the unconscious); Jung 1967: 577 (where Jung uses lunacy as an example of the invasion of the conscious mind by the unconscious).

16 But see Rosenzweig 1992.

17 See Jung 1999.

18 See Lacan 1982.

19 See Irigaray 1993b, 1999 and 1991a.

20 See Jung 1998. See Lucy Huskinson 2004; and Oliver 1994 discusses the idea of individuation in Nietzsche through Kristeva's *abjection*.

21 Andrew Samuels suggests that Lacan's work is compatible with Jung's and that 'Lacan's Symbolic and Imaginary may be aligned with Jung's archetypal theory (collective unconscious) and personal unconscious respectively' (Samuels 1985: 40). Lacan's contention that Freud took the symbolic to be external to the psyche and Lacan's subsequent development of the symbolic/imaginary/real order are evidence of this (Lacan 2002: 392). I take up and develop this theme in my concluding chapter.

1 The dreaming body

1 However, Harald Atmanspacher's work on Wolfang Pauli appears to takes Jung's and Pauli's investigations of the collective aspects of the unconscious in quantum physics very seriously. See Atmanspacher (2004).

2 Jung was interested in Nietzsche from the time he was a student. That Freud did not read Nietzsche was a source of irritation between the two men. The extent of Nietzsche's influence on Carl Jung is fully documented in his lectures (1998), which were given between 1934 and 1939. Acknowledging Jung's intellectual debt to Nietzsche is important since it will influence how Jung is read. This is especially so given recent literature which suggests that Jung had already begun to engage with some of the major issues in postmodern thinking. See, for example, Huskinson (2004), Young-Eisendrath (1997), Barnaby and D'Acierno (1990), and Hauke (2000). These are very different stories from Nagy's, which situates Jung firmly in the philosophical milieu of the nineteenth century,

trapping him, I think, in Idealism, Vitalism, and the attendant metaphysics (Nagy 1991). While it is undeniable that Jung was influenced by Plato, Kant and Schopenhauer among others, one should be careful of confusing influence with repetition and mimicry.

3 Owen Flanagan advances this view. Indeed, Flanagan proposes that 'we are always, while alive, conscious' (Flanagan 2000: 68).

4 Alvin Goldman suggests that '"[a]wareness" is just an approximate synonym of "conscious", and so is "phenomenal"' (Goldman 1997: 111). The approximateness of these words as synonyms should be stressed.

5 See Freud (1961: 15).

6 Sandor Ferenczi raised some objections to this passage. An Editor's note in Appendix A deals with those objections, although how satisfactorily, I am not sure. See Freud (1961: 60–3).

7 In discussing the notions of super- and sub-consciousness, Jung remarks that his 'concept of the unconscious leaves the question of "above" or "below" completely open, as it embraces both aspects of the psyche' (Jung 1969: 178).

8 Nietzsche argues that we need forgetfulness or else we would go mad (Nietzsche 1969: 58).

9 For an excellent reading of this problem, see Owen Flanagan's paper, 'Prospects for a Unified Theory of Consciousness or, What Dreams are Made Of', cited in Güven Güzeldere, 'The Many Faces of Consciousness: A Field Guide' (1997: 97–109).

10 Although Malcolm makes the controversial claim that a dream is an effect of telling a dream, rather than something that happens during sleep (Malcolm 1959).

11 Patricia Churchland suggests that it is necessary for psychological capacities, amongst which I assume she would include consciousness, to be understood in terms of the biological mechanisms that produce them (see her 'Can Neurobiology Teach Us Anything about Consciousness?' in Block *et al.* (Güzeldere 1997: 127)). Hence she takes an eliminativist stance towards psychological capacities, arguing elsewhere that such capacities are eliminable as folk psychology (see Alvin I. Goldman's essay 'Consciousness, Folk Psychology, and Cognitive Science' in Block *et al.* (1997)). She is not only ontologically eliminativist, but epistemologically so. If psychological capacities and conscious states can be shown to be capacities and states of the brain, then 'they' as non-physical capacities and states are eliminated from our ontology. But she is also epistemologically eliminativist, as she seems to envisage a future possible world which has refigured itself and no longer uses the terminology (e.g. consciousness) that we now use. But I am not sure how her argument is meant to be understood as she also argues that (a) 'phlogiston' is no longer used because what it was supposed to be does not exist and (b) the meanings in language can change. It seems odd to me that if there is no referent of 'consciousness' then we would continue to use the term, albeit differently. What would be the criteria for retaining some terms and eliminating others? The transformation of so-called 'folk psychology' it seems to me would be complete only with the full elimination of all folk psychological terms. That would leave language empty of almost everything that is interesting about it, metaphor, simile, allusions, analogies: poetry and all symbolic meanings. Further, she needs to be able to show that scientific language itself is more than metaphorical, more than a model built around metaphors, that it 'captures reality' or refers in a way that non-scientific language does not, and she does not do that. A Jungian reading of the relation between dreaming and theories of mind can be found in Wilkinson (2006).

12 Unlike Kant's noumena, the underlying reality behind the phenomenal appearances of objects that we experience, and which can never be known and so are unknowable, the unconscious on this story, is not a 'realm' of the unknowable.
13 The notion of objectivity that Jung uses here is related to Schopenhauer's idea of the objective. See Schopenhauer (1972: 121).
14 I thank Catherine Tang (Weng Wah), whose first language is Chinese, for pointing out that Chinese speakers talk about 'making dreams when we are asleep' (private exchange); E. R. Dodds (1956) notes that the Homeric poets took dreams to be objective facts which involved a visit – on this reading, dreams are outside the making processes of the unconscious, but are something that happens to the sleeping subject (see Ch. IV 'Dream Pattern and Culture Pattern': 102–34). And I thought, well yes, that's exactly what I and Jung partly argue.
15 Bourdieu is unhappy about the idea of the unconscious as explicated by Lévi-Strauss (Bourdieu 1977: 27 and 103), but he assesses the unconscious in a positive light as history (1977: 78–9).

2 The philosophical Jung

1 Elizabeth Spelman (1988) uses the terms 'manly soul' and 'womanly soul'. She argues that masculine nature and rational embodiment are closely linked. A manly soul is characterised by the dominance of reason and a womanly soul by the dominance of desire. A manly soul is ordered and a womanly soul is disordered. 'Rational' and 'order' are paired descriptors and 'disorder' and 'irrational' are paired descriptors, in both cases paired by sameness rather than difference. According to Plato male soldiers who are cowards have womanly or irrational souls. Badness (and madness) are bad and mad because the soul is disordered.
2 In *Inessential Woman* (1988), Elizabeth Spelman argues that bodies and souls are either matched or mismatched in Plato's metaphysics. Female bodies can be the bearers of either womanly or manly souls, and male bodies likewise can be the bearers of womanly or manly souls. You get a 'match' when female body and womanly soul are together and male body and manly soul are together.
3 I am reminded here of advice from devout Catholic clergy of my youth who taught me that when I was in doubt, I should ask the question, 'What would Jesus do here?' and then do what the answer to the question was. The moral implications of such a procedure are interesting. Imagining what someone else might do impacts on our self-understanding as autonomous individuals. I return to this (potential) problem shortly.
4 For the purposes of this book's argument, let us assume that 'masculine' and 'manliness' and 'feminine' and 'womanliness' are synonymous.
5 This is not on the face of it moral inferiority. It is rather to do with what is dominant or superior in the psyche, more like dominant and recessive in gene theory.
6 Jung's discussion of a finely differentiated Eros that results from a mother complex in a man and which gives rise to great capacity for friendship, aesthetic taste and religious sensibility sits alongside his discussion of homosexuality and Don Juanism. Jung very clearly sees the former as feminine qualities just as he sees the positive effects of Don Juanism as masculine. From this it is evident that he understands psychological attributes to be gendered along fairly traditional lines. However, I think this suggests a different reading of 'feminine' from the one I am proposing here.

7 Grace Jantzen argues that women mystics need to develop masculine or manly souls in order to be more like God (Jantzen 1995).
8 We can see this as an example of the Pythagorean Table of Opposition which Aristotle schematises in *Metaphysics*, Book 1 986a (1991). As the table is cited by Aristotle, it represents the first contrary principles (ten in number) stated by the Pythagoreans.
9 See Jay (1991: 89–106) for a feminist discussion of this point (without acknowledging Aristotle).
10 For a full discussion of the form and content of the Platonic dialogues see, for example, Richard Kraut (1992: 620–4; 1996); introductions to *The Republic* (Plato 1998) and (Plato 1992); and Annas (1981).
11 Plato's *Republic* is a discussion of the nature of justice. In his translation Waterford interprets the Greek '*dikaiosune*' as morality. Waterford comments in his Introduction (Plato 1998): 'Aristotle says (Nichomachean Ethics 1129b–1130a) that "*dikaiosune*" – the Greek word involved – refers to something which encompasses all the various virtues and is almost synonymous with "virtue" in general' (Plato 1998: xii). Likewise, Lindsay, in the Introduction to his translation (Plato 1992), asserts that 'justice (*dikaiosune*) has a wider scope than the English word might suggest . . . Justice therefore includes (what we might call morality as a whole)' (1992: x). Thus Plato's talk of the just man is our talk of the moral person. I thank Peter Corrigan for his helpful discussions here.
12 The meaning of 'guardian' in *The Republic* changes. Initially it means 'soldier', but as Plato's argument develops and from 413ff, Plato refers to the guardians as 'rulers'. But not all guardians are rulers, and the class of individuals whom Plato calls 'auxiliaries' are those individuals who have failed the test of rulership (1992: 413c–414c).
13 See, for example, Jung's 'The Archetypes and the Collective Unconscious' (1968a: 72) and 'Psychological Typology' (1971: 963).
14 Although not everyone with such a soul actually does become a guardian. Education plays a very important role in the making of a guardian. Guardians are the elite of the elite, so some during their training will not achieve the high degree of learning and integrity a guardian must have. Indeed, the guardians' education takes many years – twenty years or more (Plato 1992: 539–540b). Plato deals with education in various sections of *The Republic*, discussing what should be taught and how it should be taught. He argues that children in the republic will be educated and their talents will be 'discovered' by the guardians and nourished through the state educational system. The speakers in *The Republic* refer to 'our' children' (1992: 377b). Presumably the children to be educated are the children of the elite, some of whom will be chosen to be trained as guardians (Plato 1992: 377b, 376d–412b, 449a–471c, 521c–541b).

3 Locating identity: Individual and collective matters

1 I am not sure how to refer to myself in relation to the group of which I am a member: do I say 'they' or 'we'? Do I say 'their' and 'our' when I refer to women's positions, women's bodies, women's ideas and so on? Because I do not wish to exclude readers who are not women, I have decided to use 'they' and 'their' while noting that I am indeed a woman and that I include myself in the class of women.
2 For a good discussion of this see Susan Rowland (2002: 133–59).
3 This applies also to body colour where similar characterisations of behaviour as the expression of womanly souls (ruled by desire not reason) are equally

pejorative. It is arguable that the same is the case with class and religion, aspects of the socio-cultural situatedness of any body. The value of such meanings is differentially produced and applied, and always embodies what a collective values and disparages. But, as Kimberle Crenshaw (1991) has pointed out, these factors are better viewed as multiple intersecting perspectives which have an impact on a life rather than highlighting any specific perspective. See also Michael Vannoy Adams (1996).

4 Jung thinks of the self 'as an empirical concept . . . [which] designates the whole range of psychic phenomena in man. It expresses the unit of the personality as a whole' (Jung 1968a: 789). The concept 'self' is controversial in Jung's psychology for the way in which he articulates it, but more broadly, it is controversial in philosophy. I shall be discussing the concept in my chapter on sex/gendered embodiment.

5 An interesting issue arises here when we consider that the origin of some babies is through artificial insemination and through *in vitro* fertilisation. The mother's body is not home to a penis in such cases. So the originary site, if there is one, of the masculine must be elsewhere.

6 Michel Foucault's discussion of the hermaphrodite Adéläide-Herculine Barbin is very instructive here. See Foucault 1980: vii–xviii.

7 See 'Any Theory of the "Subject"' and 'Plato's *Hystera*' in Luce Irigaray (1985a).

8 Irigaray does not represent patriarchy as a relationship between members of a gendered society *per se*. As I read her, she understands patriarchy as the rule of the masculine paternal, which is to say the father, as bearer of the phallus, rules and is symbolically (and practically) privileged in a society of his own making. The masculine symbolic therefore encompasses patriarchy. For a discussion of patriarchy as a relationship amongst gendered members of society see Moira Gatens (1991).

9 See 'Women on the Market' and 'Commodities amongst Themselves' in Luce Irigaray (1985b).

10 Henceforth written as 'symbolic/imaginary'.

11 See 'Questions' in Luce Irigaray (1985b) and Whitford (1991) for a comprehensive discussion of Irigaray's use of the symbolic. See also 'Luce Irigaray and the Ethics of Alterity' in Grosz (1989) and Lacan (2002) 'The Function and Field of Language in Psychoanalysis', especially 'II – Symbol and Language as Structure and Limit of the Psychoanalytic Field' and 'III – The Resonances of Interpretation and the Time of the Subject in Psychoanalytic Technique'.

12 I follow Mary Midgley in my use of the 'myth' and its cognates. She says, 'Myths are not lies. Nor are they detached stories. They are imaginative patterns, networks of powerful symbols that suggest particular ways of interpreting the world. They shape its meaning' (Midgley 2004: 1). Robert Segal's *Myth: A Very Short Introduction* is an extended essay in which he critically examines various approaches to myth, but Segal also understands myth as fundamentally a story (2004: 4). His book explores the function of myth and discusses various approaches taken for example by Lucien Lévy-Bruhl, Bronislaw Malinowski and Karl Popper (among others).

13 Segal (2004: 4) discusses this kind of myth as a 'belief or credo'.

14 Margaret Atwood's novel *The Handmaid's Tale* (1986) considers the consequences of war on women's fertility and then the enslavement of fertile women who are forced to participate in bizarre, possibly even macabre, rituals of insemination and birthing.

15 The list of feminist thinkers who have done some of this work is now very long. Recent contributors to the debate are Christine Battersby (1998), Amy Hollywood

(2001), Penelope Deutscher (2002), Judith Butler (1999a), Seyla Benhabib (1999), but the question remains: how do you get the men to read the women?

16 I have a problem with reifying unconsciousness which is what we do when we use the term '*the* unconscious'. I raised this problem with Paul Bishop: 'As you know the translators of Jung always refer to the collective unconscious. I worry about the reification implicit in this translation and am wondering if it would be equally correct (or even better perhaps) to translate Jung's German "kollectiven Unbewussten" as "collective unconsciousness"?' Paul's reply was as follows: 'Jung himself often refers to "das kollektive Unbewusste" (or – dative case – dem kollektiven Unbewussten; – genitive – des kollektiven Unbewussten, etc.). In these cases, it's entirely appropriate to use the definite. If, however, Jung speaks of "kollektives Unbewusstes", then your suggested translation, collective unconsciousness, would be exactly right. In the case of das Bewusste and Bewusstes, however, it's hard to think of a translation that would differentiate, since "consciousness" would translate both (sometimes one sees "the conscious", but that always sounds a bit strange to me).' I thank Paul for this; and I follow his advice.

17 Interestingly, Jacques Lacan (2002: 392) claims that Freud knew that the unconscious (unconsciousness) was both collective and individual, that it wasn't an issue for Freud because he knew that the symbolic is located outside man and that this, Lacan claims, 'is the very notion of the unconscious'. I am not so sure that Lacan's pronouncement represents Freud's idea that the unconscious evolves through personal repression and wonder whether Lacan is interpolating some of his own views.

4 Projection: The mirror image

1 Maurice Merleau-Ponty argues that 'There is vision, touch, when a certain visible, a certain tangible, turns back upon the whole of the visible, the whole of the tangible . . . as upon two mirrors facing one another where two indefinite series of images set in one another arise which belong really to neither of the two surfaces, since each is only the rejoinder of the other . . . there is a fundamental narcissism of all vision' (Merleau-Ponty 1968: 139). Merleau-Ponty is marking the territory of vision and its interdependence on the mirror trope which, I believe, is fundamental to projection in a general sense.

2 See Meyers (2002) for a feminist reading of the mirror trope in a socio-political context.

3 Lacan's debt to Henri Wallon as an influence on his thinking is not recognised in the 1949 paper on 'The Mirror Stage as Formative of the *I* Function' (Lacan 2002).

4 Often a child will look behind the mirror to find the person whose face is in the mirror. Lacan does not mention this. But the action of looking behind the mirror suggests the child does not know whose the image is and that the child has no 'innate' knowledge of what she/he looks like or that she/he can look like anything. Rather, it suggests that for the child, where there is a human image there will be a human body attached and an actual human being. Cognitive sophistication has not developed in the child, it seems, at this point. Furthermore, the child does not appear to think symbolically when she/he takes the appearance literally, as looking for the owner of the face suggests.

5 I am ambivalent about what Lacan's account of the mirror stage is intended to show. I suspect that those who are, for example, blind from birth or those who

are sighted but have no access to mirrors or reflecting surfaces in which they can see themselves, must have a different self-concept from those who are sighted and do have such access. It does not follow from Lacan's account that they would not have any different or indeed any better self-concept, only that it might be different.

6 Rose's reference is to *Revue française de psychanalyse 4* October–December, 1949, p. 567.

7 Descartes argued that his senses had deceived him and therefore they could not be trusted as the foundation for certainty (Descartes 1984: 85). Alternatively, Lacan's child gazing into the mirror exhibits the way in which the senses interact and can be self-correcting.

8 In *Psychological Types* Jung argues that part of projection involves the projecting subject's realising that she/he is projecting. There Jung argues for a link between identity (out of which arises identification) and projection, but he maintains that '[p]rojection results from the archaic identity of subject and object, but is properly so called only when the need to dissolve the identity with the object has already arisen' (Jung 1971: 783). Jung suggests elsewhere (at 741 of the same volume) that the possibility of projection depends on identity.

9 My use of the term 'God' is deliberately ambivalent. I do not mean to suggest that the God of Plato's *Timaeus* is the very same God as that of Genesis. Each story gives us the details of creation by a creator God and the translators of each text use the capitalised 'God' rather than 'god'. I, for the moment, follow their use. In the Genesis story, God is in several places presented as a plurality, witnessed by the use of the term 'we'. I extrapolate this notion of the plural God in my discussion of the collective unconscious and conscious.

10 Jung also argues that some introjection is passive, for example, 'transference phenomena in the treatment of neuroses' (1971: 768).

11 For Hegel's account of subject and object see my Introduction and Hegel (1977: 111–19).

12 A performative is a speech act in which the act accomplishes something in the world because of the context in which the speech act is made. For example, promise making and marrying someone are speech acts that are performatives. In saying, 'I promise you X' or 'I thee wed' one does not have to do anything over and above the uttering of words (the speech act) in order to achieve the action in the world (promise making or marrying). In *Bodies that Matter* (1993: 13) Judith Butler argues that there is a 'biblical rendition of the performative, i.e., "Let there be light!"'. But it is difficult to see how it is a performative in Austin's sense since 'Let there be . . .' is a command that could fail in its effect (Austin 1962). Consider 'Let there be happiness' or 'Let them be married'. These directives need something over and beyond the command in order to be effected. In each case there is an expression of a desired end state rather than the bringing about of a state as in 'I thee marry'. Further, the requirement that there be a set of social practices in which a performative *is* a performative is missing from the biblical example. In the case of the collective, members may fail in carrying out a collective's directives. I am reading this 'failure' as an aspect of individuation.

13 The editors of *The New American Bible* (1987: 3) point out that in Genesis 2: 7, the second account of the creation of humans, 'God is portrayed as a potter moulding man's body out of clay. There is a play on words in Hebrew between *adam* (man) and *adama* (ground). *Being*: literally, "soul"' (*The New American Bible* 1987: 3). This account does not suggest that humans are made in the image of God. However, man is animated by the breath of God when God blows 'into his nostrils the breath of life, and so man became a living being'.

5 Divine reversal

1 It is significant that this comment occurs in 'Psychological Aspects of the Mother Archetype', Part 4, 'Positive Aspects of the Mother-Complex' (Jung 1968a).
2 For an interesting reflection on the relation between Kant and Jung see de Voogd (1984).
3 As Richard Kraut points out, these terms also have an ordinary everyday meaning apart from their reference to eternal abstract entities, the eternal Forms (Kraut 1992: 40).
4 Andrew Brook argues that 'Three ideas define the basic shape (cognitive architecture) of Kant's model and one its dominant method. They have all become part of the foundation of cognitive science. The mind is a complex set of abilities (functions) . . . The functions crucial for mental, knowledge-generating activity are spatio-temporal processing of, and application of concepts to, sensory inputs. Cognition requires concepts as well as percepts. These functions are forms of what Kant called synthesis. Synthesis and the unity in consciousness required for synthesis are central to cognition. These three ideas are fundamental to most thinking about cognition now. Kant's most important method, the transcendental method, is also at the heart of contemporary cognitive science. To study the mind, infer the conditions necessary for experience. Arguments having this structure are called 'transcendental arguments' (Brook 2004). For a more extended discussion of Kant's concept of the mind see Brook (1997) or Gardner (1999).
5 Jung does not commit himself to an identity theory of brain and psyche (or mind), although he does acknowledge the importance of the body, as I have already noted.
6 This could, however, also be either Platonic or Aristotelian in terms of the function of forms or ideas.
7 Jung undoubtedly adopts and adapts philosophical language and concepts here, although whether he is straightforwardly Platonic, Aristotelian or Kantian is unclear.
8 Debates about what the feminine is and whether 'it' has a referent, and related questions to do with defining 'woman', 'female', 'sex' and 'gender', abound in feminist theory. Rosemarie Tong gives a good summary of feminist debates and positions in *Feminist Thought* (1989).
9 Elisabeth Grosz argues that Luce Irigaray refers to (female) morphology and not (female) anatomy. Grosz says that she does 'not refer to the female body in biological terms, but only in so far as it is enveloped, produced and made meaningful by language' (Grosz 1990a: 144). In my view, 'female morphology' implies and is dependent upon female anatomy. That one talks about female anatomy does not imply that one is referring to a purely natural or given biological entity. Language always influences how, and what, we think, see and understand, whether we use the term 'biology', 'nature', anatomy' or 'morphology'.
10 We might think of this as a strategic anthropomorphism. It seems to be contrary to Kant's earlier arguments for an archetypal theology. Yet the latter employs 'archetype' as *idea* whereas anthropomorphic theology seems to revolve around the notion of a moral *ideal*.
11 There is serious reason to wonder at these remarks from Feuerbach if the God/man relation might be seen analogously as the man/woman relation where 'man' is 'God' and 'woman' is 'man'.
12 Compare this with the Genesis story in which the woman is produced from Adam's rib.

13 See Luce Irigaray (1985b: 140), where she announces that of course we do not know what masculine discourse is, there is no Other.
14 See Rosi Braidotti (1994: 62–70) for a discussion of this point. See also Whitford (1991: 50 and 104). For another interesting reading of 'other' in Luce Irigaray and Simone de Beauvoir, see Karen Green (2002).
15 For a fuller discussion of the mirror trope see Irigaray's essay 'Une mère de glace' (Irigaray 1985a: 168–79).
16 For her analysis of the maleness of God, of the Incarnation, and of the role Mary plays as mother of God see her essay 'Divine Women' (Irigaray 1993a). See also her essay 'The Fecundity of the Caress' (1993b) for her analysis of the role of women as the beloved and producer of a male heir for the lover.
17 See Feuerbach's *The Essence of Christianity* (1989: 137–9) and Jung's 'Archetypes of the Collective Unconscious' in Jung 1968a: 282.
18 There is an obvious reversal that takes place in this story since women bear men; they make men from their bodies, their flesh and bones.
19 'Il manque à la femme un mirroir pour devenir femme. Avoir un Dieu et devenir son genre vont de pair. Dieu est l'autre dont nous avons absolument besoin . . . Un dieu *féminin* est encore à venir . . .' (Irigaray 1987: 79). 'Woman has no mirror wherewith to become a woman. Having a God and becoming one's gender go hand in hand. God is the other that we absolutely cannot be without . . . A female god is still to come . . .' (Irigaray 1993a: 67).
20 In this she follows Simone de Beauvoir. See de Beauvoir's *The Second Sex* (1949).

6 Mimesis revisited: Demeter and Persephone

1 Irigaray uses both forms of mimesis. See Naomi Schor, 'This Essentialism which is Not One', in Burke, Schor and Whitford (1994: 67). See also Morny Joy (1990: 73–86) for a discussion of transformation and mimesis.
2 The term 'strategic' was used by Gayatri Spivak (1988: 205). For discussion of Irigaray as a strategic feminist see Margaret Whitford (1991), Elizabeth Grosz (1989) and Naomi Schor's 'Previous Engagements' in Burke *et al.* (1994).
3 Judith Butler (1990) discusses parody as a political and social tactic which has the ability to displace identities without origin and which are in fact imitative. Butler argues this in relation to drag, and comments, '*In imitating gender, drag implicitly reveals the imitative structure of gender itself – as well as its contingency*' [her italics] (1990: 136–7). The question which seems to arise here is whether or not Irigaray intends women to imitate gender (viz. sexual behaviour). Given that she is quite explicit in articulating women as sexed subjects, I do not think this is the case. The relation between the sexed subject and her female body is both fundamental and historically contingent. I think Irigaray wants women to take this very seriously. The point of her mimetic strategy seems then to be subversive and transformational; to claim and create identity rather than a strategy for deferring identity, which if I read Butler at all well is that about which she is speaking.
4 For example, see 'Heraclitus' in Jonathan Barnes (1987). See also 'Theaetetus' in Francis Macdonald Cornford (1935: 179c–186e).
5 I have in mind assumptions such as that the One should be privileged over the many, that the symbolic within which we work is neutral, that the feminine cannot be symbolised outside the symbolic because there is no other symbolic possible apart from that which we already inhabit.

6 Homer 2006 'Hymn to Demeter', trans. H. G. Evelyn-White. Online. Available HTTP. <www.lingshidao.com/waiwen/homer.htm> (accessed 03/09/2006).

7 I acknowledge the work of two of my graduate students, Leslie McLean and Fiona Utley, at this point. Leslie's and Fiona's work on rape and its ethical contexts, as they see it, is illuminating and extremely honest. I thank them for introducing me to Susan Brison's book *Aftermath: Violence and the Remaking of a Self* (2002). For anyone who would interpret rape, actual or metaphorical or mythical, as an initiatory rite, then Brison's book would be an excellent remedy, dealing as it does with the violation, loss and refiguring of the self.

8 Another example of this is the story of Antigone who buries her brother's ashes outside the walls of the city. See Irigaray (1985b, 1993b, 1994). See also Whitford (1991) for an excellent discussion of Irigaray's reading of the Antigone myth.

9 Irigaray points out that Mary, the mother of Jesus, does not appear to have a mother and that the Greek goddesses are all motherless as they emerge from primal chaos which is masculine/neutral. See Luce Irigaray (1994) and see also her 'Divine Women' (1993a), where Irigaray discusses the necessity of female genealogy to a feminine symbolic.

10 I see much of Irigaray's work in this context, ranging from mythic through to psychoanalytic and philosophic traditions. It is arguable that these traditions exist as part of the masculine–feminine symbolic. The importance of mimesis, of miming the masculine–feminine comes into play here. So I see the acknowledgement of the feminine tradition here as integral to the overall project and to mimesis.

11 Cf. Elisabeth Schüssler-Fiorenza (1983, 1992), who also proposes re-reading and retrieving women's traditions in the Christian Church, but within what I read as quite an orthodox context, in that she retains, unquestioningly, elements of orthodox Christian thinking, for example, the importance and centrality of Jesus.

7 Jung, Luce Irigaray and essentialism: a new look at an old problem

1 Many so-called essentialist assumptions (such as women are unfit to rule or that they are realised only in becoming mothers) turn, as we shall see, on popular stereotypical constructions of women. An example is the furore engendered by Australian Senator Bill Heffernan when he claimed that Opposition Deputy Leader Julia Gillard was unfit for office because she is childless and selfish: <www.theage.com.au/articles/2007/05/03/1177788310331.html>. His remarks capture something of the prejudice.

2 See, for example, Saul Kripke (1980), Hilary Putnam (1975 and 1983).

3 See Susan Rowland (2002), Christopher Hauke (2000), Roger Brooke (2000).

4 Moi claims that 'Irigaray's attempt to establish a theory of femininity that escapes patriarchal specul(aris)ation, necessarily lapses into a form of essentialism' (1991: 143).

5 Contrary to the views in *The essential difference*, Charlotte Witt's paper engages the feminist essentialist debate philosophically and provides grounds, I believe, for reading the feminist debate about essence as a debate about stereotypes.

6 Hilary Putnam (1975).

7 See Penelope Deutscher (2002).

8 See Charlotte Witt (1989) for her discussion of the population problem in relation to essence.

9 For a good discussion of Locke's analysis of essence see Roger Woolhouse (1994: 146–71).

10 On Locke's triangle see Woolhouse (1994: 159ff) and Stoljar (1995).

11 We should be aware that some feminist philosophers, notably Natalie Stoljar and Charlotte Witt, have developed interesting readings of what I am calling Internal Property Essence. They have attempted to work out how the notion of essence as internal property in relation to women can be suitably characterised within the philosophical tradition, and have developed some very interesting readings of the feminist debate. In her article 'Anti-essentialism in Feminist Theory' Witt, for example, suggests that there are two forms of gender essentialism: individual and generic gender essentialism. Individual essentialism has to do with the thesis that:

> there is some property (or properties) necessary to my being a woman, like being nurturing, or being oppressed, or having a uterus . . . [g]eneric gender essentialism holds that there is a commonality of experience or a characteristic that unites all women, a core of properties that constitutes the generic Woman and that must be satisfied if something is to count as a woman.
>
> (Witt 1995: 322)

Witt claims that (most) anti-essentialist feminists do not distinguish between the two forms, but that they do have a core argument in common. Anti-essentialist feminists equate essentialism and biologism and claim that gender is 'socially constructed rather than given by biology or nature' (Witt 1995: 324). She argues that the premise that equates essentialism and biologism is false and that 'anti-essentialism does not follow from the claim that gender essentialism is socially constructed'. Because these two premises are false, the conclusion must be false, so the core argument does not lead to the desired conclusion that anti-essentialism follows from the two premises. Witt maintains that we have to look elsewhere for reasons to take anti-essentialism on board and identifies what she calls the exclusion argument, the instability argument and the power argument. Witt thinks of anti-essentialism as having a 'first-principle status' in feminist theory which is 'a result of the illicit and tacit combination, and sometimes, conflation of these arguments' (Witt 1995: 322). The three arguments are inconsistent with each other, and Witt says that even if we consider each independently, then how persuasive we allow them to be is an open question. I am not proposing an anti-essentialist theory in this book, but am, instead, using Witt's work on Aristotle to attempt an understanding of what is liberatory for women.

12 See, for example, Teresa de Lauretis, 'The Essence of a Triangle or, Taking the Risk of Essentialism Seriously: Feminist Theory in Italy, the U.S., and Britain' in Schor and Weed (1994) and Fuss (1989).

13 The ontological or metaphysical question which relates to the nature of real essence is, generally speaking, not explored by most feminist theorists although notable exceptions to this generalisation are Sally Haslanger (1995), Natalie Stoljar (1995) and Charlotte Witt (1989 and 1995).

14 Witt argues that some 'contemporary essentialists locate in Aristotle the historical origins of their essentialist view' but notes that Kripke does not make such a connection (Witt 1989: 2).

15 Aristotle's four causes are formal (the idea of something), material (what something is made of, its matter), final (what its purpose is) and efficient (what brings it about – for example, the cobbler makes the shoes hence he brings them about). See Aristotle 1941: 'Politics' II 194b–195c).

16 As the table is cited by Aristotle, it represents the first principles (ten in number) stated by the Pythagoreans. Feminist discussions of the table and its variants can be found, for example, in Lloyd 1984: 3.

17 Natalie Stoljar's argument that the concept 'woman' is a cluster concept involves the idea that there are no essential or necessary properties which must be had by a woman but that there is a pool of properties and that 'people are women when they have *enough* of the properties relevant in the application of the concept' (Stoljar 1995: 288). Although clusters of properties are involved in Putnam's and Stoljar's arguments they are distinct arguments.

18 I am indebted to Peter Forrest for his drawing my attention to Putnam's notion of stereotype and to Drew Khlentzos for his constructive comments on this and the material below on Hilary Putnam.

19 See Crenshaw (1991); for a compelling attack on 'white feminist middle-class' appropriation of 'woman' see Moreton-Robinson (2000).

20 With such a conceptualisation of both essence and stereotype in mind, a number of issues need resolving, especially since the notion of stereotype decides meaning. If what Putnam argues is true, language that is not one's native language will also depend on familiarity with the relevant stereotype.

8 Conclusion: speaking of the collective unconscious . . .

1 Aileen Moreton-Robinson is the inspiration behind this claim. See Moreton-Robinson 2000.

Bibliography

Adams, M. V. (1996) *The Multicultural Imagination: "Race", Color, and the Unconscious*, London and New York: Routledge.

Agonito, R. (ed.) (1977) *A History of Ideas on Women: A Source Book*, New York: Putnam.

Annas, J. (1981) *Introduction to Plato's Republic*, Oxford: Oxford University Press.

Aristotle (1941) *Basic Works of Aristotle*, ed. R. McKeon, New York: Random House.

Aristotle (1991) *Metaphysics*, trans. J. H. McMahon, Buffalo and New York: Prometheus.

Artemidorus, *The Interpretation of Dreams* (*Oneirocritica*), trans. R. J. White (1975), Park Ridge, N.J.: Noyes Press.

Atmanspacher, H. (2006) 'Quantum Approaches to Consciousness', *The Stanford Encyclopedia of Philosophy* (Winter), ed. E. N. Zalta. URL = <http://plato.stanford.edu/archives/win2006/entries/qt-consciousness/>.

Atwood, M. (1986) *The Handmaid's Tale*, Boston, Mass.: Houghton Mifflin.

Austin, J. L. (1962) *How To Do Things With Words*, Cambridge, Mass.: Harvard University Press.

Barnaby, K. and D'Acierno, P. (eds) (1990) *C. G. Jung and the Humanities: Towards a Hermeneutics of Culture*, Princeton, N.J.: Princeton University Press.

Barnes, J. (1987) *Early Greek Philosophy*, Harmondsworth: Penguin.

Battersby, C. (1998) *The Phenomenal Woman: Feminist Metaphysics and the Patterns of Identity*, London: Routledge.

de Beauvoir, S. (1949) *The Second Sex*, trans. H. M. Parsley, London: Picador Books.

Benhabib, S. (1999) 'Sexual Difference and Collective Identities', in *Signs*, vol. 24, no. 4.

Bourdieu, P. (1977) *Outline of a Theory of Practice*, trans. R. Nice, Cambridge: Cambridge University Press.

Bourdieu, P. (1991) *Language and Symbolic Power*, trans. G. Raymond and M. Adamson, Cambridge: Polity Press.

Braidotti, R. (1994) 'Radical Philosophies of Sexual Difference: Luce Irigaray', in *Polity Reader in Gender Studies*, Cambridge: Polity Press.

Brentano, F. (1973) *Psychology from an Empirical Standpoint*, trans. A Rancurello, D. Terrell and L. McAlister, London and New York: Routledge.

Brison, S. (2002) *Aftermath: Violence and the Remaking of the Self*, Princeton, N.J.: Princeton University Press.

Brook, A. (1997) *Kant and the Mind*, Cambridge: Cambridge University Press.

Brook, A. (2004) 'Kant's View of the Mind and Consciousness of Self', in E. N. Zalta (ed.), *The Stanford Encyclopaedia of Philosophy*, Stanford: Stanford University Press. Online. Available HTTP <http://plato.stanford.edu/archives/win2004/entries/kant-mind/> (accessed 18/8/06).

Brooke, R. (ed.) (2000) *Pathways into the Jungian World: Phenomenology and Analytical Psychology*, London and New York: Routledge.

Bullfinch, T. (1979) *Bullfinch's Mythology Illustrated*, New York: Avenal Press.

Burke, C., Schor, N. and Whitford, M. (eds) (1994) *Engaging with Irigaray*, New York: Columbia University Press.

Butler, J. (1990) *Gender Trouble: Feminism and the Subversion of Identity*, New York: Routledge.

Butler, J. (1993) *Bodies that Matter: On the Discursive Limits of 'Sex'*, New York and London: Routledge.

Butler, J. (1999a) *Gender Trouble*, 2nd edn, New York and London: Routledge.

Butler, J. (1999b) *Subjects of Desire: Hegelian Reflections in Twentieth Century France*, New York: Columbia University Press.

Burnham, J. (1971) 'From Mesmer to Medical Psychology', in *Isis* vol. 62, no. 4, 527–9.

Chanter, T. (1995) *Ethics of Eros: Irigaray's Re-Writing of the Philosophers*, New York: Routledge.

Cixous, H. and Clément, C. (1996) *The Newly Born Woman*, trans. B. Wing, Minneapolis and London: University of Minnesota Press.

Cornford, F. (1935) *Plato's Theory of Knowledge*, New York: Kegan Paul.

Crenshaw, K. (1991) 'Mapping the Margins: Intersectionality, Identity Politics and Violence against Women of Color', in *Stanford Law Review*, vol. 43, no. 6, 1241–99.

Crombie, I. M. (1962) *An Examination of Plato's Doctrines. Vol. 1 Plato on Man and Society*, London: Routledge; New York: The Humanist Press.

Dennett, D. C. (1977) 'Are Dreams Experiences?', in *Philosophical Essays on Dreaming*, Ithaca and London: Cornell University Press.

Descartes, R. (1984) *Descartes: Selected Philosophical Writings*, trans. Cottingham, Stoothoff and Murdoch, Cambridge: Cambridge University Press.

Descartes, R. (1996) *The Philosophical Writings of Descartes*, trans. and ed. by J. Cottingham, Cambridge: Cambridge University Press.

Deutscher, P. (2002) *A Politics of Impossible Difference: The Later Works of Luce Irigaray*, Ithaca and London: Cornell University Press.

Deutscher, P. (1994) '"The Only Diabolical Thing about Women . . .": Luce Irigaray on Divinity', in *Hypatia*, vol. 9, no. 4, ed. N. Frankenberry and M. Thie.

De Voogd, S. (1984) 'Fantasy versus Fiction: Jung's Kantianism Appraised', in Renos K. Papadopoulos and G. S. Saayman (eds) *Jung in Modern Perspective*, Hounslow: Wildwood House.

Dick, P. K. (2002) 'We Can Remember it for You Wholesale', in *Selected Stories*, New York: Pantheon.

Dodds, E. R. (1956) *The Greeks and the Irrational*, Berkeley and Los Angeles: University of California Press.

Ellenberger, H. (1970) *The Discovery of the Unconscious: The History and Evolution of Dynamic Psychiatry*, New York: Basic Books.

Feuerbach, L. (1989) *The Essence of Christianity*, trans. G. Elliot, New York: Prometheus Books.

Flanagan, O. (2000) *Dreaming Souls: Sleep, Dreams, and the Evolution of the Conscious Mind*, Oxford and New York: Oxford University Press.

Foucault, M. (1954) 'Dream, Imagination, and Existence', in K. Hoeller (ed.) (1993) *Dream and Existence*, Atlantic Highlands, N.J.: Humanities Press.

Foucault, M. (1980) *Herculine Barbin: Being the Recently Discovered Memoirs of a Nineteenth-Century French Hermaphrodite*, trans. R. McDougall, New York: Pantheon Books.

Foucault, M. (2002) *The Archaeology of Knowledge*, trans. A. M. Sheridan Smith, London and New York: Routledge.

Foucault, M. and Binswanger, L. (1993) *Dream and Existence*, Studies in Existential Psychology Psychiatry, Atlantic Highlands, N.J.: Humanities Press International.

Fox, M. (2005) *The Accessible Hegel*, New York: Prometheus Books.

Freud, S. (1961) *Standard Edition of the Complete Psychological Works of Sigmund Freud. Vol XIX (1923–1925) The Ego and the Id and Other Works*, trans. J. Strachey, Anna Freud, A. Strachey and A. Tyson, London: The Hogarth Press and the Institute of Psychoanalysis.

Freud, S. (1995) *The Freud Reader*, ed. P. Gay, London: Vintage Books.

Fuss, D. (1989) *Essentially Speaking: Feminism, Nature and Difference*, New York and London: Routledge.

Gallop, J. (1982) *Feminism and Psychoanalysis: The Daughter's Seduction*, London and Basingstoke: Macmillan Press.

Gardner, S. (1999) *Kant and the Critique of Pure Reason*, London and New York: Routledge.

Gatens, M. (1991) *Feminism and Philosophy: Perspectives on Difference and Equality*, Indiana: Indiana University Press.

Giegerich, W. (2005) '"Conflict/Resoultion," "Opposites/Creative Union" versus Dialectics, and The Climb Up the Slippery Slope', in W. Giegerich, D. Millar and G. Mogenson (2005) *Dialectics and Analytical Psychology*, New Orleans, La.: Spring Books.

Goldman, A. I. (1997) 'Consciousness, Folk Psychology, and Cognitive Science', in N. Block, O. Flanagan and G. Güzeldere (eds), *The Nature of Consciousness: Philosophical Debates*, Cambridge, Mass., and London, England: MIT, 111–25.

Gray, Frances (forthcoming 2008) 'Plato's Echo: A Feminist Re-figuring of the Anima', in L. Huskinson (ed.), *Dreaming the Myth Onwards, New Directions in Jungian Therapy and Thought*, London/Hove: Routledge.

Green, K. (2002) 'The Other as Another Other', in *Hypatia*, vol. 17, no. 4, 1–15.

Griswold, C. (2005) 'Plato on Rhetoric and Poetry', in E. N. Zalta (ed.), *The Stanford Encyclopaedia of Philosophy*, Stanford: Stanford University Press. Online. Available HTTP; <http: //plato.stanford.edu/archives/sum2005/entries/plato-rhetoric/> (accessed 12/6/04).

Grosz, E. (1989) *Sexual Subversions: Three French Feminists*, St Leonards: Allen and Unwin.

Grosz, E. (1990a) *Jacques Lacan: A Feminist Introduction*, London and New York: Routledge.

Grosz, E. (1990b) 'A Concluding Note on Essentialism', in S. Gunew (ed.), *Feminist Knowledge, Critique and Construct*, London and New York: Routledge.

Grube, G. M. A. (1980) *Plato's Thought*, London: Athlone.

Güzeldere, G. (1997) 'The Many Faces of Consciousness: A Field Guide', in N. Block, O. Flanagan and G. Güzeldere (eds), *The Nature of Consciousness: Philosophical Debates*, Cambridge, Mass., and London: MIT, 1–67.

Hallett, G. L. (1991) *Essentialism: A Wittgenstein Critique*, Albany: State University of New York Press.

Haslanger, S. (1995) 'Ontology and Social Construction', in *Philosophical Topics*, vol. 23, no. 2 (Fall), 95–125.

Hauke, C. (2000) *Jung and the Postmodern: The Interpretation of Realities*, London and Philadelphia: Routledge.

Hegel, G. W. F. (1977) *Phenomenology of Spirit*, trans. A. V. Miller, Oxford: Oxford University Press.

Heidegger, M. (1984) *Being and Time*, trans. J. Macquarrie and E. Robinson, Oxford: Blackwell.

Hirsh, E. and Olsen, G. (1996) 'Je-Luce Irigaray: A Meeting with Luce Irigaray', trans. E. Hirsh and G. Brulotte. Online. Available HTTP <www.cas.usf.edu/JAC/163/irigaray.html>.

Hollywood, A. (2001) *The Soul as Virgin Wife: Mechthild of Magdeburg, Marguerite Porete and Meister Eckhart*, Notre Dame and London: University of Notre Dame Press.

Homer (2006) 'Hymn to Demeter', trans. H. G. Evelyn-White, Online. Available HTTP <www.lingshidao.com/waiwen/homer.htm> (accessed 03/09/2006).

Hume, D. (1962) *A Treatise of Human Nature: Book One*, London and Glasgow: W. M. Collins Sons.

Huskinson, L. (2004) *Nietzsche and Jung: The Whole Self in the Union of Opposites*, Hove: Brunner-Routledge

Irigaray, L. (1985a) *Speculum of the Other Woman*, trans. G. C. Gill, Ithaca and New York: Cornell University Press.

Irigaray, L. (1985b) *This Sex Which Is Not One*, trans. C. Porter with C. Burke, Ithaca and New York: Cornell University Press.

Irigaray, L. (1987) *Sexes et Parentés*, Paris: Les Éditions Minuit.

Irigaray, L. (1991a) *Marine Lover of Friedrich Nietzsche*, trans. G. C. Gill, New York: Columbia University Press.

Irigaray, L. (1991b) *The Irigaray Reader*, ed. M. Whitford, Malden and Oxford: Blackwell.

Irigaray, L. (1992) *Elemental Passions*, trans. J. Collie and J. Still, New York: Routledge.

Irigaray, L. (1993a) *Sexes and Genealogies*, trans. G. C. Gill, New York: Columbia University Press.

Irigaray, L. (1993b) *An Ethics of Sexual Difference*, trans. C. Burke and G. C. Gill, New York: Cornell University Press.

Irigaray, L. (1993c) *Je, tu, nous:Towards a Culture of Difference*, trans. A. Martin, New York and London: Routledge.

Irigaray, L. (1994) *Thinking the Difference for a Peaceful Revolution*, trans. K. Montin, New York: Routledge.

Irigaray, L. (1999) *The Forgetting of Air*, trans. Mary Beth Mader, London: The Athlone Press.

Irigaray, L. (2000) *To be Two*, trans. M. M. Rhodes and M. F. Cocito-Monoc, London and New Brunswick, N.J.: Athlone Press.

Irigaray, L. (2002) 'Between East and West: From Singularity to Community', trans. S. Pluhacek in *European Perspectives: A Series in Social Thought and Cultural Criticism*, New York: Columbia University Press.

Jantzen, G. M. (1995) *Power, Gender and Christian Mysticism*, Cambridge: Cambridge University Press.

Jay, N. (1991) 'Gender and Dichotomy', in S. Gunew (ed.), *A Reader in Feminist Knowledge*, London and New York: Routledge.

Joy, Morny (1990) 'Hermeneutics and *Mimesis*', in *Studies in Religion*, vol. 19, no. 1. (Winter 1990), 73–86.

Jung, C. G. Except where indicated, all references are, by volume and paragraph, to *The Collected Works of C. G. Jung* (1953–91) (CW), ed. H. Read, M. Fordham and G. Adler, trans. R. F. C. Hull, London: Routledge; Princeton, N.J.: Princeton University Press.

Jung, C. G. (1973), vol. 2, trans. L. Stein.

Jung, C. G. (1961), vol. 4.

Jung, C. G. (1966, 2nd edn), vol. 7.

Jung, C. G. (1967, 2nd edn), vol. 5.

Jung, C. G. (1968a, 2nd edn), vol. 9, Pt I.

Jung, C. G. (1968b, 2nd edn), vol. 9, Pt II.

Jung, C. G. (1964, 2nd edn), vol. 10.

Jung, C. G. (1969, 2nd edn), vol. 8.

Jung, C. G. (1970, 2nd edn), vol. 14.

Jung, C. G. (1971), vol. 6.

Jung, C. G. (1977), vol. 18

Jung, C. G. (1990) *Psychology and the East*, trans. R. F. C. Hull, Princeton, N.J.: Princeton University Press.

Jung, C. G. (1998) *Seminar on Nietzsche's Zarathustra*, Princeton, N.J.: Princeton Bollingen.

Jung, C. G. (1999) *Encountering Jung on Death and Mortality*, Princeton, N.J.: Princeton University Press.

Jung, C. G. (1999) *The Psychology of Kundalini Yoga*, ed. S. Shamdasani, Princeton, N.J.: Princeton University Press.

Jung, C. G. (2002) *Dreams*, trans. R. F. C. Hull, London and New York: Routledge.

Kant, I. (1930) *Critique of Pure Reason*, 2nd edn, trans. N. Kemp Smith, London: Macmillan.

Kant, I. (1934) *Religion within the Limits of Reason Alone*, trans. T. M. Greene and H. H. Hudson, La Salle: Indiana Open Court.

Kant, I. (1999) *Critique of Pure Reason*, trans. P. Guyer and A. W. Wood, Cambridge: Cambridge University Press.

Kant, I. (1997) *Prolegomena to Any Future Metaphysics that Will Be Able to Come Forward as Science with Selections from The Critique of Pure Reason*, trans. G. Hatfield, Cambridge: Cambridge University Press.

Kant, I. (2005) *Notes and Fragments*, trans. and ed. T. Green and H. Hudson, Cambridge: Cambridge University Press.

Kojève, A. (1996) *Introduction to the Reading of Hegel: Lectures on the Phenomenology of Spirit*, trans. James H. Nicholls, Ithaca and London: Cornell University Press.

Kraut, R. (ed.) (1992) *The Cambridge Companion to Plato*, Cambridge: Cambridge University Press.

Kraut, R. (1996) 'Plato', in R. Audi (ed.), *The Cambridge Dictionary of Philosophy*, Cambridge: Cambridge University Press.

Kripke, S. A. (1980) *Naming and Necessity*, Oxford: Blackwell.

Lacan, J. (1982) *Jacques Lacan and the École Freudienne: Feminine Sexuality*, ed. J. Mitchell and J. Rose, trans. J. Rose, Basingstoke and London: Macmillan.

Lacan, J. (1999) *On Feminine Sexuality, the Limits of Love and Knowledge: The Seminar of Jacques Lacan, Book XX, Encore*, trans. J.-A. Miller and B. Fink, New York and London: W. W. Norton and Co.

Lacan, J. (2002) *Ecrits*, trans. B. Fink, H. Fink and R. Grigg, New York and London: W. W. Norton.

de Lauretis, T. 'The Essence of a Triangle, or Taking the Risk of Essentialism Seriously: Feminist Theory in Italy, the U.S., and Britain', in N. Schor and E. Weed (eds) (1994) *The essential difference*, Bloomington: Indiana University Press.

Levinas, I. (1996) *Basic Philosophical Writings*, ed. A. Peperzak, A. Citchley and R. Bernasconi, Bloomington and Indianapolis: Indiana University Press.

Lloyd, G. (1984) *The Man of Reason: 'Male' and 'Female' in Western Philosophy*, London: Methuen.

Locke, J. (1947) *An Essay Concerning Human Understanding*, Oxford: Clarendon Press.

Lorraine, T. (1999) *Irigaray & Deleuze Experiments in Visceral Philosophy*, Ithaca and London: Cornell University Press.

Macdonald, M. (1997) 'Sleeping and Waking', in *Philosophical Essays on Dreaming*, Ithaca and London: Cornell University Press.

Malcolm, N. (1959) *Dreaming*, London: Humanities Press.

Merleau-Ponty, M. (1962) *Phenomenology of Perception*, trans. C. Smith, London: Routledge and Kegan Paul.

Merleau-Ponty, M. (1964) *Signs*, trans. R. C. McCleary, Evanston, Ill.: Northwestern University Press.

Merleau-Ponty, M. (1968) *The Visible and the Invisible*, trans. A. Lingis, Evanston, Ill.: Northwestern University Press.

Meyers, D. T. (1994) *Subjection and Subjectivity: Psychoanalytic Feminism and Moral Philosophy*, New York and London: Routledge.

Meyers, D. T. (2002) *Gender in the Mirror: Cultural Imagery and Women's Agency*, Oxford and New York: Oxford University Press.

Midgley, M. (2004) *The Myths We Live By*, London and New York: Routledge.

Mill, J. S. (1957) *Utilitarianism*, Indianapolis: Bobbs-Merrill.

Moi, T. (1985) *Sexual Textual Politics: Feminist Literary Theory*, London and New York: Routledge.

Moreton-Robinson, A. (2000) *Talkin' up to the White Woman: Indigenous Women and Feminism*, St Lucia: University of Queensland Press.

Nagel, T. (1974) 'What is it Like to be a Bat?', in *Philosophical Review*, 83; reprinted in N. Block, O. Flanagan and G. Güzeldere (eds), *The Nature of Consciousness* (1997), Cambridge, Mass., and London: MIT.

Nagy, M. (1991) *Philosophical Issues in the Psychology of C. G. Jung*, Albany: State University of New York Press.

New American Bible, The (1987), Nashville, Atlanta, London, Vancouver: Thomas Nelson.

Nietzsche, F. (1967) *The Birth of Tragedy and The Case of Wagner*, trans. W. Kaufmann, New York: Vintage Books.

Nietzsche, F. (1969) 'Second Essay: Guilt, Bad Conscience, and the Like', in *On the Genealogy of Morals*, trans. W. Kaufmann and R. J. Hollingdale, New York, Vintage Books.

Nye, A. (1986) 'French Feminism and Philosophy of Language', in *Noûs*, vol. 20, no. 1, 45–51.

Oliver, Kelly (1994) 'Nietzsche's Abjection', in *Nietzsche and the Feminine*, ed. P. Burgard, Charlottesville and London: University Press of Virginia.

Papadopoulos, Renos K. and Saayman, G. S. (eds) (1984) *Jung in Modern Perspective*, Hounslow: Wildwood House.

Plato (1970a) *The Dialogues of Plato Volume 1: The Apology & Other Dialogues*, trans. B. Jowett, London: Sphere Books.

Plato (1970b) *The Dialogues of Plato Volume 2: The Symposium and Other Dialogues*, trans. B. Jowett, Aylesbury: Sphere Books.

Plato (1970c) *The Dialogues of Plato Volume 3: Timaeus and Other Dialogues*, trans. B. Jowett, Aylesbury: Sphere Books.

Plato (1992) *The Republic*, trans. A. D. Lindsay, London: Everyman.

Plato (1998) *The Republic*, trans. R. Waterfield, Oxford: Oxford University Press.

Plato (2003) *The Last Days of Socrates*, trans. H. Tredennick and H. Tarrant, London: Penguin.

Putnam, H. (1975) 'The Meaning of Meaning', in *Mind, Language and Reality*, Cambridge and New York: Cambridge University Press.

Putnam, H. (1983) 'Possibility and Necessity', in *Realism and Reason: Philosophical Papers vol. 3*, Cambridge, New York, New Rochelle, Melbourne, Sydney: Cambridge University Press.

Rockmore, T. (2003) *Before and After Hegel: A Historical Introduction to Hegel's Thought*, Indianapolis: Hackett Publishing Co.

Rosenzweig, S. (1992) *Freud, Jung, and Hall the Kingmaker: The Historic Expedition to America (1909)* with G. Stanley Hall as Host and William James as Guest, Seattle, Toronto, Bern, Göttingen: Hogrefe & Huber Publishers.

Rowland, S. (2002) *Jung: A Feminist Revision*, Cambridge: Polity Press.

Samuels, A. (1985) *Jung and the Post-Jungians*, London, Boston, Melbourne and Henley: Routledge & Kegan Paul.

Samuels, A. (1993) *The Political Psyche*, London and New York: Routledge.

Schopenhauer, A. (1972) *Essays and Aphorisms*, trans. R. J. Hollingdale, Middlesex, Baltimore, Ringwood: Penguin Books.

Schor, N. (1994) 'Introduction' in *The essential difference*, New York: Brown University.

Schor, N. and Weed, E. (eds) (1994) *The essential difference*, Indianapolis, IN: Indiana University Press.

Schroeder S. (1997) 'The Concept of Dreaming: On Three Theses by Malcolm', in *Philosophical Investigations*, vol. 20, no. 1.

Schüssler-Fiorenza, E. (1983) *In Memory of Her: A Feminist Theological Reconstruction of Christian Origins*, London: SCM Press.

Schüssler-Fiorenza, E. (1992) *But She Said: Feminist Practices of Biblical Interpretation*, Boston, Mass.: Beacon Press.

Segal, R. (2004) *Myth: A Very Short Introduction*, Oxford: Oxford University Press.

Shepherdson, C. (2003) 'Lacan and Philosophy', in J.-M. Rabaté (ed.), *The Cambridge Companion to Lacan*, Cambridge Companions to Literature. Cambridge: Cambridge University Press.

Shorter, B. (1987) *An Image Darkly Forming*, London and New York: Routledge.

Spelman, E. (1988) *Inessential Woman: Problems of Exclusion in Feminist Thought*, Boston, Mass.: Beacon Press.

Spivak, G. (1988) *In Other World: Essays in Cultural Politics*, New York and London: Routledge.

Spivak, G. (1994) 'In a Word: Interview', in *The essential difference*, New York: Brown University.

Stoljar, N. (1995) 'Essence and the Concept "Woman"', in *Philosophical Topics*, vol. 23, no. 2.

Summers, A. (1994) *Damned Whores and God's Police*, Ringwood, Australia: Penguin.

Taylor, C. (1975) *Hegel*, Cambridge: Cambridge University Press.

Taylor, C. (1989) *Sources of the Self: The Making of Modern Identity*, Cambridge Mass.: Harvard University Press.

Tong, R. (1989) *Feminist Thought: A Comprehensive Introduction*, London: Unwin Hyman.

Vattimo, G. (1993) *The Adventure of Difference: Philosophy after Nietzsche and Heidegger*, trans. C. Blamires and T. Harrison, Cambridge: Polity Press.

Walker, A. (1992) *Possessing the Secret of Joy*, New York, San Diego, London: Harcourt Brace Jovanovich.

Weber, J. C. (1966) 'Feuerbach, Bach and Theological Methodology', in *The Journal of Religion*, vol. 1, no. 1.

Whitford, M. (1991) *Luce Irigaray: Philosophy in the Feminine*, London and New York: Routledge.

Witt, C. (1989) *Substance and Essence in Aristotle: An Interpretation of Metaphysics VII–IX*, Ithaca and London: Cornell University Press.

Witt, C. (1995) 'Anti-Essentialism in Feminist Theory', in *Philosophical Topics*, vol. 23, no. 2.

Wittgenstein, L. (1994) *The Wittgenstein Reader*, ed. A. Kenny, Oxford, UK and Cambridge, USA: Blackwell.

Wittgenstein, L. (2001) *Philosophical Investigations*, trans. G. Anscombe, Oxford and Malden: Blackwell.

Woolhouse, R. (1994) 'Locke's Theory of Knowledge', in V. Chappell (ed.), *The Cambridge Companion to Locke*, Cambridge: Cambridge University Press.

Young, I. M. (1990) *Justice and the Politics of Difference*, Princeton, N.J.: Princeton University Press.

Young, I. M. (1994) 'Gender as Seriality', in *Signs*, vol. 19, no. 31.

Young-Eisendrath, P. (ed.) (1997) *The Cambridge Companion to Jung*, Cambridge: Cambridge University Press.

Index